A POPULAR CRIMINOLOGY OF YOUTH JUSTICE

Analysing the representation of youth crime and justice-involved children in popular fictional films, this book explores how what we see on screen contributes to the perceptions of youth justice in society, policy, and practice.

Putting forward the argument that fictional representations have a real-world impact on the opportunities available to children, each chapter in the book focuses on a different genre or type of film and considers the ways in which justice-involved children have been demonised, stereotyped, and harmed by their portrayal on the big screen. From James Dean and the birth of "monstrous youth" in *Rebel Without A Cause* to the current, more nuanced portrayals as seen in *The Young Offenders*, the book examines films throughout history and across different cultures. In doing so, it demonstrates how portrayals of justice-involved children have contributed to the social understanding of what youth crime is and who is to blame for it, and highlights how we can use this knowledge to better understand and support children.

By combining youth justice theory with media analysis, *A Popular Criminology of Youth Justice: Youth on Film* makes a novel contribution to both fields and will be of great interest to students and researchers in the areas of youth crime, youth justice, and the media.

Jessica Urwin is a Lecturer in Criminology at the University of Leicester, UK and a Senior Fellow of the Higher Education Academy. After gaining a BSc in Psychology from Coventry University, Jessica worked in secondary schools with at-risk young people and completed research for the National Youth Agency. This led her to complete an MRes in Social Work at De Montfort University prior to undertaking her PhD. She currently teaches Criminology programmes at both undergraduate and postgraduate levels.

Routledge Studies in Crime, Culture and Media

Routledge Studies in Crime, Culture and Media offers the very best in research that seeks to understand crime through the context of culture, cultural processes and media.

The series welcomes monographs and edited volumes from across the globe, and across a variety of disciplines. Books will offer fresh insights on a range of topics, including news reporting of crime; moral panics and trial by media; media and the police; crime in film; crime in fiction; crime in TV; crime and music; 'reality' crime shows; the impact of new media including mobile, Internet and digital technologies, and social networking sites; the ways media portrayals of crime influence government policy and lawmaking; the theoretical, conceptual and methodological underpinnings of cultural criminology.

Books in the series will be essential reading for those researching and studying criminology, media studies, cultural studies and sociology.

True Crime and Women
Writers, Readers, and Representations
Edited by Lili Pâquet and Rose Williamson

Social Media and Criminal Justice
Xiaochen Hu and Nicholas P. Lovrich

A Popular Criminology of Youth Justice
Youth on Film
Jessica Urwin

A POPULAR CRIMINOLOGY OF YOUTH JUSTICE

Youth on Film

Jessica Urwin

LONDON AND NEW YORK

Designed cover image: Jessica Urwin

First published 2025
by Routledge
4 Park Square, Milton Park, Abingdon, Oxon OX14 4RN

and by Routledge
605 Third Avenue, New York, NY 10158

Routledge is an imprint of the Taylor & Francis Group, an informa business

© 2025 Jessica Urwin

The right of Jessica Urwin to be identified as author of this work has been asserted in accordance with sections 77 and 78 of the Copyright, Designs and Patents Act 1988.

All rights reserved. No part of this book may be reprinted or reproduced or utilised in any form or by any electronic, mechanical, or other means, now known or hereafter invented, including photocopying and recording, or in any information storage or retrieval system, without permission in writing from the publishers.

Trademark notice: Product or corporate names may be trademarks or registered trademarks, and are used only for identification and explanation without intent to infringe.

British Library Cataloguing-in-Publication Data
A catalogue record for this book is available from the British Library

ISBN: 978-1-032-51618-9 (hbk)
ISBN: 978-1-032-51620-2 (pbk)
ISBN: 978-1-003-40315-9 (ebk)

DOI: 10.4324/9781003403159

Typeset in Sabon
by SPi Technologies India Pvt Ltd (Straive)

CONTENTS

Preface and Acknowledgements   *viii*

1   Introduction   1

Popular Criminology and Youth Justice 3
The Purpose and Remit of This Book 9
Structure of This Book 13
A Note on Language 15
Film List 16
References 17

2   "You Wanna Start a Rumble?": The Birth of Problem Youth   22

Problem Youth Films as Spectacle 26
Explanations of Offending? 30
Public Responses and the Legacy of Problem Youth 39
Film List 42
References 42

3   "This Ain't a Girl Scout Camp!": Policing and
    Imprisoning Youth   46

Children are Overpoliced and Criminalised 48
Police Narratives About Children 50
Children's Response to Police 53

vi Contents

Imprisoning Children 59
Film List 64
References 65

4 "I Killed the Teen Dream! Deal with It!":
Gender, Violence, and Crime 70

Girl World as a Site of Violence 74
Commodification of Girls Violence 76
Class and Consequences 80
Film List 84
References 85

5 "I'm Not a Ghetto Boy, I Just Live in Deptford":
Urban 'Realities', Ethnicity, and Cities 89

Cities as Place of Fear 90
Blackness as a Risk Factor 97
The Perpetuation of Fear 102
Film List 105
References 106

6 "Thank You for Respecting Me and My Family's
Privacy": True Youth Crime, Sensationalism,
and Fictionalisation 111

Sensationalised Truth 113
Fictionalised Truth 117
Consuming Truth 122
Film List 126
References 127

7 "You Won, Justice was Done, Who Cares?":
Children in the Courtroom 131

Youth Court Dramas 133
The Innocent–Dangerous Dyad 135
Innocent Children in Dangerous Situations 141
Film List 143
References 144

Contents **vii**

8   "Now That I Know You, I Can't Really NOT
    Know You": Child First Films   148

    Showing Children as Children 153
    Building Pro-Social Identity 157
    Diverting from Stigma 162
    A Child First Future 168
    Film List 170
    References 170

9   Conclusion   177

    The Youth Crime Film 179
    A Popular Criminology of Youth Justice 185
    Film List 188
    References 188

Index   192

PREFACE AND ACKNOWLEDGEMENTS

This book emerged as a result of two things: teaching media analysis to criminology undergraduate students and running the ESRC Festival of Social Science film screening events in partnership with Phoenix Leicester. Teaching means I am forced to answer questions I had never thought of and always seems to spark new ideas. My students asked me why film matters, and the answer was so long it needed a full monograph. Students also told me that they struggled in finding readings that analysed film from a youth justice perspective, so this book is an attempt to fill that gap. In running film screening events for the ESRC Festival of Social Science I realised how much I love talking about film and that other people found what I had to say about it interesting, which made me think that a book about it might be worth reading. In doing these things it became clear to me that youth justice was a piece missing from the broader conversation about crime and media. This led me to contribute a chapter to the Elgar Research Handbook on Youth Criminology, calling for a popular criminology of youth justice to be developed. That work was one of the most enjoyable writing experiences I had had up to that point and made me want to be the person to create the thing I was calling for. That is what led to this book. I hope it achieves some of the things I have aimed for it to do.

I must inform readers that this is not intended to be a comprehensive guide to youth justice on film and does not include every film that features youth justice throughout history. Films were selected based on subject matter, public reception, and in some cases; availability. There are some works I wanted to include that didn't quite fit with the remit of this book (sorry *Mean Girls*), but my hope is that by highlighting the need to develop a popular criminology of youth justice, there will be a clear space for these to be discussed in future.

Preface and Acknowledgements **ix**

Additionally, I'm very aware that this book is limited by my own knowledge and awareness of film, and I look forward to seeing future research that considers these issues on a global scale, as I'm sure that filmmakers around the world have addressed these issues in interesting and diverse ways.

Before progressing into the book proper, I must thank several people. Firstly, Emily and Olivia. The motivational group chat was a genuine help, and I am so very grateful for your support and friendship. Secondly, the Write Club gang! Writing with you all made the process far more fun and was a great help in finding and maintaining motivation. For anyone considering writing a book, I strongly recommend running a writing group; it means you're forced to sit down and put words on paper, and you meet some brilliant people.

Also great thanks to everyone who read drafts, suggested films to watch, and listened to me talk through my ideas. My goal for writing this book was to not cry about it, and I've been successful in that due support the support of friends, family, and colleagues; thank you all so much. A big thanks also to Phoenix Leicester, my favourite cinema. Many of the films I talk about in this book I know of because I watched them at Phoenix and I spent several hours sitting in the café bar writing and enjoying the excellent coffee and cakes. Support your local indie cinema!

None of my work would get done without the support of my partner, Les. Thank you so very much for encouraging me, supporting me, and putting up with me taking over the kitchen to write. You're the best person I know.

1

INTRODUCTION

Three teenage boys clad in black leather jackets walk with purpose down a crowded, graffiti-covered street. They don't adjust their stride for oncomers, walking three abreast, taking up the whole pavement. People walking in the opposite direction are knocked aside, and a child's toy pram is kicked out of the way and sent into the road. The trio approaches a group of teens sitting on the steps outside their home. Flick knives appear, a fight ensues, and the trio seem to repeatedly stab one of the boys. The girls scream as the trio run off pursued by sirens and a boy lies dead on the steps of his home.

This is the opening scene of *The Young Savages* (1961), a film where three teenagers are accused and tried for attempted murder. However, the images it uses could be from a contemporary crime drama, simply change the biker jackets for hoodies or tracksuits. How we present crime in media is powerful, influencing our perceptions of "real" crime and our sense of safety in the world (Jewkes, 2015). Often this imagery tries to shock audiences, as a way of keeping attention or heightening drama, and a frequent way to create this shock is to present children as the source of crime. Society has always wanted to know why people commit crimes, and children's criminal activity is a consistent source of fear (Kort-Butler and Hartshorn, 2011), as it potentially suggests that some people are "born bad" or that a criminal life cannot be avoided. However, many of our ideas about youth crime have come from media like *The Young Savages*, or the myriad of "problem youth films" (Doherty, 2002) that have followed rather than actual engagement with justice-involved children. These films have created and maintained a set of cultural ideas about justice-involved children (see note on terminology at the end of this chapter for an explanation of this phrasing), often utilising stereotypes, promoting inaccuracies, or assuming that systems of justice for

DOI: 10.4324/9781003403159-1

children are the same as those for adults. This means that understanding the media presentation of youth justice is hugely important. The imagery of crime evokes ideas that have been created, recreated, and reinforced throughout media and across society, ultimately impacting upon youth justice policy and practice. This book aims to deconstruct this imagery, to understand how and why these ideas have been maintained within society, and the role of fictional media within youth justice.

Youth crime has been a continual concern within society, meaning it is also a subject ripe for depiction on film. From 1950s moralising through to coming-of-age comedies; children's involvement with crime and justice has always been a popular topic for film. However, this is not a distinct genre, with depictions of justice-involved children spanning dramas, thrillers, horrors, comedies, and more. The ways in which we view justice-involved children often depend upon what their crime is, what their background is, and what cultural ideas we hold about them. This shows the intersection between media representation and real-world views of justice-involved children, which can then impact upon how those children are treated by the world around them. Whether this is heightened panics over knife crime (see Chapter 5), minimising the crimes of girls through comedy (see Chapter 4), or challenging the stereotypes of justice-involved children (see Chapter 8) film impacts upon justice in practice.

Understanding how films impact justice-involved children in reality requires considering not only the context and presentation of films, but also audience reactions, and how these reactions may have influenced societal conceptions of justice-involved children, as well as youth justice policy and practice. There cannot be a direct line drawn between the films that this book discusses and the outcomes in specific cases, or the development of legislation, however, these films contribute more broadly to the societal conception of crime and justice, including how it should be responded to, thus warranting study. Hayward (2009) states that all criminologists should be aware of and actively consider how the "story of crime" is created, and this book aims to contribute to this.

"Youth" is a social category rather than a biological marker of age (Case, 2018). It is distinct from childhood and adulthood, a liminal space in which a transition from one stage to the other occurs. Whilst there are differences in how youth is defined, this book considers 10–18-year-olds, and films that focus on characters within this age range. As a society we do not generally teach children how to become adults, instead expecting them to absorb this information from being in society (MacDonald and Shildrick, 2007). This means that both adults and children's perceptions of what youth should be like are often informed by individual experiences, discussion with peers, and media. This is not to say that audiences uncritically absorb the messages presented in media, but that this is part of the information that is incorporated into the social construction of these categories (Buckingham, 1993). This is an idea that has long existed, Plato's concept of mimesis acknowledges that whilst artworks are not true representations of reality and cannot create knowledge, they create a version of reality that is absorbed into societal thought (Plato, 380AD, 2008). This means that to truly understand how "youth" and children are understood and responded to by society on both an individual and general level, we need to analyse the messages within media representations.

There is much wonderful scholarship that has already been carried out in this field, in particular the work of the Centre for Contemporary Cultural Studies (CCCS), and the cultural criminology of Ferrell, Hayward and Young (Ferrell et al., 2008; Hayward, 2016; Hayward and Young, 2004). This work has addressed media presentation of subcultures (Cohen and Short, 1958), the role of subculture in children's lives (Hall and Jefferson, 2006), and the construction and experiences of deviancy (Cohen, 1965). A vast majority of this work looks at these issues through the lens of class (Blackman, 2005). Indeed, youth studies often specifically focuses on the experiences of working-class children, which leads to an overlap with youth justice research. However, when this work looks at youth it is in general, without specifically focussing on criminal and criminalised behaviours. This book aims to address this, by developing a popular criminology of youth justice. Looking specifically at representations of justice-involved people in commercially released films, this book considers the messages about youth justice that are created, perpetuated, and challenged, as well as the response to these media, in social, political, and practice contexts.

Popular Criminology and Youth Justice

Based upon the work of Rafter and Brown (2011) popular criminology considers the discourses about crime and justice presented in media (with a focus on audio/visual media) and how this relates to criminological theory and public perception, thus changing both. By studying the overlap between academic criminology and popular culture, we recognise the fuzziness of the boundaries between the two, allowing us to better understand the influence they each have on the other (Deflem, 2010). It is in this space that popular criminology emerges. The work of popular criminology is to examine the narratives of crime and justice that are presented, maintained, and challenged through film, considering this in relation to criminological theory. Popular criminology is a developing area within the broader field of cultural criminology (King, 2013). Initially, discussions about popular criminology related to "true crime" media, which often presents itself as an authority on what happened in specific cases, on a parallel with academic research (Rawlings, 1998). There are debates and varying opinions about

4 A Popular Criminology of Youth Justice

the validity and usefulness of these "true crime" works (Bruzzi, 2016; Yardley et al., 2019), however, what cannot be ignored is the function these works play in society.

True crime media has been consistently publicly popular in society and has evolved with trends in reporting style, format, and technology (Bruzzi, 2016). From newspaper reports on Jack the Ripper to Netflix documentaries about serial killers, there is a fascination in the public with the representation of crime, and research suggests that engagement with this type of media becomes infused into public opinion about crime and justice (Bruzzi, 2016; Yardley et al., 2017, 2019). Peay (1998) and Rawlings (1998) discussed the impact of popular crime media on academic criminology, highlighting that these issues cannot be considered outside of the context of late modernity and populism. And this is the context in which we must still consider representations of youth justice. Peay (1998) argued that true crime media's focus on individual cases, which are often highly shocking or unusual, creates a distorted impression of crime in society, normalising biased perceptions about the frequency of violence. This then can be manipulated for the purposes of penal populism, as in the case of Michael Howards' rhetoric about justice-involved children following the James Bulger case (Green, 2008). However, not all crime media falls within the genre of true crime. Fictional popular media representing crime has these same cultural impacts, thus warranting study. Rafter and Brown (2011) developed the field of popular criminology, widening the scope to consider fictional media representations of crime and justice as well as factual ones. This has led to popular criminology being utilised in a variety of ways, from analysing representations of justice in children's cartoons (Kort-Butler, 2012, 2013), to considering media and practice links in the representation of sex offenders (Kohm and Greenhill, 2011; Rafter, 2007), to encouraging criminologists to think about the borders of the subject and how criminology relates to the public (Akrivos and Antoniou, 2019; Silva, 2019).

Popular criminology's consideration of fictional media representations of crime and justice must acknowledge the context of late modernity. One change within media that this has brought is the move towards postmodernism. Film now is more likely to emphasise the context of a character's behaviour, showing the impact of psycho-socio-political factors, aiming to develop sympathy from the audience (King, 2013). This is a clear difference from the true crime media that Rawlings (1998) and Peay (1998) were discussing. This also means that popular criminology's analysis of media needs to take into account not only the work itself (images and text), but the context in which it was created and released, and the social response to this. Media messages cannot be considered in isolation, and it is the work of popular criminology to examine those messages and consider their impact not only in broader society, but in relation to criminological theory and research as well

(Hayward, 2009). Taking media such as film seriously is a key aspect of this. As Rafter and Brown suggest, "Dismissing these accounts as voyeurism or schlock limits our understanding of their social functions" (2011:5). This does not mean assuming all media is serious or literal, popular criminology recognises the enjoyment of watching crime from a safe position and that presentations of crime and justice can be joyful, funny, and endearing as well as dramatic. This also acknowledges the role of poetic license, a main aim of film is to tell a story, and so liberties may need to be taken with timelines, plot points or characterisation. But it does mean recognising film and broader media as a legitimate source, as this is where a large section of the public gains information about and develops knowledge of crime and justice. Even if film is not accurate, it may still contain truths. This means that to have a complete picture of the function of crime and justice in society, we must look at the narratives and stories we tell about crime and justice.

Popular criminology has pedagogical elements, using film as a teaching tool to elucidate the complexities of criminological theory (Atherton, 2013). Rafter and Brown's *Criminology Goes to the Movies* (2011) is the key text in this regard, with each chapter using a specific film as an example of a criminological theory. Subsequent work within popular criminology has built upon this, theorising how representations across media relate and respond to criminological theory, and how these messages may impact viewers (Akrivos and Antoniou, 2019; Dowler et al., 2006; King, 2013). This book doesn't explicitly use popular media in a pedagogical manner, instead focusing on the deconstruction of underlying messages in film and their implications for youth justice.

Popular criminology is a subset of cultural criminology, and it is necessary to set out this distinction here to clarify the theoretical position and contribution of this book. Cultural criminology looks at criminal activity within the context of broader culture, including media (Presdee, 2000). Whereas popular criminology looks purely at media, without necessarily being linked to "real world" crime. Whilst this book does discuss the similarities and differences between youth justice on screen and in practice, it will not be discussing specific cases or making causal links between depictions of justice-involved children on film and criminal(ised) behaviours of children in reality. Much cultural criminological work considering youth has looked at youth culture and subculture. This has developed an understanding of children (in Britain in particular) considerably, but also presents children and youth culture as a form of "becoming", focusing on subculture as being transitory or a "phase". Whilst work has looked at adults in subculture, or alternative forms of adulthood (Hodkinson, 2016; Howe et al., 2015), the broader narratives surrounding youth are ones of temporariness, transition, and transformation allowing children to conceptualise the adults that they are going to be.

6 A Popular Criminology of Youth Justice

Cultural criminological work on youth frequently discusses deviance and criminalisation, but does not necessarily address criminal behaviours, or the impacts of criminal justice. Some of the criticisms of the CCCS are relevant here, the singular focus on class frames almost all deviant or criminal activity as a form of resistance (Blackman, 2005). However, research has found children engage in criminal activity for a wide range of reasons; from boredom to gaining opportunities, to fun. Separating deviance from criminality is important because whilst deviant behaviour is socially punished (and may become criminalised), we have developed social, legal, and organisational structures to address criminal behaviours. The impact of involvement with these structures can alter a person's entire life and future, whereas deviance can be transitioned out of, or the trappings of subculture can be taken off. For justice-involved children, youth studies approaches often don't explain or fully represent this aspect of their lived experiences. However, youth justice might. The youth justice perspective does not mean perceiving justice-involved children as "criminal". This is something that youth justice research has criticised for a long time, and more recent research promotes Child First views (Case and Hazel, 2023; Drakeford, 2009), which actively advocate against labelling children as criminal, even moving towards abolitionism (see Chapter 8).

Youth justice combines aspects of criminology, psychology, sociology, and social work. Aiming to understand children's criminal behaviour and what is an appropriate way for society to formally respond to this behaviour, youth justice research has considered many areas of children's lives that youth studies does not. However, this often focuses on practice, not considering the impact and relationship between fictional media and criminal justice. This means that there is a gap in how research understands children, where the cultural and criminal overlap. This book aims to respond to that gap, by considering youth justice theories in relation to cultural representations of justice-involved children.

Children and their behaviours have consistently been perceived as a problem throughout history, with various philosophers, politicians and cultural commentators bemoaning the declining state of youth (Roche et al., 2004). In this way, youth has always been perceived as challenging and as having the potential to destabilise the status quo. Children's testing of social boundaries (much in the way that babies and toddlers test the physical boundaries of the world) is frequently seen by the adults around them as inherently challenging the validity of those boundaries and questioning their worth. Bemoaning these children's behaviours is a way of re-establishing the social order, through belittling or undermining the supposedly rebellious behaviours of youth. This also acts as a form of social control, setting out what is and isn't an acceptable way for children to behave (Muncie, 2008). From Aristotle stating that children are "high-minded because they have not yet

Introduction **7**

been humbled by life" (Ruggeri, 2017) to David Cameron declaring that "teamwork, discipline, duty" are part of the "solution" to the "problem of alienated, angry children" (Cameron, 2011), for as long as there have been adults, they have been decrying the declining standard of children. Many of these concerns reoccur throughout history; fighting, swearing, drinking, and talking back to adults are frequent complaints (Roche et al., 2004). These gripes often relate to the increasing independence given to children. They are no longer "children" but not yet "adults". "Youth" is still beholden to parents and carers, but able to make more of their own choices. The concerns of adults often represent their fears in giving up control of the children in their lives; allowing them more control over themselves (Cohen, 1965). The social control of children is a common theme through many of the films discussed in this book, and is in essence, one of the aims of youth justice. The "problem" of youth is solved if/when these children become law-abiding, conforming, adults.

Research considering justice-involved children in media has predominantly looked at factual media, such as TV news, newspapers and websites, and documentaries (Boldison, 2006; Jupp et al., 2011; Mejias and Banaji, 2019). This has continually found that there are two main categories into which the representation of children falls: innocent victims and dangerous offenders (Case, 2018; Roche et al., 2004). These two categorisations have been found throughout history, particularly the idea of the dangerous offender (Evans, 2005). Within the cultural narrative of children as a problem, there is the spectre of social control (Donoghue, 2011). For children who do not conform to societal mores, the negative judgements and punishments (both social and legal) are amplified. This can be seen in much of the work around subculture (Hollingworth, 2015), the criminalisation of children's activities (MacDonald and Shildrick, 2007; Shildrick and MacDonald, 2006), and the demonisation of justice-involved children (Baldry et al., 2018; Creaney, 2012). News media in particular prioritises stories of youth deviance as this has an additional shock factor that draws interest (Wayne et al., 2008). The idea that "innocent children" can become "dangerous offenders" is something that society focuses on, with the idea that by understanding these transformations we can prevent them from occurring in others. However, the presentation in these stories is almost always lacking nuance, and re-presenting pre-existing narratives of deviance, meaning that understanding is not developed, but the status quo of youth being characterised as a problem is maintained.

Populism and political change is a constant point of conversation within youth justice. The public conversation regarding children has historically tended towards the negative as already discussed. However, this negative characterisation of children impacts some more than others. Children who are justice-involved are more likely to be considered as vulnerable (Brooks-Wilson, 2020; Goldson, 2000). Whether this is due to developmental

8 A Popular Criminology of Youth Justice

differences, mental health needs, learning differences, abuse or neglect, or other adverse childhood experiences, justice-involved children are typically considered particularly in need (Goldson, 2000). These needs are often not met by societal structures and existing resources, and the coping mechanisms that these children then develop are often criminalised (Briggs, 2013). Whether this is self-medicating through substance misuse (Hammersley et al., 2006), violent or aggressive behaviours (Jennings et al., 2012), or participating in alternative subcultures (Selfhout et al., 2008), the children who are criminalised are frequently already on the fringes of society or have been excluded in some way. This makes their criminalisation even more damaging, and only furthers the sense of exclusion (Gray, 2007; MacDonald and Shildrick, 2007). When films depict or represent justice-involved children, the public responses to this often further exclude them from cultural narratives. Whilst some of the films discussed within this book are aimed at children, the majority are created with an adult audience in mind. Additionally, these films in general are made by adults, many use the perspective of adult characters as the lens through which young characters are perceived and are discussed in the public space by adults. The narratives about justice-involved children often exclude actual justice-involved children from contributing to or commenting on them. This only furthers the exclusion that these children feel. Youth criminology's focus on news media means that the fictional narratives and stories of justice are overlooked. These are often more important in how societal discourse develops and have a profound influence upon public opinion (Buckingham, 1993; Jewkes, 2015). This means that we must consider how these stories of justice are created, maintained, and challenged within society; meaning we need a popular criminology of youth justice.

Much research has identified the impact and importance of stories upon culture (Dowler et al., 2006; Surette, 2015). Presdee (2000) has discussed that emotional responses to stories can be used as a form of capital, particularly by the non-wealthy. The threat of moral outrage is powerful and can be weaponised as a means of gaining or maintaining political power (Presdee, 2000). This relationship is something that has been well discussed in relation to moral panics (Altheide, 2009; Cohen, 2011) and cycles of criminalisation. However, in relation to justice-involved children this cannot be said to be the case. The long-standing historical concern about the decaying of children's morals means this does not fit the criteria of a moral panic, as it is a persistent concern within society. This makes films representing justice-involved children particularly important. They are depicting a contentious group of people who are already the subject of societal ire, and a sympathetic portrayal can be seen as being soft on crime whereas focusing on violence and negative aspects is often perceived as sensationalist and glamourising violence. The polarised (and polarising) responses to these films do not necessarily stay in the realms of pop culture discussions. Films and the stories they present sometimes act as lightning rods for public concern, becoming the centre of a discussion that is actually much broader. This can then contribute to political responses, particularly populist approaches focused on criminalisation (Green, 2008). Films are not only stories we tell for entertainment, but have cultural, social, and political impacts as well. Understanding the messages within these stories, and their impacts is key to establishing and developing the popular criminology of youth justice.

The Purpose and Remit of This Book

This book looks specifically at youth crime on film from a youth justice perspective. This involves asking the following questions:

1 What messages are portrayed in films about justice-involved children?
2 How have these messages reflected and/or reinforced hegemonic narratives about youth justice?
3 What does this emphasise for the treatment of justice-involved children in society?

In asking these questions this book aims to establish and develop a popular criminology of youth justice. As discussed throughout this chapter, popular criminology provides a necessary space to examine media created as commercial entertainment products from a criminological perspective, particularly considering the relationship with criminological theory. This work has not yet explicitly considered youth justice and given the clear relationship between public opinion and concern regarding children and youth justice policy, it is essential to understand how representations of youth justice may impact upon these conversations. As this is a newer area of work, this book does not intend to be the *only* work on this topic. Rather, I hope it encourages others to create work in this area, particularly considering other cultures and youth justice approaches. The purpose of this book is to highlight the need for a popular criminology of youth justice and further the conversation.

The films selected for and discussed throughout this book are by no means the totality of films representing youth crime, justice, and justice-involved children. Selections have been made based on the age of characters, their behaviours, the age of the film, the influence and reception of the film. These factors mean that all the films discussed feature children aged 10–18 who carry out criminal activity. Films that display children behaving in ways that may be perceived as deviant but aren't necessarily criminal are not considered here. There is already a wealth of scholarship looking at representations of deviance that readers may enjoy (Cohen, 1965; Cohen and Short, 1958; Goode and Ben-Yehuda, 1994; Wiley and Esbensen, 2016). The films selected

10 A Popular Criminology of Youth Justice

from this range are exemplars of these works, it would not be possible to discuss them all. Some films have been included due to their cult status, cultural impact, or the public response to their release, as well as consideration of accessibility and availability. The films discussed throughout are a small sample of representations of justice-involved children on film, and the Western bias of these must be acknowledged. The films drawn upon in this book are primarily American and British, with some representation of works from France, Germany, and Scandinavia. This bias is due to firstly knowledge of films, I am British, and so am more familiar with works aimed at British audiences. Secondly, the focus on cultural implications within Critical Discourse Analysis (CDA), meaning I am not equipped to fully understand the cultural impact of films from and within countries I have little experience of, and I would not feel comfortable doing so. There are scholars better placed across the globe to carry out that work. It's not possible to discuss *every* film that depicts justice-involved children, but I have endeavoured to include a range that showcases different perspectives across time, includes diversity of depictions of class, race and gender, and addresses the key issues of youth justice on film.

The films considered throughout this book have been analysed using CDA. CDA emphasises not only the micro aspects of a text such as the messages it presents about a specific subject, but also the macro impacts this has upon cultural and political spaces (Denscombe, 2010). In this application, CDA is considering what implicit cultural messages and ideas about justice-involved children are being presented in commercial films at an individual level, and what influence or impact this has had upon broader cultural considerations of justice-involved children and youth justice in society. The films considered throughout this book have been analysed individually, but the messages found within them have been contrasted and considered in relation to the other films analysed, to gain an overall picture of the cultural representation of youth justice.

This approach has drawn upon scholarship from media studies, as there is a consistent and well-developed tradition of using CDA to analyse various types of texts, including film (Chepinchikj and Thompson, 2016; Stokes, 2021). CDA goes beyond a surface-level analysis, not simply taking the words and images presented in films at face value. Consideration of the implications of the film, the cultural context in which it was created and received, and the cultural response to this is also considered. This is broadly in line with Rose's (2016) approach to film analysis, which draws upon CDA and visual analysis. Whilst this book does not claim to be a visual criminology, it would be remiss not to draw upon visual analysis and acknowledge its use in deconstructing film.

Rose (2016) argues that there are four sites where the meaning of an image is made, and all must be considered in an effective analysis of that image.

These four sites are: the site of production, the image itself, the site of publication/promotion, and the audience's response. This takes a holistic view of a work, considering not only the piece itself, but its creation, audience interaction, and the broader cultural response. This fits well with CDA, which examines texts to understand what discourse is embedded within them, and what the implications of this are within the broader social context (Wodak and Meyer, 2009). Whilst CDA primarily is concerned with language in both spoken and written forms (Locke, 2004), applying this to other forms of media such as film is becoming increasingly common (Asseel, 2020; Bateman, 2017; Gatling et al., 2015). Applying CDA to film within Rose's framework means considering the following factors for each film included in the sample:

- Language: Spoken/written, but also visual language, such as scenery, costuming and staging. The visual language of a film can convey information to an audience by using broader social tropes, signifiers, and stereotypes. For example, wearing a sub-cultural costume tells the audience a lot about a character instantly, impacting the perception of what they say and do.
- Process: Commercial film creation is a large and long process. The works discussed in this book will have been through extensive processes of creation, editing, and responding to notes from producers, financers, editors, and censors. This means that nothing is included in a film unconsciously, and those processes of choice are essential to understanding the ideas being put across. For the purposes of this work this includes consideration of actor and director interviews and comments on the process of creating the film, information about censor requests and responses, and film standards and codes at the time of release. This aspect also allows consideration of the impact of capitalism and late modernity on the film process, as social concerns and priorities impact what can and can't be shown, or what is viewed as "palatable" for a general audience.
- Response: The advertising of the film, the public response, the critical response, and the academic responses all impact the broader influence or perception of films. Those held as "classics" only reached such status through the mediation of viewer responses, impacting the cultural legacy of films, and what is embedded within the social discourse. Within this book the response is considered through reviews by critics, media articles discussing public responses to films, and academic discussion of the films. Whilst this is not a true reflection of public opinion, it is a reflection of the social response on a broad scale, allowing the understanding of what has influenced the discourse about justice-involved children.

Through analysis of these factors for each film considered within the book, a picture can be developed of what discourses are being promoted to audiences

12 A Popular Criminology of Youth Justice

about justice-involved children and youth justice systems, and if this promotion is successful. Locke (2004) argues that creators assume the audience is complicit in understanding the opaque or underlying discourse within their work, partly from understanding of the same social constructions and cultural discourses. However, we will see throughout this book where the discourses within films may have been misinterpreted by audiences, or the broader capitalist response to the film obscures this message, retaining the status quo. The language of the film alone is not enough to capture these aspects, so the CDA must include the process and response aspects to develop a full understanding.

One aspect which will not be considered in detail in this book is the mode and site of consumption. For films, there are two main sites of consumption; cinemas and the home (Buckingham, 2021). The cinema was originally the only place where one could view films and quickly became a staple place of public entertainment (Buckingham, 2021). However, the rise of streaming services has changed the way in which many films are presented, with some companies now forgoing cinema releases in favour of the potentially wider streaming audience. Research has looked at audience responses to streaming (Wayne and Uribe Sandoval, 2021), however, it is not yet clear if this impacts upon how the messages within media are interpreted or responded to. Therefore, in this work we are not necessarily considering the site of consumption itself in detail, instead focusing on the promotion of the film; what is used to draw in audiences and encourage them to watch, and the broader cultural responses to films. Film promotion is not always an accurate reflection of the film itself, often relying on genre conventions to develop audience interest (Finsterwalder et al., 2012). However, film promotion does often distil some of the key messages of a film into simple visual materials. These messages also often draw on existing cultural tropes, to gain an audience's interest. Considering this in relation to the film itself is important to understand the expectations of an audience, and to show differences in presentation. For example, different demographics of justice-involved children are often presented differently in films, and the marketing emphasises this.

CDA's qualitative nature means we must address the question of subjectivity. I do not claim that the analysis and interpretation of the films discussed in this book are objective or unequivocable. However, this does not mean that the analysis is without value. By unpicking the narratives presented within these films even through the lens of one possible interpretation, one facet of the perception of justice-involved children in society is uncovered. By furthering the popular criminology of youth justice and adding to this work, the area will only be strengthened. It is hoped that within each chapter the reasoning for the interpretations given is clear to the reader, and even if they would not have come to the same conclusion, the process is clear and logically sound.

Introduction **13**

The methods used throughout this book are a mix of approaches from criminology and media studies. However, the theoretical underpinning is a purely criminological one. Specifically utilising youth justice perspectives. By combining methodologies and theories from different disciplines, it is hoped that this book promotes interdisciplinary work relating to youth justice and shows the importance of acknowledging the cultural impact of fictional media. Combining a youth justice theoretical standpoint CDA as an approach to analysing films allows the popular criminology of youth justice to develop with a clear foundation.

Structure of This Book

This book has been split into chapters that each focus on a specific issue or area of criminal justice. This is to make it easier to find information relevant to the reader's interests, and to allow in-depth consideration of how these subjects are addressed in film. Some topics run through all the chapters, such as race and ethnicity, class, and gender, but may have particular prominence in specific chapters. For example, race is discussed in almost every chapter, but Chapter 5 in particular gives a detailed analysis of the representation of minority ethnicity children and Chapter 4 has a more explicit focus on representations of girls' criminal behaviours.

Chapter 2 looks at the birth of problem youth, starting with the 1950s "juvenile delinquency" films that introduced to a mass audience many of the tropes and stereotypes about justice-involved children that remain today. This chapter considers *Rebel Without A Cause* (1955) in detail, and how James Dean has become the icon of cool, angst-ridden youth. Rebel is the most well-known of these early problem youth films, but it is by no means alone. This chapter also considers *Blackboard Jungle* (1955) and *The 400 Blows* (1959) amongst others to show the embedding into the social consciousness the idea that children can change from innocent well-behaved children into monstrous teenagers. These problem youth films cemented into society the pre-existing fear of youth using media iconography, setting in motion the tropes, narratives and stereotypes which are still present in films today, and this chapter analyses these messages to understand the foundations of youth crime on film.

Chapter 3 focuses on representations of criminal justice processes relating to children, namely policing and imprisonment. "Cop films" are their own distinct genre and one of the most consistently popular in cinema. We love to see the bad guys get caught, and justice be served. However, this narrative doesn't quite fit when the bad guys are children. This means that films about policing youth take a slightly different angle, often showing police and other authority figures as saviours. *21 Jump Street's* (2012) depiction of police interactions with children is a key focus of this chapter, contrasting the

14 A Popular Criminology of Youth Justice

on-screen depiction with the realities of the criminalisation of children. This chapter also considers how punishment is portrayed on-screen, ranging from classic dramatic depictions such as *Scum* (1979) to more genre-focused films such as *Holes* (2003). These films are considered in relation to what messages are being presented about how youth crime should be responded to and the role of punitive populism in the public sphere.

Chapter 4 focuses on how gender impacts upon media's presentation of crime. Looking at key examples of bad girl films such as *Heathers* (1988), *Jawbreaker* (1999) and *Thirteen* (2003), this chapter breaks down the intersection of class, violence, and the performance of femininity. Simultaneously mocking and maintaining negative stereotypes about girls' interactions and relationships, these films create a visual language for girls' criminality that equates style with success and implies that girls can avoid criminal justice consequences.

Chapter 5 discusses how social realism has been used in films depicting justice-involved children in cities, and how the development of the urban film perpetuates stereotypes of Black criminality. By considering British urban films of the 2000s, this chapter focuses on ethnicity and how this intersects with both class and the perception of cities as dangerous places. Considering *Bullet Boy* (2004), *Kidulthood* (2006), and *Blue Story* (2020) in the context of risk-based frameworks allows a clear view of the changing construction of justice-involved children, and youth justice's response to them.

Being "based on a true story" is a frequent feature of cinema, and Chapter 6 looks at films where real cases have informed or acted as the inspiration for fictional(ised) films. Considering how these films blur the lines between truth and entertainment and how the depiction of justice-involved children changes when there are real people at the centre of the story gives an important position on how we view youth crime in society. This chapter looks in depth at films that address real events or concerns regarding justice-involved children. *The Bling Ring* (2013), *Badlands* (1972), and *County Lines* (2019) are all discussed in detail, to analyse how some of the discourses about youth crime are presented and how this can develop sympathy in audiences for justice-involved children, but the film screen's treatment of these cases as exceptional may not impact broader cultural ideas about youth justice.

Chapter 7 returns to the processes of youth justice, focusing on courtrooms and the processes of punishment. Legal dramas are a well-developed genre (Elkins, 2006) and a subset of these focus on justice-involved children. This chapter considers how "justice" is depicted on film and what implications this has for public opinion, policy, and practice. The majority of the public will not have the opportunity to enter a courtroom and so film is one of the main ways in which the public gains information about this aspect of criminal justice. This chapter discusses the embedding of cultural narratives of justice in films such as *12 Angry Men* (1957), and how this has developed

Introduction **15**

over time via *The Whole Truth* (2016), *Primal Fear* (1996), and *The Client* (1994). This discussion contrasts with the ideas presented in Chapter 2, as courtroom films build upon the innocent-dangerous dichotomy creating an innocent-dangerous dyad. This builds on stereotypes of justice-involved children causing further harm.

Popular criminology links criminological theory with the ideas presented in film, and Chapter 8 looks at how more recent developments in youth justice theory have made their way into the cultural discourse. This can be seen in *The Young Offenders* (2016) and *Scrapper* (2023), which present a realistic but positive portrayal of justice-involved children. These films are illustrative of the move towards Child First (Case and Hazel, 2023; Drakeford, 2009) youth justice, which emphasises that the children represented in youth crime films are in fact children, and the complexity of their lives has had a profound impact upon their justice-involvement. Developing the ideas in the previous chapter, here we consider how these Child First films differ from their forebears. Justice-involved children are depicted without the narrative of hopelessness from previous films, policing and courts are not valorised or demonised, but shown in a nuanced way, and the children themselves are shown as being childlike. This presentation shows the impact of change due to the theoretical developments, and how the cultural conversation regarding justice-involved children has developed from the stereotyped views of the 1950s. This also shows the development of film, moving away from the quasi-propaganda of problem youth films, allowing a more nuanced depiction of children.

Finally, Chapter 9 brings together the ideas and discussions that have run throughout the whole book. Considering how justice-involved children are depicted and who they are depicted as being, how the processes of justice are depicted (policing and courts), how this relates to youth justice in practice, and what this means for the treatment of children in society, this chapter comes back to our overall questions about youth justice on film. Whilst popular media's aim is to entertain, we cannot overlook the ways in which it informs, constructs, and maintains social ideals which have real-world impacts upon how our social and criminal justice systems are run. And so, we consider, can popular media create justice?

A Note on Language

Youth justice is a key area of criminology, public policy, politics, and practice. As such a wide range of terminologies have been developed to refer to the systems, behaviours, and children within and around youth justice. Within this work the terms "young offender", "juvenile delinquent", "deviant", "criminal" will generally not be used, with the term "justice-involved child" being used instead. The reason for this choice is due to various research showing the harm

16 A Popular Criminology of Youth Justice

caused by stigmatising terminology that attributes criminal behaviours as being inherent within a person, or part of their identity (Creaney, 2012; Fraser and Atkinson, 2014; Wiley et al., 2013). The term justice-involved child instead acknowledges that involvement with justice is not necessarily permanent, and that "justice" itself is a socially constructed system to respond to particular behaviours that have been deemed unacceptable or undesirable. There are strong reasons to use the term "child" rather than "young person" (Haines and Case, 2017), particularly to emphasise vulnerability and lack of social capital, and so this is used throughout this book. All the chapters focus on those under the age of 18, which generally conforms to internationally recognised definitions of "childhood" (United Nations, 1989). Whilst during the teenage years, children develop a greater sense of agency and often receive increased responsibility or rights, meaning "child" may not always feel appropriate to that individual, it is important that institutions recognise their continued status as children and use the appropriate terminology.

Films discussed in this book will have the release date included with the first mention in each chapter. A full list of all the films mentioned is included at the end of each chapter.

Film List

12 Angry Men (1957)
21 Jump Street (2012)
Badlands (1972)
Blackboard Jungle (1955)
Blue Story (2020)
Bullet Boy (2004)
County Lines (2019)
Heathers (1988)
Holes (2003)
Jawbreaker (1999)
Kidulthood (2006)
Primal Fear (1996)
Rebel Without A Cause (1955)
Scrapper (2023)
Scum (1979)
The 400 Blows (1959)
The Bling Ring (2013)
The Client (1994)
The Whole Truth (2016)
The Young Offenders (2016)
The Young Savages (1961)
Thirteen (2003)

Introduction **17**

References   •

Akrivos D and Antoniou AK (2019) Conclusion: Popular criminology revisited. In: Akrivos D and Antoniou AK (eds) *Crime, Deviance and Popular Culture*. Palgrave Studies in Crime, Media and Culture. Cham: Springer International Publishing, pp. 335–338. Available at: https://link.springer.com/10.1007/978-3-030-04912-6_14 (accessed 4 January 2023).

Altheide DL (2009) Moral panic: From sociological concept to public discourse. *Crime, Media, Culture* 5(1): 79–99. SAGE Publications.

Asseel D (2020) *Seeing the unseen. Euphemism in animated films: a multimodal and critical discourse analysis*. PhD. Lancaster University. Available at: https://doi.org/10.17635/lancaster/thesis/1112 (accessed 8 February 2023).

Atherton M (2013) Teaching through film: Utilizing popular criminology in the classroom. *Journal on Excellence in College Teaching* 24(2): 77–99.

Baldry E, Briggs DB, Goldson B, et al. (2018) 'Cruel and unusual punishment': An inter-jurisdictional study of the criminalisation of young people with complex support needs. *Journal of Youth Studies* 21(5): 636–652. Routledge.

Bateman JA (2017) Critical discourse analysis and film. In: John Flowerdew and John E. Richardson (eds) *The Routledge Handbook of Critical Discourse Studies*. Oxon: Routledge, pp. 596–608.

Blackman S (2005) Youth subcultural theory: A critical engagement with the concept, its origins and politics, from the Chicago school to postmodernism. *Journal of Youth Studies* 8(1): 1–20. Taylor & Francis Group.

Boldison L (2006) *'Hoodies': A New Moral Panic?: An Examination of Media Representations of Crime, Youth Subcultures, Moral Panics and the Application of the Moral Panic Theory to Media Reporting of 'Hoodies' in Britain's National Newspapers*. Leicester: University of Leicester.

Briggs DB (2013) Conceptualising risk and need: The rise of actuarialism and the death of welfare? Practitioner assessment and intervention in the youth offending service. *Youth Justice* 13(1): 17–30. SAGE PublicationsSage UK: London, England.

Brooks-Wilson S (2020) Rethinking youth justice journeys: Complex needs, impeded capabilities and criminalisation. *Youth Justice* 20(3): 309–327.

Bruzzi S (2016) Making a genre: The case of the contemporary true crime documentary. *Law and Humanities* 10(2): 249–280.

Buckingham D (ed.) (1993) *Reading Audiences: Young People and the Media*. Manchester; New York: New York, NY, USA: Manchester University Press; Distributed exclusively in the USA and Canada by St. Martin's Press.

Buckingham D (2021) *Youth on Screen: Representing Young People in Film and Television*. Cambridge; Medford: Polity.

Cameron D (2011) UK riots: David Cameron's statement in full. Available at: http://www.telegraph.co.uk/news/uknews/crime/8693134/UK-riots-David-Camerons-statement-in-full.html (accessed 22 November 2012).

Case S (2018) *Youth Justice: A Critical Introduction*. Abingdon, Oxon; New York, NY: Routledge.

Case S and Hazel N (eds) (2023) *Child First: Developing a New Youth Justice System*. Cham: Palgrave Macmillan.

Chepinchikj N and Thompson C (2016) Analysing cinematic discourse using conversation analysis. *Discourse, Context & Media* 14: 40–53.

18 A Popular Criminology of Youth Justice

Cohen AK (1965) The sociology of the Deviant Act: Anomie theory and beyond. *American Sociological Review* 30(1): 5–14. [American Sociological Association, Sage Publications, Inc.].

Cohen AK and Short JF (1958) Research in delinquent subcultures. *Journal of Social Issues* 14(3): 20–37.

Cohen S (2011) Whose side were we on? The undeclared politics of moral panic theory. *Crime, Media, Culture* 7(3): 237–243. SAGE Publications.

Creaney S (2012) Targeting, labelling and stigma: Challenging the criminalisation of children and young people. *Criminal Justice Matters* 89(1): 16–17.

Deflem M (2010) Introduction: The criminology of popular culture. In Deflem M (ed) *Popular Culture, Crime and Social Control (Sociology of Crime, Law and Deviance, Vol. 14)*. Leeds: Emerald Group Publishing Limited, pp. ix–xi. https://doi.org/10.1108/S1521-6136(2010)0000014003.

Denscombe M (2010) *The Good Research Guide*. Berkshire: Open University Press.

Doherty TP (2002) *Teenagers and Teenpics: The Juvenilization of American Movies in the 1950s*. Rev. and expanded ed. Philadelphia: Temple University Press.

Donoghue J (2011) Anti-social behaviour orders: A culture of control? *British Journal of Criminology* 51(6): 1063–1065.

Dowler K, Fleming T and Muzzatti SL (2006) *Constructing crime: Media, crime, and popular culture. Canadian Journal of Criminology and Criminal Justice* 48(6): 837–850.

Drakeford M (2009) Children first, offenders second: Youth justice in a devolved Wales. *Criminal Justice Matters* 78(1): 8–9.

Elkins JR (2006) Popular culture, legal films, and legal film critics. *Loyola of Los Angeles Law Review* 40: 745.

Evans K (2005) Young people in the media: A dangerous and anti-social obsession. *Criminal Justice Matters* 59(1): 14–15. Taylor & Francis Group.

Ferrell J, Hayward K and Young J (2008) *Cultural Criminology: An Investigation*. Los Angeles; London: SAGE.

Finsterwalder J, Kuppelwieser VG and de Villiers M (2012) The effects of film trailers on shaping consumer expectations in the entertainment industry—A qualitative analysis. *Journal of Retailing and Consumer Services* 19(6): 589–595.

Fraser A and Atkinson C (2014) Making up gangs: Looping, labelling and the new politics of intelligence-led policing. *Youth Justice* 14(2): 154–170. SAGE Publications Inc.

Gatling M, Mills J and Lindsay D (2015) Representations of middle age in comedy film: A critical discourse analysis. *The Qualitative Report*. Epub ahead of print 3 December 2015. https://doi.org/10.46743/2160-3715/2014.1256

Goldson B (2000) Children in need or young offenders? *Child & Family Social Work* 5(3): 255–265.

Goode E and Ben-Yehuda N (1994) *Moral Panics: The Social Construction of Deviance*. Oxford: Blackwell Publishing Ltd. Available at: https://books.google.co.uk/books?hl=en&lr=&id=SbY2Mksi1kcC&oi=fnd&pg=PR7&dq=moral+panics+the+social+construction+of+deviance&ots=KK05FQ_jiU&sig=1mPhnoXnXBcYQb9kgdmlfEpgbqE (accessed 2 February 2017).

Gray P (2007) Youth justice, social exclusion and the demise of social justice. *The Howard Journal of Criminal Justice* 46(4): 401–416.

Green DA (2008) *When Children Kill Children: Penal Populism and Political Culture.* Oxford: OUP. Available at: https://books.google.com/books?id=QIvp2Jg7yRkC& pgis=1 (accessed 13 November 2015).

Haines K and Case S (2017) Putting children first in the youth justice system. In: *Positive Youth Justice*. Bristol: Policy Press, pp. 125–176.

Hall S and Jefferson T (eds) (2006) *Resistance through Rituals: Youth Subcultures in Post-War Britain*. 2nd ed., Rev. and expanded ed. London; New York: Routledge.

Hammersley R, Reid M and Minkes J (2006) Treatment for substance use problems among young offenders: Difficulties and dilemmas for implementation and evaluation in the UK. *Educational and Child Psychology* 23(2): 41–53.

Hayward K (2009) Visual criminology: Cultural criminology-style: Keith Hayward makes the case for 'visual criminology'. *Criminal Justice Matters* 78(1): 12–14.

Hayward K (2016) Cultural criminology: Script rewrites. *Theoretical Criminology* 20(3): 297–321.

Hayward K and Young J (2004) Cultural criminology: Some notes on the script. *Theoretical Criminology* 8(3): 259–273.

Hodkinson P (2016) Youth cultures and the rest of life: Subcultures, post-subcultures and beyond. *Journal of Youth Studies* 19(5): 629–645. Routledge.

Hollingworth S (2015) Performances of social class, race and gender through youth subculture: Putting structure back in to youth subcultural studies. *Journal of Youth Studies* 18(10): 1237–1256.

Howe TR, Aberson CL, Friedman HS, et al. (2015) Three decades later: The life experiences and mid-life functioning of 1980s heavy metal groupies, musicians, and fans. *Self and Identity* 14(5): 602–626. Psychology Press Ltd.

Jennings WG, Piquero AR and Reingle JM (2012) On the overlap between victimization and offending: A review of the literature. *Aggression and Violent Behavior* 17(1): 16–26.

Jewkes Y (2015) *Media and Crime*. London: SAGE.

Jupp E, Gaitskell J, Escrig J, et al. (2011) *Unbalanced Negative Media Portrayal of Youth*. Leicester: National Youth Agency.

King N (2013) Calling Dirty Harry a liar: A critique of displacement theories of popular criminology. *New Review of Film & Television Studies* 11(2): 171–190. Routledge.

Kohm SA and Greenhill P (2011) Pedophile crime films as popular criminology: A problem of justice? *Theoretical Criminology* 15(2): 195–215.

Kort-Butler LA (2012) Rotten, Vile, and Depraved! Depictions of criminality in superhero cartoons. *Deviant Behavior* 33(7): 566–581. Taylor & Francis Group.

Kort-Butler LA (2013) Justice League?: Depictions of justice in children's superhero cartoons. *Criminal Justice Review* 38(1): 50–69. SAGE PublicationsSage CA: Los Angeles, CA.

Kort-Butler LA and Hartshorn KJS (2011) Watching the detectives: Crime programming, fear of crime, and attitudes about the criminal justice system. *The Sociological Quarterly* 52(1): 36–55. Blackwell Publishing Inc.

Locke T (2004) *Critical Discourse Analysis*. Continuum Research Methods Series. London; New York: Continuum.

MacDonald R and Shildrick T (2007) Street corner society: Leisure careers, youth (sub)culture and social exclusion. *Leisure Studies* 26(3): 339–355. Routledge.

Mejias S and Banaji S (2019) Backed into a corner: Challenging media and policy representations of youth citizenship in the UK. *Information, Communication & Society* 22(12): 1714–1732. Routledge.

Muncie J (2008) The `punitive turn' in Juvenile justice: Cultures of control and rights compliance in Western Europe and the USA. *Youth Justice* 8(2): 107–121.

Peay J (1998) The power of the popular. *The BSC Online Journal* 1: 1–11. The British Criminology Conferences: Selected Proceedings.

Plato (380AD, 2008) *The Republic*.Translated by Waterfield R Oxford: Oxford University Press.

Presdee M (2000) *Cultural Criminology and the Carnival of Crime*. London; New York: Routledge.

Rafter N (2007) Crime, film and criminology: Recent sex-crime movies. *Theoretical Criminology* 11(3): 403–420. SAGE Publications Ltd.

Rafter NH and Brown M (2011) *Criminology Goes to the Movies: Crime Theory and Popular Culture*. New York: New York University.

Rawlings P (1998) Crime Writers: Non-Fiction Crime Books. *The BSC Online Journal* 1: 1–25. The British Criminology Conferences: Selected Proceedings. Volume 1: Emerging Themes in Criminology.

Roche J, Tucker S, Thomson R, et al. (eds) (2004) *Youth in Society: Contemporary Theory, Policy and Practice*. 2nd ed. London; Thousand Oaks, Calif: SAGE.

Rose G (2016) *Visual Methodologies: An Introduction to Researching with Visual Materials*. 4th ed. London: SAGE Publications Ltd.

Ruggeri A (2017) People have always whinged about young adults. Here's proof. Available at: https://www.bbc.com/worklife/article/20171003-proof-that-people-have-always-complained-about-young-adults (accessed 8 February 2023).

Selfhout MHW, Delsing MJMH, Ter Bogt TFM, et al. (2008) Heavy metal and hip-hop style preferences and externalizing problem behavior: A two-wave longitudinal study. *Youth and Society* 39(4): 435–452.

Shildrick T and MacDonald R (2006) In defence of subculture: Young people, leisure and social divisions. *Journal of Youth Studies* 9(2): 125–140. Taylor & Francis Group.

Silva JR (2019) Mass shooting films: Myths, academic knowledge, and popular criminology. *Victims & Offenders* 14(2): 239–264.

Stokes J (2021) *How to Do Media and Cultural Studies*. 3rd ed. Thousand Oaks: SAGE Publishing.

Surette R (2015) Thought bite: A case study of the social construction of a crime and justice concept. *Crime, Media, Culture* 11(2): 105–135. SAGE Publications.

United Nations (1989) Convention on the Rights of the Child. Available at: https://www.ohchr.org/en/professionalinterest/pages/crc.aspx (accessed 5 August 2020).

Wayne M, Henderson L, Murray C, et al. (2008) Television news and the symbolic criminalisation of young people. *Journalism Studies* 9(1): 75–90. Taylor & Francis Group.

Wayne ML and Uribe Sandoval AC (2021) Netflix original series, global audiences and discourses of streaming success. *Critical Studies in Television*: 17496020211037259: 1–20. SAGE Publications.

Wiley SA and Esbensen FA (2016) The effect of police contact: Does official intervention result in deviance amplification? *Crime and Delinquency* 62(3): 283–307. SAGE Publications Inc.

Wiley SA, Slocum LA and Esbensen FA (2013) The unintended consequences of being stopped or arrested: An exploration of the labeling mechanisms through which police contact leads to subsequent delinquency. *Criminology* 51(4): 927–966.

Wodak R and Meyer M (eds) (2009) *Methods of Critical Discourse Analysis*. 2nd ed. Introducing qualitative methods. London; Thousand Oaks [Calif.]: SAGE.

Yardley E, Kelly E and Robinson-Edwards S (2019) Forever trapped in the imaginary of late capitalism? The serialized true crime podcast as a wake-up call in times of criminological slumber. *Crime, Media, Culture: An International Journal* 15(3): 503–521. SAGE Publications Ltd.

Yardley E, Wilson D and Kennedy M (2017) "TO ME ITS [SIC] REAL LIFE": Secondary victims of homicide in newer media. *Victims & Offenders* 12(3): 467–496. Routledge.

2

"YOU WANNA START A RUMBLE?"

The Birth of Problem Youth

As discussed in Chapter 1, children have essentially always been the subject of societal ire. This largely stems from the very visible challenge to the status quo that children represent. However, this is framed not as younger generations having different priorities or views but as being worse than their forebears. Either through declining morals, increased delinquent behaviour, or lack of drive, children are often societally characterised by adults as being less able, less hardworking, and overall less than the adults around them. These concerns are often a fundamental aspect of the innocent-dangerous dichotomy (Case, 2018), particularly in relation to which children are placed in each category. The divide between innocent and dangerous has been found consistently across time (Goldson, 2020) and is still a main feature of reporting about children today (Mejias and Banaji, 2019). However, the classification of innocent or dangerous is not based solely on behaviour. Class, gender, and race/ethnicity all play a role in this, as do the cultural concerns of the time. Of children displaying the same undesirable behaviours, girls are more likely to be considered as "innocent victims" (unless they are lower class), minority ethnicity children are more likely to be considered as "dangerous", and those with greater class status are more likely to be considered as "innocent" (Case, 2016). The way in which these factors intersect often means that there is a proto-underclass of children who will always be considered as dangerous, regardless of what they do or what happens to them due to factors out of their control.

The way in which "dangerous youth" is constructed stems from social, cultural, political, and historical factors. However, there is a clear link between these ideas and the problem youth films of the 1950s. Largely coming from America, these films capitalised upon the pre-existing ideas of

DOI: 10.4324/9781003403159-2

"You Wanna Start a Rumble?" **23**

dangerous youth in conjunction with the explosion of youth culture's visibility following social changes after World War II (Buckingham, 2021). Following World War II children's lives were different across large sections of the world. With many countries reducing or removing requirements for national service and increasing social support programmes (Osgerby, 2020) this meant that children had greater choice in how to use their time. Previously, there was a much clearer progression between childhood and adulthood, with little transitional space between the two. Leaving education meant entering the workforce and creating and/or providing for a family. Taking on the responsibilities of adulthood meant leaving behind childhood, and with it any delinquent behaviours, lest you become a criminal. Social recognition of this new liminal age saw the term "teenager" becoming common parlance (Buckingham, 2021; Osgerby, 2020). The comparative freedom given to teenagers and young adults after the war meant that they had more disposable income, more free time, and more opportunities socially, educationally, and professionally. This allowed teenagers to develop their personal interests more openly, and spaces started to cater to this market, with soda shops playing popular rock "n" roll music, drive-ins showing youth-oriented films, and more cinema catering to the "youth market" (Buckingham, 2021). Teenagers had not only become socially prominent, but they had become a demographic to be capitalised upon.

Cultural media such as film is always in conversation with the culture from which it emerges (Bateman, 2017), and during the 1950s this meant film responding to both teenager's desire to see films that represented their experience and the concerns of the adults around them about the perceived declining standards of children. The result of this was the problem youth film (also referred to as juvenile delinquency or JD films). These films depicted the trials and tribulations of growing up, but whilst there might be some similarities with the coming-of-age film we know today, problem youth films focused on children who were on the verge of failing to become successful adults, often engaging in crime and delinquency. The most culturally enduring of these films is *Rebel Without A Cause* (1955), but there were a slew of others both before and after this. *Rebel* and *The Wild One's* (1953) popularity was the instigator for several copycat films all of which focused on children in the transition to adulthood and the various fights, scrapes, and problems they faced. *The Bad Seed* (1959), *The Violent Years* (1956), *I Was a Teenage Werewolf* (1957), *The Delicate Delinquent* (1957), and *The Cry Baby Killer* (1958) all capitalised on the social concerns about juvenile delinquency and the rise of youth culture to gain audiences with both adults and teens (Buckingham, 2021). These films established and embedded the tropes of problem youth into society.

The 1950s problem youth film is not a distinct genre, but there are a number of hallmarks of this type of film. Gangs, flick knives, drag racing,

24 A Popular Criminology of Youth Justice

ineffectual parents, kindly policemen, and existential angst are common tropes of problem youth films (Doherty, 2002). Often set in schools; particularly reform schools; characters will break free of the constraints of conformity and hang out in streets, parks, or abandoned buildings to listen to music, dance, drink, and have fun. There may be drag racing for those who have cars, there will certainly be fights with both peers and authority figures. Parents and teachers will despair of the children who cannot be controlled, whilst those children will despair of the adults who do not understand them. The main character (often a 16–18-year-old boy) will have a "dark night of the soul" and regret their harmful actions, vowing by the end of the film to make things right by settling down, doing what's right and conforming to what is expected of them. The settings for these films are primarily inner cities, which are graffiti-covered, litter-strewn, and filled with low-quality housing where children do not have space for themselves. The "gang" characters often wear leather jackets and biker boots, all the young characters listen to rock "n" roll, dancing is a favoured activity, and relationships with parents, teachers and police are strained. These films in general have created the model for how we view teenagerhood, and many of these tropes have persisted both within and outside film.

The problem youth film is a major source of the culturally enduring stereotypes and ideas about justice-involved children, and many subsequent narratives have been based on the foundations laid by these films. To consider how youth crime, justice, and justice-involved children are considered in films from any subsequent era, it is essential to acknowledge the background context of the problem youth film. The reason these films have had such a long-standing impact is partially due to the poignancy and enjoyability of the stories they tell, partially due to their quality in acting, direction and staging, and partially due to the confluence of capitalism, consumerism, and mass culture during the time of their release.

The 1950s saw both an economic and technological boom which led to greater spending, particularly on electronics and appliances such as labour-saving devices within the home, such as vacuum cleaners, refrigerators, and electric hairdryers. Implicitly, this cemented within society the idea that the way to a better life is through consumption. This also gave people (particularly women) more free time to engage in mass culture, through activities like trips to the cinema (Driscoll, 2011). This period of broad social changes (in America and Europe particularly) coincided with political change, we see moves towards capitalist positions cemented during this period alongside the idea that prosperity is financial in nature (Driscoll, 2011). This means that the perceived path to adulthood shifted; previously having a family and children was seen as "success", whereas post-war there is a more explicit focus on *providing* for your family and comparison to others. For children and teenagers, this meant that there was a greater expectation of academic success to support entry into well-paying jobs and progression once a job was achieved. This type of social control was always present within society, however, during the post-war period, "success" had a visible element, for example being able to afford new technology, fashionable clothes, or cars. For children, this meant that the freedoms and choice they were now given, came with the price of social conformity. For those who resisted or wanted to retain more of the liminal space of the "teenager", there were accusations of delinquency and familial concern, ideas which were popularised through now the more accessible commodity of problem youth films.

Problem youth films in the 1950s were a hit with audiences and production companies (Doherty, 2002). For adult audiences, these films highlighted the spectacle that they read about in the news and the messages of these films often tried to explain why problem behaviour occurs and provide ways to respond to it (Buckingham, 2021). For adult audiences this almost filled the same niche as horror films, providing a safe environment in which to engage with and understand their fears. Producers capitalised upon this, and these films began to more heavily feature violence, particularly in the form of knife fights and drag racing, leading to battles with censors (Biltereyst, 2007; Simmons, 2008). For young audiences, these films were one of the first occasions they had seen their lives (or something resembling them) depicted in film, and so were an immediate point of interest. Youth-oriented films previously have been more wholesome and family-appropriate (Doherty, 2002), the problem youth film did not shy away from the tumultuous experience of growing up and thus won the attention of children (Buckingham, 2021). Simmons (1995) highlights the sense of ownership that children felt over these films at the time.

> In the era of Father Knows Best, Rebel was the first motion picture to express our world rather than theirs. More than any other, it captured our youthful torment, our restless natures, our craving for acceptance
> *(Simmons, 1995: 63)*

It also helped that problem youth films also featured rising Hollywood stars, rock "n" roll soundtracks, and new fashions. All of which piqued the interest of children and made cinemas and drive-ins an enjoyable place to spend their free time. For producers, having two audience demographics made problem youth films profitable, and they became in essence a subgenre. Whilst the boom of these films was in the 1950s, with many classics of the genre being released in this time, we see the problem youth film lasting well beyond this period. The 1960s saw a continuation of the tropes and conventions already established, the 1970s started to subvert some of these within the context of counter culture (see Chapter 2), the 1980s saw a return to the narratives of violence, along with more diversity, including girls in these stories

26 A Popular Criminology of Youth Justice

(see Chapter 4). The 1990s was almost a second boom of the problem youth film, with moralising concerns about the downfall of society and the need for strong institutions, and the 2000s capitalised on the pessimism of the seemingly unchanging nature of the way in which justice-involved children are considered within society (see Chapter 5). Whilst there are differences in storytelling, characterisation, and narrative (as will be discussed in future chapters), all these narratives and tropes can be traced back to the problem youth films of the 1950s. This chapter focuses on "classics" of the genre which have become highly influential in both film and broader society; *Rebel Without A Cause* (1955), *Blackboard Jungle* (1955), and *The Young Savages* (1961). We will also consider the more explicitly fantastical view of the problem teen as depicted in *I Was a Teenage Werewolf* (1957), and the social realism of *The 400 Blows* (1959).

Problem Youth Films as Spectacle

Problem youth films focused on the spectacular aspects of youth crime and "juvenile delinquency". Media in general has been noted for this, from gangster films to news reports (Jewkes, 2015). Presdee (2000) refers to this as the "carnival of crime", questioning how this impacts upon the boundaries between the popular imagination of criminality and the actual responses to criminal behaviour. If media such as fictional film so frequently presents violence and serious crime as a spectacle to be enjoyed, what does this imply for audiences? Presdee posits that this may make audiences complicit in criminalisation by enforcing the message that crime is ok to consume as entertainment, but not engage in. However, for it to be consumed as entertainment it is required for *someone* to engage in crime, furthering the notion of an underclass who are not accepted by society but are exploited for their entertainment and the maintenance of the status quo (Presdee, 2000).

Problem youth films capitalised on this, with some scholars classing these films as "exploitation pictures" (Doherty, 2002). *Reefer Madness* (1936) is a problem youth film that has achieved cult status due to its camp presentation of drug use and is often the standout example of the "teensploitation" genre. However, problem youth films of the 1950s were generally more nuanced in their depiction of children's lives, with many incorporating then-current psychological, sociological and criminological theories into their overall messaging about the explanations for criminal behaviours. *Rebel Without A Cause* (1955) is potentially the most well-known of the problem youth films, having gained an enduring cultural legacy. In this film Jim Stark (James Dean) faces a crisis of identity as he stands on the cusp of adulthood. Jim is trying to become his own person and understand how he wants to live his life. He is dissatisfied with the role models around him; his father is emasculated and indecisive, his teachers are indifferent and passionless, and Inspector Fremick

(Edward Platt) whilst kind, is not realistic about what it is like to be a teenager. Jim is heavily focused on how others perceive him, wanting to be seen as a "real man" and not a "chicken". *Rebel* was wildly popular upon release, with Dean's portrayal being a key selling point. Another key selling point was the portrayal of violence in the film. The knife fight and "chickee run" are key features of the marketing for the film as seen in the posters, lobby cards, and trailers (Baker, 2005).

The knife fight in *Rebel* is one of the most remembered scenes, particularly its location at Griffith Park Observatory. This location has become a shorthand within film since *Rebel*, with this being the place where characters experience turning points in their lives or make decisions about their futures whilst gazing at the LA skyline (Slocum, 2005). *Rebel's* chickee run inspired subsequent films to include drag racing as a way of depicting both the excitement and danger of being a teen (Baker, 2005). Within *Rebel* Jim readily agrees to participate in the chickee run, where he and classmate/rival Buzz (Corey Allen) both drive at high speed towards a cliff, to see who will "chicken out" first. The other characters are all excited by this, coming to watch and Buzz's girlfriend Judy (Natalie Wood) is visibly thrilled to be calling the start of the race. The acceptance and excitement about the run by all the teen characters frame this type of activity as commonplace, implying that children are careless with their lives and will gamble them for fun. The only worried character is Plato (Sam Mineo), a bullied outsider who sees Jim as a friend. Buzz does not survive the chickee run, a strap of his biker jacket having been caught on the door handle of the car meaning he could not jump out and escape the fall over the cliff. This is a minor detail, but that the trappings of subculture (a biker jacket) contribute to Buzz's death is indicative of the implicit messaging within *Rebel*, that deviance, delinquency, and non-conformity is akin to throwing your life away.

Many problem youth films feature a transformative element, as characters progress from innocent children to dangerous teens. This transformation is one of the key sources of spectacle in these films. Nowhere is this more explicit than *I Was A Teenage Werewolf* (1957). The main character, Tony (Michael Landon), is an authority-avoidant teenager who attends school, has a group of friends, a girlfriend, and a loving father. However, Tony hates being told what to do, and wants to make choices on his own terms. This is a problem for the adults around him, who refer Tony for psychiatric "adjustment", which turns out to be experimental treatment to "transform him and unleash the primitive instincts that lie within". These primitive instincts are that of a wolf, and Tony transforms into a werewolf who violently attacks his peers and is uncontrollable. This is rather heavy-handed symbolism but shows how teens were viewed as animalistic and entirely unrelated to children or adults. Within *I Was A Teenage Werewolf* there is a lot of discussion about the process of "adjustment" which is the aim of Tony's

28 A Popular Criminology of Youth Justice

treatment, and this makes clear that the aim of this is to make him controllable and conforming. Tony has always achieved high grades, but his "deportment" is the concern of his teachers, and his college application is framed as being dependent not upon his academic performance or ability, but on his behaviour. The police in trying to find the cause of Tony's transformation speak to his father, who says that he never had behavioural problems with Tony, because he knew how to ask Tony to do things in "the right way" so that he obeyed, which in essence was explaining why something had to be done and asking politely, rather than assuming compliance as a given.

The transformation in *Teenage Werewolf* is played as horrifying, using Phillip Scheer's makeup effects to showcase the grotesque nature of Tony's inner "savage beast". Whilst this is a literal transformation, the idea that becoming a teenager involves a transformation into a monster of some description has become embedded into cultural ideas about growing up. Parents in particular were concerned that their innocent children would transform into dangerous offenders, and that this would be permanent and irreversible. Following *Teenage Werewolf* there were a slew of similar films such as *I Was A Teenage Frankenstein* (1957) and was a direct influence for *An American Werewolf in London* (1981), *Teen Wolf* (1985) and *Ginger Snaps* (2000). The idea that the teen years are troubled and troubling has become a fundamental aspect of their construction, and with it the idea that justice-involved children are a danger to be controlled and contained.

The idea of transformation into the "dangerous offender" comes with the question of if this transformation is permanent. The werewolf trope specifically highlights the potentially temporary nature the undesirable or negative behaviours, only happening on three days each month. Many problem youth films showcase transformation even if this is not into an overt or supernatural monster; Mrs Stark in *Rebel Without A Cause* cries asking what happened to her son, when did he change into this rebellious teen. However, problem youth films showed two outcomes of transformation: conformity or death. The stark contrast between the two outcomes is due to the Hays Code and the requirements of film censors (Bittereyst, 2007; Simmons, 1995, 2008). During the 1950s it was unacceptable for films to portray criminals "getting away with it", alongside a slew of other requirements for depicting romance, sexuality, drinking and so on (Simmons, 2008). Censors were particularly vigilant regarding teen films and depictions of teenagers, fearing the influence they may have on children more broadly (Bittereyst, 2007). For American films, the Cold War also had an impact upon how stories could be told, as film exports were viewed as a method of promoting American culture, and how films would reflect the strength of America was a key consideration (Bittereyst, 2007). For *Blackboard Jungle* in particular, due to its more explicit depiction of delinquency, this led to a fierce debate about where and if the film should be shown (Golub, 2015).

"You Wanna Start a Rumble?" **29**

Censors required transformed teens to face consequences by the end of the film, to emphasise to audiences that crime doesn't pay and that state institutions have the required strength to respond to hooligans, ruffians, and teen wolves. The transformed teen faces one of two paths: conforming to the expectations of society and becoming an adult or death at the hands of law enforcement, rival gangs, or the self. These two paths brought the subtext of the problem youth film to the forefront, deviance and criminal-justice involvement can be a phase on the way to adulthood, put away when becoming an adult, however, for those who do not choose to do so, their lives will be short, painful and on the outside of society. Criminals and non-conformists don't get happy endings. Censors insisted upon these endings for characters, the gun carrying, puppy drowning Plato (Sam Mineo) could not survive *Rebel Without A Cause* due to his queerness, criminality, and to act as the catalyst for Jim's reformation (Slocum, 2005). In one version of the script, Jim was shot alongside Plato by police during the climax of the film (Baer, 1999), however, this would have removed the chance of redemption for all of the characters and so was changed, leading to Jim's acquiescence to the "traditional" life path set out by society. Artie West (Vic Morrow) in *Blackboard Jungle* doesn't die at the end but is thoroughly chastised by his now patriotic and conforming classmates, and runs away from the school, with the implication being that he will not return. Now confirmed to a life of crime it is implied that Artie will not be successful, happy, or long-lived. Tony in *I Was a Teenage Werewolf* receives the worst fate. Victim of unethical experiments, his transformation was not a choice, and not under his control, but still, Tony is shot dead by police in the closing scene of the film. With the monstrous teen dead, there is no more story to tell.

The risk of transformation into a "dangerous offender" permeates these films but this is not presented as hopeless. "Juvenile delinquency" can be a transitional stage in the process of *becoming* an adult (Gooch, 2019). Jim Stark reforms at the end of *Rebel Without A Cause*, taking off his red jacket (the symbol of his non-conformity) and introducing Judy, now his girlfriend, to his parents. Artie West's classmates in *Blackboard Jungle* become engaged with education, showing a way out of their delinquency. The other teens in *I Was A Teenage Werewolf* learn from Tony's cautionary tale to avoid disruptiveness and questioning the adults around them. The process of "adjustment" discussed in *I Was a Teenage Werewolf* is something that other teens pick up on naturally, whereas others like Jim, Artie, and Tony have not automatically absorbed and agreed to. Problem youth films make the need for this "adjustment" explicit but show it as achievable. These films all use shocking incidents to promote adjustment; the death of a friend, violence in the classroom, the general dangers of being an outsider to society. There was debate during the 1950s and 1960s about the messages of these films, with some

30 A Popular Criminology of Youth Justice

critics saying their violence was a dangerous influence on children and others lauding the hopeful message they gave on how to respond to "juvenile delinquency" (Golub, 2009; Walker, 2010). Whilst transformation and the "monstrous youth" archetype have become embedded into film and are still used today, the notion of hope has not always been consistent (as will be discussed in Chapter 5).

One of the main cultural messages that problem youth films cemented into society was the idea of "youth" and/or the teenage years as a transitional space in which to find and cement your identity before settling into adulthood. The American bias of these films suggests markers of adulthood as achieving a romantic relationship or marriage, getting a good education and a steady, respectable job. That these aspects all allow individuals to fit into the capitalist roles of consumers, workers, and subjects may be coincidental but given the highly censored and restrictive requirements for these films to be released, this is telling of the priorities of American post-war culture (Biltereyst, 2007). The rambunctious teenage years being permissible only if the child completes their transformation into a well-behaved, compliant adult is evident in problem youth films, as is the underlying theme within them of social control.

Explanations of Offending?

Within problem youth films there are consistent narratives about the causes of offending and how offending should be responded to. Many of these films were highly explicit in this messaging, with the opening credits of *Blackboard Jungle* being the clearest example.

> Today we are concerned with juvenile delinquency—its causes—and its effects. We are especially concerned when this delinquency boils over into our schools. The scenes and incidents depicted here are fictional. However, we believe that public awareness is a first step toward a remedy for any problem.

There were three main types of explanations for offending behaviour given in these films, a lack of strong educational institutions, a lack of strong family relationships, and surprisingly, social determinants of crime such as poverty and the role of authority figures.

Education

Blackboard Jungle is explicitly focused on education, taking place within a reform school, and telling the story of novice teacher Richard Dadier's (Glenn Ford) adjustment to working with delinquent students who are characterised by his colleagues as "animals" and "savages". Throughout the film, education and the support of teachers are presented as the solution to "juvenile delinquency". Two of the student characters; Artie West (Vic Morrow) and Gregory Miller (Sidney Poitier) are contrasted against each other, one as redeemed and the other as irredeemable. Artie West wears a biker jacket and boots, showing his gang affiliation clearly and acting as a leader of disruption in the classroom. He is also the main instigator of many of the problems Mr Dadier faces throughout the film, such as being assaulted by a gang, his wife being sent threatening letters, and being reported to the headmaster for using racial slurs in the classroom. However, Dadier's focus is primarily on Miller, who he initially perceives as a delinquent instigator but comes to respect, encouraging him to remain in education. The redemption of Miller at the end of the film, with his deciding to remain in education is framed as a triumph for Dadier's approach to teaching. However, that the same approach did not impact West in the same way is taken as a failure on West's part, shown as him in essence "choosing" the delinquent lifestyle rather than a failure of Dadier's to reach him. The overriding message of the film is that redemption is possible for those who "earn it" through engagement with existing systems and that those who choose not to conform should be shunned and excluded.

Blackboard Jungle's emphasis on the status quo and engagement with education is reflective of the political narratives of the time, emphasising that tough reform schools were the right place to deal with troublesome children, and that deviance was a choice (Walker, 2010). However, aspects of its message on how to support and reform children ring a little hollow. Gregory Miller's character at the start of the film, does not enjoy school, seeing it as a means to an end but he isn't necessarily delinquent. We never see the character engaging in criminal behaviour, and he lacks many of the markers of criminality. In fact, we see that he has multiple protective factors in place. Miller is the leader of a gospel singing group, he works as a mechanic's assistant and intends to become a mechanic upon leaving school, he engages with his local community, and has a supportive family. However, Dadier (and the audience) assume he is delinquent because he does not explicitly like school, and more importantly (but not said explicitly within the film), because he is Black. Dadier makes it his mission to reform his pupils, with the idea that if he can reach Miller, he can reach all of them. The "redemption" of Gregory Miller is false, as this character would have been fine regardless. Early in the film Dadier tries to encourage the class to engage, saying that if they do, they could become carpenters, electricians, builders, and mechanics. Working in the trades is the only aspiration he can see for them, and this is something that Miller has already achieved on his own. Remaining in school is positive for Miller, but it is not necessarily the success story that the film's surface-level presentation suggests. It is in the comparison of Miller and West, that the film's true message regarding children becomes clear; the aim is social

32 A Popular Criminology of Youth Justice

control. Both Miller and West are viewed as difficult and delinquent at the start of the film, partially because they don't agree with what they are told, and don't naturally conform to social expectations. For both boys, this lack of conformity stems from rejection by society. West is angry at a world that offers him no opportunities other than a life of drudgery and servitude, where his needs were never considered let alone met.

> *Oh. You know, a year from now, the army comes by, and they say, 'ok, Artie West, you get into uniform, and you be a soldier, and you save the world, and you get your lousy head blowed right off'. Or maybe—maybe I get a year in jail, and maybe when I come out, the army, they don't want Artie west to be a soldier no more. Maybe what I get is—is out.*

This is a relatively accurate representation of many current justice-involved children. A majority of those who have had contact with youth justice systems are victims of abuse or neglect (Fox et al., 2015), have care experiences (McElvaney and Tatlow-Golden, 2016), additional learning needs (Brooks-Wilson, 2020), mental health needs (Stallard et al., 2003), and impoverished backgrounds (Brooks-Wilson, 2020). This is a group of children who are clearly "in-need" and these needs are heavily linked to a lack of structural support (Baldry et al., 2018; Case and Haines, 2004; Goldson, 2000). For children like Artie West, whether in the 1950s or today, it seems that the world has rejected them right from the start, and so crime appears to be a reasonable response; a way of getting something back from a situation in which they are always losing. Dadier's focus on Miller and judgement of West is subtly reflective of issues within youth justice in practice, where those with the greatest level of need often are perceived as "difficult", leading to the unconscious prioritisation of "easy wins" such as cases like Gregory Miller.

Gregory Miller similarly is rejected by society and must seek alternative means to success. However, this is not because of his class, but his race. Being a Black child in the 1950s America was inherently a position of lower status, lack of opportunities, of being oppressed and excluded (Walker, 2010). Sidney Poitier's casting in the film as Miller was viewed by some as controversial, due to Poitier's involvement with Committee for the Negro in the Arts, and leftist organisations campaigning for civil rights (Walker, 2010). The character of Miller is a child who recognises his exclusion from mainstream society, including mainstream education, on the basis of his race and so focuses on his own community. Within the film we see Miller leading other young Black boys as part of a singing group, we see him receive support from his Uncle, who provides him with employment opportunities. We see Dadier visit his neighbourhood, and there is a marked difference between here and the streets that West refers to as his "classroom". We see Dadier's surprise

"You Wanna Start a Rumble?" **33**

upon discovering the intelligence and potential of Miller, however, this is played as Miller developing into this person, opposed to Dadier finally seeing the person that Miller is, removed from his own expectations of what Black children are like.

Blackboard Jungle presents education as an answer to offending behaviour. However, the actions of the teacher characters in the film are not necessarily focused on education as the development of knowledge. Many of the actions of the teachers (Dadier included) are about developing pupils' capacity for conformity and reducing resistance to social control. The focus is on getting the pupils to sit still and be quiet during lessons, to engage in the tasks set without questioning their purpose, and to develop them into effective members of the workforce upon graduating.

You've got to have discipline and that means obedience.

The idea that working-class children are more resistant to social control is a consistent theme of the film. *Blackboard Jungle* is set in North Manual High School, where the principal, teachers, and even students seem resigned to the idea that these children are unteachable. At one point Dadier visits his former mentor, who works at a public school where the children are middle-class, polite, and well-behaved. Dadier notes the difference in what is expected here, saying "anyone can teach kids like these", meaning kids who already know how to "behave" and whose parents have instilled in them the value of education. This section was added to the script to appease censors, who wanted to show that not all American schools were like North Manual High (Golub, 2015). For the children at North Manual High, the jobs they are expected to obtain don't require academic qualifications, their families don't have academic qualifications, and their teachers treat them like criminals. All the teachers bemoan their pupil's behaviour, saying "what's the point of teaching if the kids don't care about an education", but it's clear why these children don't value school; it's a place that doesn't offer them opportunity beyond the lowest expectations and doesn't offer them any real value beyond learning how to fit in with the future that maintains a status quo in which they are lesser.

The narrative of education as an answer to offending has had something of a contested history within criminology. Whilst there is evidence showing that participation and educational attainment are correlated with reduced offending behaviours (McVey, 2016), suggesting justice-involved children "stay in school" will not necessarily lead to improved outcomes. For many of this group, education is a difficult place to be, due to additional learning needs, the hidden curriculum, and negative perceptions resulting from labelling (Arnez and Condry, 2021; Hayden, 2008; Shafi, 2019). Education can be supportive, however, this is most effective where there are trusting

34 A Popular Criminology of Youth Justice

relationships with teachers, inclusive curriculums, and accessible pedagogies (Griffith et al., 2018; Shafi, 2019). However, the narratives presented in problem youth films suggest that children need to change to fit in, rather than systems becoming more accommodating. We see elements of this in *Rebel Without A Cause*; Jim Stark participates in education, but his childish jokes at the planetarium are taken as evidence of his lack of interest. Similarly, Tony in *I Was A Teenage Werewolf* gets good grades, but questions the structures around him, thus earning the ire of his teachers. Throughout these films the risk of criminalisation is presented as an individual choice, regardless of circumstances.

Parents and Family

After education, one of the biggest factors in explaining why children become involved in criminal activity was (and still is) parenting. Within problem youth films, the relationship to adults is central. The teenage characters' perception of themselves as different from their parents, and the lack of understanding between parents and children is the source of many of the conflicts within these films. The idea that parents are responsible for their children has been consistent within society. However, this is somewhat divisive (Holt, 2009). Whilst parents are responsible for the care of their children, the question of whether they should be held responsible for the actions of their children is culturally bound and changes over time. This can be seen in various legislative changes that punish parents for the crimes of their children (Le Sage and De Ruyter, 2008). During the era of problem youth films, the general attitude was that children were becoming unreasonable and uncontrollable as they transformed into "teens" (Doherty, 2002). This impacted upon the censors' approach to reviewing many problem youth films, there was a concern that seeing delinquent youth on screen would cause young audiences to become wild themselves. A particular example of this is the possibly apocryphal tale of one of the first screenings of *Blackboard Jungle*. It was reported that as "Rock Around The Clock" played during the opening credits, children in the auditorium became excited to the point of riot, started ripping up seats, and causing havoc (Simmons, 2008). The veracity of this story has not been verified, but its survival and retelling meant that the image of uncontrollable, delinquent youth was perpetuated and linked explicitly to cinema.

The idea that the transformation into a "teen" was uncontrollable exempted parents from responsibility for the actions of their children. In problem youth films this view is both bolstered and contradicted. In many of the American films, parents look on in consternation as their children misbehave, unable to comprehend how this could have happened. An exemption to this is Danny DiPace's mother in *The Young Savages*, who continually

"You Wanna Start a Rumble?" **35**

supports her son and advocates for his innocence based only on her belief that her son wouldn't harm someone else. A contradiction of the view of helpless parents came from European films, such as *The 400 Blows* (1959), as we will see later in this chapter. The American view of youth crime was exported around the world, as an example of both how serious the problem was and how it could be solved (Golub, 2015). One of the solutions that these films suggest, is strong relationships with parents and family, with this being most clearly set out in *Rebel Without A Cause*.

Rebel Without A Cause has become the exemplar of the genre of problem youth films. Due to both the style, themes, and production of the film itself, but also the impact of the death of its star, James Dean. *Rebel* has become cemented within popular culture as a representation of the tribulations of the teenage years, with Dean's angsty portrayal of Jim Stark becoming a model for many future representations. Having characters wear a red jacket whilst visiting Griffith Park Observatory during a time of crisis has almost become overused to the point of cliché in film and TV. However, one of the more interesting aspects of *Rebel* is how it represents families. All three of the main characters, Jim (Dean), Judy (Natalie Wood), and Plato (Sal Mineo) have difficult relationships with their families, and this informs their attitudes and choices. The family situations of each character differ; however, all three children end up in the same situation. At the beginning of *Rebel* each of the three main characters has been picked up by police, and in this initial scene the tensions in their family relationships become clear. Plato is cared for by the housekeeper, his mother having left the home. He had been arrested for drowning puppies. Judy ran away from home because her father was cold to her, viewing their relationship differently now she is 16. Jim was arrested for public drunkenness, and the different reactions of his parents are clearly the main conflict in Jim's life. Mrs Stark (Ann Doran) views Jim's actions as very serious and a sign that he is uncontrollable but wants the situation to be covered up to avoid social embarrassment. Mr Stark (Jim Backus) views Jim's behaviour as youthful exuberance and nothing to be worried about. He does still try to bribe the police officer with cigars to avoid a fuss though. This difference in perception confuses Jim, he doesn't know if what he has done is wrong or not, and this leads to his famous declaration that "you're tearing me apart". The squabbling of his parents and a lack of clarity about what is expected of him is a key struggle for Jim. He is trying to understand what type of adult he wants to become, and the role models available to him are his hen-pecked father, and a kindly, but often unavailable police officer.

Within *Rebel* we see different parental responses to children's behaviour. Jim's mother tries to control both her son and the narrative around him. It is insinuated that the Stark family moved to this town to escape the reputation and consequences of Jim's poor behaviour. She expects her son to be

36 A Popular Criminology of Youth Justice

compliant and not question the adults around him, whilst simultaneously not giving him much visible support. Jim's father tries to help his son by talking out his problems, however, the lack of clear answers leaves Jim to try and find his own solutions. The Stark's parenting in *Rebel* is not showed positively, however, whilst this is the cause of Jim's angst, it is not portrayed as the reason for his behaviour. For Plato, there is a much clearer link between parenting and criminality. Plato's mother left their home, and Plato's behaviour in the films is a clear response. He steals his mother's gun, he squats in an abandoned mansion, and his attachment to Jim and Judy is all an attempt to try to create the family that he lacks in his home. He doesn't trust the adults around him, as those who were responsible for him have left. The scene in the mansion shows how the characters view their parents, as they "play house", pretending to be adults discussing their own children.

> *If you have children—Oh I hate the word!—or if you decide to adopt one—they can carry on and you'll never even notice. In fact, if you lock them in you never have to see them again, much less talk to them.*

The tensions between childhood and adulthood are resolved at the end of the film, with a traumatic event giving Jim the certainty that he needs. When faced with delinquency and death, he decides that it is better to conform. Judy, having found a loving relationship in Jim seems to no longer feel the need to strive for her father's approval. However, the future for these characters does not necessarily seem bright. They have chosen to avoid delinquency, to instead conform to the expectations of adults. But the adults around them do not seem happy, their own conformity has brought them a comfortable but inauthentic life. This is potentially what Jim and Judy will become. *Rebel*'s central conflict is Jim's quest to become an adult whilst remaining authentic (Baer, 1999), and at the end of the film the answer he has is that this is not possible, that those who stand out, like Plato and Buzz, will die. The complexities of parenting and families are linked to this, with doing as your parents ask and settling down and having a family of your own being seen as the way to avoid the untimely end of the delinquent. Within *The Young Savages* all but one of the young characters have no visible parents. This is similar within *Blackboard Jungle*, with one of the teachers decrying that "gang leaders have taken the place of parents". Throughout all these films is the idea that a strong family unit will safeguard children against criminality. And whilst there is evidence to suggest that this is the case (Aldridge et al., 2011; Le Sage and De Ruyter, 2008), in the context of the problem youth film, this narrative around families is more about social control than safeguarding. Crime must be stopped to protect society, rather than to protect children.

Authority Figures

The problem youth perspective on factors relating to criminality is shown most clearly in *The Young Savages* (1961). The film focuses on Assistant District Attorney Hank Bell (Burt Lancaster), who is prosecuting three children for murder. As he tries to find information relating to the case, the lives of the three boys are clearly depicted as being ones based in hardship. However, Bell explicitly dismisses "social oppression theories" as the cause of their behaviour, suggesting that it is a choice to behave in this way instead. It is only the fact that one of the boys is the son of his former girlfriend that causes Bell to look more closely at the situation and to consider the possibility that they may not be guilty. The film sets a clear difference between the three children accused of the crime. Arthur Reardon (John Davis Chandler) is a 17-year-old who is framed as being calculating, manipulative, and the leader of the gang. Anthony Apasto (Neil Burstyn) is 16, illiterate, and continually referred to as "stupid". Finally, Danny DiPace (Stanley Kristien) is 15, quiet, and has a strong advocate in his mother, who asks Bell to protect her son. These three children are almost emblematic of the stereotypes of juvenile delinquents. The truly bad kid in Arthur, the easily manipulated child who doesn't know any better in Anthony, and the innocent Danny who was subjected to peer pressure but hasn't actually done anything wrong. The neighbourhood in which the boys live is impoverished, graffiti-covered, and renowned as being dangerous. Bell came from this neighbourhood as well but views his ability to leave and "make something of himself" as proof that anyone can. A common feature of problem youth films is the character of a kindly adult who comes to better understand the lives of the children around them. Bell in *Savages*, Dadier in *Jungle*, and Inspector Fremick in *Rebel*. These characters are presented as the arbiters of morality and often hold positions of power over the younger characters. These adults decide which children are deserving of redemption, and which are truly dangerous or beyond help.

The relationship with adults in these films is important, because it sets out an idea of how those in positions of power or authority should respond to justice-involved children. Whilst these films are fictional, they had profound social and cultural impacts at the time, informing public opinion about youth crimes. It's also clear that these films were noted by politicians and policy makers. The discussion around the international release of *Blackboard Jungle* and *Rebel Without A Cause* was explicitly about how this would impact America's standing and reputation internationally (Golub, 2015), and the censoring of both films came from purely political concerns about how people would respond to the ideas and images of children acting independently (Simmons, 2008). Having these kindly adult characters conveyed the message that the institutions of the state such as police and education were fair,

38 A Popular Criminology of Youth Justice

supportive, and aiming to protect both children and communities. This implicitly sets up the idea that these institutions should be trusted, because the individuals that comprise them are trustworthy. In a modern context this message seems almost laughable, and many of the problem youth films of the 1950s have become perceived as camp for their naïve, simplistic presentation of justice and morality (Driscoll, 2011).

Having positive and trusting relationships with adults is seen as a key protective factor against offending behaviour (Case and Haines, 2015). These relationships can come from many different areas, such as schools, mentors, youth workers, social workers, and more (Payne et al., 2020; Pedersen et al., 2009; Pryce et al., 2021). However, the main aspect of these relationships is the support that they provide to the child. This often requires non-judgemental approaches and for the child to feel that they can be honest and disclose when they need support, particularly around criminal justice (Barry, 2017). In *The Young Savages* Bell is surprised when Danny doesn't want to speak to him and refuses to tell him what happened. He expected that this child would implicitly trust and look up to him due to his position and authority. This attitude contributes to his acceptance of what he is told by members of the rival gang The Horsemen, he assumes they are telling him the truth because they respect him. However, this wasn't the case and the information they tell him is not a full account. Bell's surprise at not being trusted seems naïve to a modern audience; of course a child will not immediately trust the person prosecuting them for murder; however, it is reflective of the values of the time; that adults are inherently trustworthy and those with power have earned it. This attitude has not been maintained within society, and currently trust in police and other institutions is particularly low (Borrero, 2001). For children, adults within the police and criminal justice are frequently perceived as a source of danger rather than trust, and stop and search rates, information about strip-searching of children, and evidence of abuse within the secure estate suggest that this distrust is not unjustified (Flacks, 2020; Griffith and Larson, 2016; Puffett, 2016).

Within *The Young Savages* a lot of the narrative focuses on the community that the characters are from and that the crime took place in. Harlem in New York had a poor reputation at the time, and the film (and book it was based upon) took full advantage of this to establish poor communities as a contributing factor in offending behaviour. The homes of the characters are cramped, with large families living in 1-bedroom tenements. The general attitude of the community is that the area is dangerous, and it was a matter of time before the gang activity led to a death. There is a general distrust of the police, with many people unwilling to disclose information. Throughout the film Bell mentions that this is the neighbourhood he grew up in, and it is clear that this has impacted his attitudes. His wife (who appears to have had a middle-class childhood), is ardently against the idea of capital punishment and frequently undermines Bell's position. He views her as an idealist, unrealistic, and unaware of the "real world" having been sheltered from neighbourhoods like Harlem. This class narrative is interesting and doesn't tend to appear as explicitly in the other problem youth films. This is perhaps because many of these films were aimed at the middle classes, who were better able to afford trips to the cinema (Buckingham, 2021). However, within *The Young Savages* the class issues are not presented as mitigating factors, but instead as an explanation for why children become involved in crime. This reaffirms the idea of deserving and underserving poor, that there are working-class people like Bell who work their way out of their situation and the others are using their situation as an excuse. This message in 1950s America was particularly prevalent, linked to the bootstrap mentality and the rise of capitalism post-war (Driscoll, 2011). The idea that you could work your way out of poverty means that the state is justified in not providing support and that remaining in poor conditions is the fault of the individual. This then justifies harsh punishments for children involved in crime.

Public Responses and the Legacy of Problem Youth

James Dean has become an icon of rebelliousness, cool, and angst partially because of his role in *Rebel*. However, within *Rebel* the character of Jim isn't particularly rebellious. Coming from a middle-class home, Jim has two parents who, whilst they have difficulties in communicating with him, clearly love and care for him; he attends school, has a car, and appears to have options in the future. Whilst the police are aware of him, Jim is seen as harmless by them, and simply struggling to find his way. By the end of the film, Jim has resolved his internal conflict and it appears he is content to conform to the standards set out by society. Whilst Jim is the main character, he is not truly a *rebel*. Instead, it is those around him that are genuinely rebelling against societal expectations. Buzz and his gang seem committed to their criminal pathway, even after Buzz's death they maintain their dislike of police, and loyalty to their subculture. Plato is potentially the most rebellious character in the film. He carries a gun, breaks into abandoned homes, and drowns puppies. Most significantly, Plato is coded as gay. Nicholas Ray was quite explicit about this in his direction, telling Sam Mineo to "look at him [James Dean] the way she [Natalie Wood] does" (Baer, 1999). The colour red is significant throughout the film, with Dean's jacket, Wood's cape and lipstick, and Mineo's socks all being bright red. However, in the final scene of the film it's commented on how Plato is wearing odd socks, one red, one black. This is another signal of his queerness, his difference, as well as a nod to how he was not cared for by those around him. Plato in his death is zipped into Jim's red jacket, the signifier

40 A Popular Criminology of Youth Justice

of his rebellion. In death, Plato will be forever a rebel, never being given the opportunity to conform even if he wanted to.

In the public imagination, it is not Plato who has become an icon though, it is Jim. This is partially spurred by the death of James Dean shortly after the film's completion. The characterisation of Dean and the film itself has achieved mythic status in society, becoming a template for media representation of teenagers in general, but particularly for those who are justice-involved. The violence and spectacle of *Rebel* were sensationalised, not only since its release, but at the time as well. Advertisements for the film proclaimed it a "challenging drama of today's juvenile violence!" and that Dean portrayed "a bad boy from a good family". This further pushed the idea that this transformation into delinquency could happen to any child regardless of their circumstances. The censoring of problem youth films acted upon this presumption as well, with many of the cuts being more stringent than other genres, simply because children were more likely to be in the audience (Simmons, 1995). Action like this has almost legitimised the idea that films can cause children to become dangerous or violent, despite there being very little evidence to support this view (Jowett et al., 1996).

Not all public responses mirrored the American narrative of problem youth. Whilst many countries were experiencing similar social concerns regarding children and the transition to adulthood, globally media did not all respond with sensationalism and commodification. The French coming-of-age film *The 400 Blows* (1959) presents quite a different picture of justice-involved children. *The 400 Blows* follows Antoine, a 13-year-old living in Paris with his mother and stepfather. The film's director François Truffaut specifically aimed to make a social realist film that reflected his own experiences as a child. In describing the film, he said that "nothing is invented" (Carr, 2022). The film follows Antoine over the course of a week in which he is expelled from school, runs away from home, is caught trying to return a stolen typewriter and is sent to an observation centre. The film mirrors many of the issues within American problem youth films, such as education, parenting, and poverty. However, the idea of social control is made explicit within *The 400 Blows* and presented as something that should be rebelled against. Antoine is portrayed sympathetically; his actions are shown as a result of the circumstances he is put in by the adults around him. This makes it very different from American problem youth films. *The 400 Blows* also features one of the youngest characters in this type of film. Whilst the American works tend to focus on older teenagers (16–18), *The 400 Blows* focuses on a 13-year-old. Whilst the age difference may explain the difference in characterisation, the cultural difference is also a factor. France has consistently had a higher age of criminal responsibility than America (Knox, 2019), which may contribute to the differing constructions of justice-involved children. The filmmaking culture in France also has a significant impact. *The 400*

Blows is considered as one of the landmark French New Wave films, and the New Wave's rejection of traditional filmmaking to embrace narrative ambiguity, realism, and direct addresses to the audience can all be seen in this work. This sets this film apart from American problem youth films, which were created under the studio system, heavily overseen by censors and produced specifically to make money, rather than as artistic statements (Hogan, 2012). *The 400 Blows* is not sensationalist in its approach and presents its "juvenile delinquent" character as a child. Antoine has not transformed into a monster; he is reacting to a monstrous world around him.

Within *The 400 Blows* Antoine attends school but is not academically successful. However, he does enjoy learning, within the film he is particularly taken with the poetry of Balzac. Antoine's teachers are strict and do not recognise creativity or curiosity outside of the lessons set. There is an emphasis on being well-behaved. The teacher worries for the future based on his perception of the class, saying "what'll France be in 10 years?". He holds the idea that people cannot change, and that those who are poor, childish, or lack academic prowess at the age of 13 will always do so. However, unlike the teachers in *Blackboard Jungle*, he is portrayed as mean and hostile. Antoine's passion for Balzac is shown as valuable and something to be encouraged, but he doesn't receive this encouragement from the adults in his life.

Antoine's parents are also presented differently than the adults in American problem youth films. Antoine's mother clearly sees her son as an inconvenience, and in need of controlling. When asked by a police officer if she wants to take her son home, she replies "he'd have to promise to change completely. Perhaps you could frighten him". There are no kindly authority figures within *The 400 Blows*. Police and the staff at the observation centre are professional, however, they are indifferent to Antoine and the other children in their care. Throughout the film Antoine is searching for freedom; to learn about what he is interested in, to spend his time as he wishes, and to visit the seaside. The use of the sea as a metaphor for freedom runs throughout the film, and in the final scenes we see Antoine escaping the observation centre, running to the beach, and upon seeing the sea, stares directly into the camera with an expression of sadness and confusion. He has reached what he perceived as freedom, but it doesn't give him any answers or route to a better life. Ultimately, *The 400 Blows* presents a hopeless message, that youth's search for meaning is fruitless as becoming an adult is a process of accepting the chaos of the world around you. This is a stark contrast to the conformist message of American problem youth films, instead asking us to confront the philosophical challenge of not how to be a child or adult, but how to be a person in an uncaring world.

The 400 Blows has become a classic film and is viewed as a cinematic masterpiece. The same cannot be said of the other problem youth films this chapter discusses. Whilst *Rebel* and its American contemporaries have an enduring cultural legacy, it is approached with something of a sense of camp;

42 A Popular Criminology of Youth Justice

the sensationalism having not aged well and seeming quite tame in comparison to depictions of violence in subsequent films. However, from all these films, the stereotypes of problem youth have developed and their cult(ural) status has allowed these ideas to be maintained within society. The problem youth film of the 1950s cemented within society a cultural ideal of what being a teenager is like. That many of these films focused on delinquency strengthened the existing idea of dangerous youth, and created the fear that any child could transform into a delinquent. The popularity of these films and their cultural legacy means that these ideas have been maintained and perpetuated. Subsequent films have referenced them, they have influenced our perception and response to other media, and generally acted as a template for the construction of justice-involved children. The melodrama, spectacle, and fantastical elements of these films mean that this template is sensationalised, and not reflective of the realities of justice-involved children's lives. However, the legacy of these films has had an impact on how society views justice-involved children and how they should be responded to.

Film List

An American Werewolf in London (1981)
Blackboard Jungle (1955)
Ginger Snaps (2000)
I Was A Teenage Frankenstein (1957)
I Was a Teenage Werewolf (1957)
Rebel Without A Cause (1955)
Reefer Madness (1936)
Teen Wolf (1985)
The 400 Blows (1959)
The Bad Seed (1959)
The Cry Baby Killer (1958)
The Delicate Delinquent (1957)
The Violent Years (1956)
The Wild One (1953)
The Young Savages (1961)

References

Aldridge J, Shute J, Ralphs R, et al. (2011) Blame the parents? Challenges for parent-focused programmes for families of gang-involved young people. *Children & Society* 25(5): 371–381.

Arnez J and Condry R (2021) Criminological perspectives on school exclusion and youth offending. *Emotional and Behavioural Difficulties* 26(1): 87–100. Routledge.

Baer W (1999) On Rebel Without A Cause: A conversation with Stewart Stern. *Michigan Quarterly Review* XXXVIII(4): 580–594.

Baker D (2005) Rock Rebels and Delinquents: The emergence of the Rock Rebel in 1950s 'Youth Problem' films. *Continuum* 19(1): 39–54. David Baker.

Baldry E, Briggs DB, Goldson B, et al. (2018) 'Cruel and unusual punishment': An inter-jurisdictional study of the criminalisation of young people with complex support needs. *Journal of Youth Studies* 21(5): 636–652. Routledge.

Barry M (2017) '*Youth Offending, Youth Transitions and Social Recognition': Rethinking Youth Justice Policy and Practice*. Ministry of Justice [Portugal]. Epub ahead of print 21 December 2017.

Bateman JA (2017) Critical discourse analysis and film. In: John Flowerdew and John E. Richardson (eds) *The Routledge Handbook of Critical Discourse Studies*. Oxon: Routledge, pp. 596–608.

Biltereyst D (2007) American juvenile delinquency movies and the European censors: The cross-cultural reception and censorship of the Wild One, Blackboard Jungle, and Rebel Without a Cause. In: Timothy Shary and Alexandra Seibel (eds) *Youth Culture in Global Cinema*. Austin: University of Texas Press, pp. 9–26.

Borrero M (2001) The widening mistrust between youth and police. *Families in Society* 82(4): 399–408. Families International Inc.

Brooks-Wilson S (2020) Rethinking youth justice journeys: Complex needs, impeded capabilities and criminalisation. *Youth Justice* 20(3): 309–327.

Buckingham D (2021) *Youth on Screen: Representing Young People in Film and Television*. Cambridge; Medford: Polity.

Carr J (2022) Notebook Primer: François Truffaut on Notebook | MUBI. Available at: https://mubi.com/notebook/posts/notebook-primer-francois-truffaut (accessed 21 April 2023).

Case S (2016) Negative Youth Justice: Creating the youth crime 'problem'. Available at: https://www.cycj.org.uk/negative-youth-justice-creating-the-youth-crime-problem/ (accessed 21 April 2023).

Case S (2018) *Youth Justice: A Critical Introduction*. Abingdon, Oxon; New York, NY: Routledge.

Case S and Haines K (2004) Promoting prevention: Evaluating a multi-agency initiative of youth consultation and crime prevention in Swansea. *Children and Society* 18(5): 355–370.

Case S and Haines K (2015) *Positive Youth Justice: Children First, Offenders Second*. London: Policy Press.

Doherty TP (2002) *Teenagers and Teenpics: The Juvenilization of American Movies in the 1950s*. Rev. and expanded ed. Philadelphia: Temple University Press.

Driscoll C (2011) Modernism, cinema, adolescence: Another history for teen film. *Screening the Past* 32: 2–21. Epub ahead of print 1 January 2011.

Flacks S (2020) Law, necropolitics and the stop and search of young people. *Theoretical Criminology* 24(2): 387–405. SAGE Publications Ltd.

Fox BH, Perez N, Cass E, et al. (2015) Trauma changes everything: Examining the relationship between adverse childhood experiences and serious, violent and chronic juvenile offenders. *Child Abuse & Neglect* 46: 163–173.

Goldson B (2000) Children in need or young offenders? *Child & Family Social Work* 5(3): 255–265.

44 A Popular Criminology of Youth Justice

Goldson B (2020) Excavating youth justice reform: Historical mapping and speculative prospects. In: *The Howard Journal of Criminal Justice* 59(3): 317–334.

Golub A (2009) They turned a school into a jungle! How the blackboard jungle redefined the education crisis in Postwar America. *Film & History: An Interdisciplinary Journal of Film and Television Studies* 39(1): 21–30. Center for the Study of Film and History.

Golub A (2015) A transnational tale of teenage terror: The Blackboard Jungle in global perspective. *Journal of Transnational American Studies* 6(1): 1–11.

Gooch K (2019) 'Kidulthood': Ethnography, juvenile prison violence and the transition from 'boys' to 'men'. *Criminology & Criminal Justice* 19(1): 80–97.

Griffith AN and Larson RW (2016) Why trust matters: How confidence in leaders transforms what adolescents gain from youth programs. *Journal of Research on Adolescence* 26(4): 790–804.

Griffith AN, Larson RW and Johnson HE (2018) How trust grows: Teenagers' accounts of forming trust in youth program staff. *Qualitative Psychology* 5: 340–357. US: Educational Publishing Foundation.

Hayden C (2008) Education, schooling and young offenders of secondary school age. *Pastoral Care in Education* 26(1): 23–31. Routledge.

Hogan E (2012) Boyhood, abuse, and adult intervention in the 400 blows (Truffaut 1959), small change (Truffaut 1976), and pellet (Mañas 2000). *Journal of Children in Popular Culture* 4(1): 28–43.

Holt A (2009) (En)Gendering responsibilities: Experiences of parenting a 'young offender'. *The Howard Journal of Criminal Justice* 48(4): 344–356.

Jewkes Y (2015) *Media and Crime*. London: SAGE.

Jowett G, Jarvie IC and Fuller-Seeley K (1996) *Children and the Movies: Media Influence and the Payne Fund Controversy*. Cambridge studies in the history of mass communications. Cambridge [England]; New York, NY, USA: Cambridge University Press.

Knox E (2019) The 400 blows and juvenile courts featured practice perspectives: Review. *Children's Legal Rights Journal* 39(3): 288–293.

Le Sage L and De Ruyter D (2008) Criminal parental responsibility: Blaming parents on the basis of their duty to control versus their duty to morally educate their children. *Educational Philosophy and Theory* 40(6): 789–802. Routledge.

McElvaney R and Tatlow-Golden M (2016) A traumatised and traumatising system: Professionals' experiences in meeting the mental health needs of young people in the care and youth justice systems in Ireland. *Children and Youth Services Review* 65: 62–69. Elsevier Ltd.

McVey M (2016) Re-engaging disconnected youth: Transformative learning through restorative and social justice education. *International Review of Education* 62(5): 647–649. Springer Netherlands.

Mejias S and Banaji S (2019) Backed into a corner: Challenging media and policy representations of youth citizenship in the UK. *Information, Communication & Society* 22(12): 1714–1732. Routledge.

Osgerby B (2020) Teen Revolution: The Rise of Post-War Subcultures | Museum of Youth Culture. Available at: https://museumofyouthculture.com/teen-intro-three/ (accessed 4 April 2023).

Payne B, Hobson J and Lynch K (2020) 'We just want to be treated with respect!': Using restorative approaches and the dramatic arts to build positive relationships between the police and young people. *Youth Justice*: 21(3) 255–274. SAGE Publications Inc.

Pedersen P, Woolum S, Gagne B, et al. (2009) Beyond the norm: Extraordinary relationships in youth mentoring. *Children and Youth Services Review* 31: 1307–1313.

Presdee M (2000) *Cultural Criminology and the Carnival of Crime*. London; New York: Routledge.

Pryce J, Deane KL, Barry JE, et al. (2021) Understanding youth mentoring relationships: Advancing the field with direct observational methods. *Adolescent Research Review* 6(1): 45–56.

Puffett N (2016) Urgent call for staffing overhaul to make youth custody safer. *Children and Young People Now* 2016(2): 8–9. Mark Allen Group.

Shafi AA (2019) The complexity of disengagement with education and learning: A case study of young offenders in a secure custodial setting in England. *Journal of Education for Students Placed at Risk (JESPAR)* 24(4): 323–345. Routledge.

Simmons J (1995) The censoring of rebel without a cause. *Journal of Popular Film and Television* 23(2): 56–63. Taylor & Francis Group.

Simmons J (2008) Violent youth: The censoring and public reception of The Wild One and The Blackboard Jungle. *Film History: An International Journal* 20(3): 381–391. Indiana University Press.

Slocum JD (2005) *Rebel Without a Cause: Approaches to a Maverick Masterwork*. Ithaca, United States: State University of New York Press. Available at: http://ebookcentral.proquest.com/lib/leicester/detail.action?docID=3407694 (accessed 4 July 2022).

Stallard P, Thomason J and Churchyard S (2003) The mental health of young people attending a Youth Offending Team: A descriptive study. *Journal of Adolescence* 26(1): 33–43.

Walker A (2010) 'Blackboard jungle': Delinquency, desegregation, and the cultural politics of 'Brown'. *Columbia Law Review* 110(7): 1911–1953. Columbia Law Review Association, Inc.

3

"THIS AIN'T A GIRL SCOUT CAMP!"

Policing and Imprisoning Youth

The most visible aspects of the criminal justice system in both media and practice, are policing and prisons. These two institutions form the main imagery associated with criminal justice, however, a majority of individuals will never interact with them. This means that for most people, their main source of education regarding criminal justice is media. Research has highlighted the influence of media upon public opinions of criminal justice (Jewkes, 2005), and the relationship between both fictional and factual media (Dowler et al., 2006; Waid-Lindberg et al., 2011). In regards to policing and prisons, media representation is particularly important. From *Dixon of Dock Green* (Reiner, 2010), to *Porridge* (Jewkes, 2005), to *Life on Mars* (Garland and Bilby, 2011), TV representation of criminal justice has long been a focus of academic and public discussion. There is such a level of interest in the stories of police and prisons and associated imagery that they have become their own genres. "Cop films" range from serious to comedic, and have spawned subgenres (e.g. buddy cop films, police procedurals). The focus in "cop films" is generally on the lives and experiences of police, and their endeavours to protect the public (Brown, 1993). Prison films tend towards drama, and often focus on the harshness of the conditions, the injustice of a particular character's imprisonment, or attempts at escape (Hedges, 2014). However, there is diversity within the genre, such as the children's film *Paddington 2* (2017), showcasing the importance of kindness in rehabilitation, and the ongoing debate as to whether or not *The Shawshank Redemption* (1994) should be classified as a prison film or a drama that happens to take place in a prison (Mason, 2003; O'Sullivan, 2001). There has been a wealth of research considering the imagery of police and prisons in media, however the majority of this has focused on adults. The findings show that there are

DOI: 10.4324/9781003403159-3

consistent presentations of police and prisons on film, which sets out specific messages for public consumption about our justice systems (Bennett, 2006; Brown, 1993; Hedges, 2014; Wilson and O'Sullivan, 2005).

A majority of films about policing and prisons feature adults as the subjects of criminal justice. This means that the stories can revel in the complexity of the issues they depict; violence, corruption, and injustice. Wilson and O'Sullivan (2004) and Rafter (2000) have both discussed the purpose of these films, arguing that their narratives broadly support the status quo where justice is restored and authority reasserted. The narratives of "justice restored" and "authority reasserted" are clearly acceptable when applied to adults; maintaining the commonly held conception that punishment is "just" and that criminals need to be controlled. This allows some of the stereotypes of the police and prison genre to become complex and nuanced: the hero cop can use brutal force if it gets results, or the corrupt warden's actions can be justified by past trauma (Bandes, 2021; Reiner, 2010). *The Green Mile* (1999) manages to combine all these elements whilst also telling a supernatural story and developing sympathy for those incarcerated. Policing and prison stories fundamentally present a moral simplicity; they are about catching and punishing wrongdoing by bad people. However, when these stories feature children, there is a profound change. When the bad person being presented is a child, this creates a paradox. Is this child an "innocent victim" or a "dangerous offender"? Chapter 2 discusses the transition between these two categories and the way in which they have become cultural mainstays. But if as the problem youth film suggests, the transition into "dangerous offender" may not be reversible, this conflicts with the traditional narratives of policing and punishment films, where justice is restored and authority reasserted (Wilson and O'Sullivan, 2004). Additionally, the violence, corruption, and moral ambiguity of policing and prison films seem out of place or uncomfortable when applied by adult characters in positions of power to children. The conventions of the prison and police film can seem unsightly when their subject is a child, causing audiences to question the validity of criminal justice. This is sometimes used to great effect within these films, with *Scum* (1979) being a seminal example. However, prison and police films are still entertainment products, there is a need to maintain a wide audience, which often results in avoiding presenting extremes in a realistic way. This means that police and prison films focused on justice-involved children have developed their own conventions that allow these stories to be told without alienating audiences.

Firstly, we must consider the context in which police and prison films about justice-involved children are made. As these films have a strong impact upon public opinions of these institutions (Jewkes, 2005; Rafter, 2000), considering the difference between what is presented and reality is important. Whilst it is highly unlikely that many people interpret fictional films as wholly representative of reality, there is evidence that we "discount towards the middle" (Wilson and O'Sullivan, 2004), ignoring the aspects of these media that we think are sanitised or sensationalised, and unconsciously believing what remains, such as the underlying themes of the film. An example of this is the cultural conception of "prison rape" which has largely emerged from fictional media (Levan et al., 2011). Whilst sexual assaults do occur in prisons (Ahlin, 2019), their continued presentation in prison films has made this into a genre convention, often linked to power dynamics, punishment, and establishing character relationships (Levan et al., 2011). This idea has taken on cultural status, which doesn't necessarily reflect the realities of prison, whilst also maintaining the cultural notion that prisons *should* be horrific and those within them should be subjected to continual punishment. This is an example of what O'Sullivan and Wilson call "sins of omission as well as commission" (Wilson and O'Sullivan, 2004: 15), where prison films can not only overlook the realities of criminal justice but create new realities which then are within the public lexicon.

Children are Overpoliced and Criminalised

For children, their existences are quite heavily policed. Partially due to the cultural conflation of youth and deviance, children are rarely free to inhabit public space without being policed. The idea of "hanging out" being disruptive to society (Whyte, 1993) was reflected in the problem youth films of the 1950s, leading to their characters hanging out in abandoned buildings, woods, and other unconventional spaces. This is something that has been maintained in subsequent films, partially based upon film writers, directors, and creators' own experiences of childhood and youth, where they were not allowed to take up space, their hobbies were seen as deviant, and they were consistently told by police to stop doing what they were doing, even when they were not in contravention of the law. *Mid90s* (2018) is a good example of how this can impact children; a group of skateboarders are consistently told to leave areas by police, simply for engaging in a sport that is not viewed as acceptable by the adults around them. This makes the characters dislike police and authority figures in general, as they continually prohibit them from participating in society.

For children in reality, there is consistent evidence to suggest that they are overpoliced, and that imprisonment is harmful (Crawford, 2009; Goldson, 2005; Jackson et al., 2019). Of all recorded crimes, 16% involve children and young adults (aged 10–25) as perpetrators (Youth Justice Board, 2023). However, routine police activities often focus on children disproportionately, despite being a much smaller criminal presence. Of police stop-and-searches, approximately 17% are carried out on under-18s, with only 8% of these leading to an arrest (Alliance for Youth Justice, 2022). For children who are also of minority ethnicity, this over-policing becomes ever-present in their lives, with stop and search data suggesting that minority ethnicity boys are far more likely to be stopped than their white counterparts (Bowling and Phillips, 2007; Flacks, 2018). During the first lockdown due to COVID-19 in 2020, Black boys accounted for over two-thirds of the Metropolitan Police's stop and searches of under-18s (Alliance for Youth Justice, 2022). Being in public spaces puts children at risk of police involvement. For those who are arrested, questioned, or receive further police involvement, evidence suggests that procedures to safeguard children are not followed or carried out effectively. A quarter of children strip-searched by police did not have an appropriate adult present (Davies, 2022), the questions and language used by police are often not altered to be understandable to children (Griffiths et al., 2011), and additional needs such as mental and physical health and speech and language needs, are not considered by arresting and questioning officers (Ellem and Richards, 2018; Jackson et al., 2019). These procedural injustices have been well documented in both academic and public spheres, making it unsurprising that children have low levels of trust in police (Gooch and von Berg, 2019; Payne et al., 2020).

Regarding the custodial estate, we similarly find the realities for justice-involved children to be bleak. Whilst the number of children given custodial sentences has been reducing over time (Youth Justice Board, 2023), questions remain about the appropriateness of any imprisonment of children (Blagg, 2012; Goldson, 2005). Research has generally found the use of custody to be harmful to children (Bateman, 2011; Case and Hazel, 2020) and those who have experienced custody have recounted a variety of difficulties that are side-effects of being in custody that have long-term impacts upon their lives (Taflan and Jalil, 2020). From strained family relationships (Young and Turanovic, 2022), reduced access to education (Case and Hazel, 2020), a lack of mental health support (Independent Police Complaints Commission, 2014), to exposure to violence from both peers and staff (Haydon, 2020), putting children into custody seems inherently linked not to rehabilitating them into law-abiding young adults, but prioritising punitiveness over all else. The result of this is that children who experience custodial sentences are more likely to remain in criminal pathways than those who receive community sentences (Abrams, 2005; Bateman, 2010; Youth Justice Board, 2023) and are more likely to develop more serious criminal behaviours. This also is to say nothing of the social impacts of imprisonment, which often leads to exclusion from society even after a sentence is finished and the "debt to society" repaid (MacDonald, 2006). Imprisoning children perpetuates the existence of a criminal underclass which can be utilised as evidence of the need for punitive criminal justice systems. That this cycle tends to target children from marginalised communities is suggestive of broader injustices (McFarland et al., 2019).

50 A Popular Criminology of Youth Justice

Police Narratives About Children

The image of police in fictional media takes different forms. Ranging from the friendly, neighbourhood policeman (Martin, 2023), to the loose cannon who gets results (Garland and Bilby, 2011), to dirty cops or disaffected superiors (Bandes, 2021), there are a variety of stereotypes that cop films give us. The utility and accuracy of these stereotypes have been questioned by researchers and the impact upon public ideas of what police officers should be, cannot be understated (Linnemann, 2019). One of the most prevailing images of police in film is that of the "hero cop". Hero cops are those who always seek out justice, sometimes going to extreme lengths to get the right outcome (Reiner, 2010). *Hot Fuzz* (2007) subverts this stereotype, by having hero cop Nicholas Angel (Simon Pegg) be viewed as an overachiever by both his peers and superiors in the Metropolitan Police, needing to be reassigned to another area to avoid skewing their statistics. When reassigned to the village of Sandford, Angel struggles to adapt to neighbourhood policing, and the concerns of the community. Amongst these concerns are "dog muck", "crusty jugglers", and "thieving kids". These concerns are reflective of the general distrust of children in society (as discussed in Chapter 2), but are unfounded, given the numerous boasts from both residents and police officers that there isn't any crime in Sandford. The community's response to children existing in public space is contradictory; they are asked to move on by police officers, accused of graffitiing without evidence, and only two children are allowed into the local shop at a time to prevent theft. However, simultaneously underage drinking is allowed in the local pub to "keep the young'uns out of trouble". Angel is the exception in Sandford in many ways, including how he views children. He does not see them as exempt from the law, penalising underage drinking, however, does not over-police them for merely being in public spaces. Angel even engages the help of the young villagers in the final standoff of the film, asking them to cover up CCTV cameras with spray paint. Children are not particularly significant within the film, however, the adult characters' reactions to them are indicative of how children have been treated within society.

Angel's portrayal of the hero cop archetype doesn't see him interact with children much, and when he does it is either clearly acting "by the book" to uphold the law or viewing them as members of the community who can support his broader goal of restoring justice. However, hero cops on screen generally don't interact with children at all. This character archetype is a mainstay of films and television (Bandes, 2021) however to show the "hero cop" policing children would be contradictory; criminalising children isn't heroic. For many police films, the interactions with children are focused on helping, development, or rescue. In many instances these films use comedy as a way of reducing the tensions between the contrast of children in criminal justice

"This Ain't a Girl Scout Camp!" **51**

systems. Throwing police into situations where they have to look after young children in particular is a source of comedy in films. *Kindergarden Cop* (1990), and *Cop and A Half* (1993) are examples of this; the serious, strait-laced police officer learning from children that there is a world outside of their work. However, within these films the children are not "criminal", finding a balance between the usual depiction of detection and arrest; which in practice with both adults and children can be quite violent and ruthless (Haydon, 2020); with the expected approach to children can be difficult and many films use comedy to achieve this.

21 Jump Street (2012) is a comedy "buddy cop" film that centres on an investigation into drug dealing with a high school. The two main characters Schmidt (Jonah Hill) and Jenko (Channing Tatum) are police officers who are assigned to an undercover investigation within the school because they look young enough to pass as teenagers, despite being 25 years old. In the beginning of the film, Schmidt and Jenko are shown to be terrible at their job. Jenko overuses force and does not know the Miranda warning (a statement of rights) and Schmidt is intimidated by suspects to the point where he is incapable of making an arrest. It is clear that this investigation is the last chance for Schmidt and Jenko and if they do not succeed in finding out who is supplying drugs to dealers within the school they will lose their jobs. The film heavily plays on stereotypes, utilising them as shortcuts for the audience to understand the characters, but also making fun of this conceit. Schmidt has "book smarts" and Jenko has "street smarts" with both characters developing additional skills over the course of the film. Captain Dickson (Ice Cube) even acknowledges his own stereotype of "angry black captain" explicitly and tells Schmidt and Jenko to "embrace your stereotypes", using this as a way to blend into the student body.

Stereotypes are most heavily used to depict the teenage characters of the film. When Schmidt and Jenko first enter the school they look at the different cliques and groups, categorising them into familiar stereotypes and subcultures. However, their lack of knowledge of current youth culture means they soon fall into unfamiliar territory. "Jocks" and "nerds" are easily spotted but hipsters are unknown, and the pair quickly make faux pas by using homophobic slang that was commonplace when they were young but is not viewed as acceptable anymore. *Jump Street* does not seem to acknowledge that many of the characters that Jenko and Schmidt interact with are children. At one point in the film they host a party, to ingratiate themselves with the drug dealers within the school. In preparation for this they buy lots of alcohol and take a pound of marijuana from the police station evidence room. It is not commented on at all that in trying to bust a drug ring, they have become suppliers themselves and see no problem with this. Additionally, there is a level of force that is used by Jenko in particular that is questionable. Upon first entering the school he punches a student in the face, and at the party

52 A Popular Criminology of Youth Justice

both he and Schmidt get into a fight with a large group of teenagers. The violence is played for laughs, with Schmidt pulling a knife from his back and saying "When did I get stabbed? That's awesome!". One of the most glaring issues within the film is the romantic sub-plot between Schmidt and Molly (Brie Larson), who is a student at the school. The pairing of a teenage girl and a 25-year-old man is not addressed at all in the film, except for Captain Dickson's initial briefing stating "Keep that dirty dick inside your pants. Don't fuck no students, don't fuck no teachers". An additional issue with this relationship is that Schmidt is undercover, using an assumed identity. Whilst the addition of this sub-plot to the film is very in-keeping with the raunchy comedy style of films at the time, in light of the assaults committed by undercover police against women who believed they were developing real relationships (Stephens Griffin, 2021), playing this for laughs rings a little hollow.

Jump Street is somewhat self-aware of its relationship to and the legacy of police films and teen films. The school Principal is named Dadier, in a nod to *Blackboard Jungle's* (1955) main character, and the film hits many of the action-cop film tropes, such as car chases, shoot-outs, explosions, and ending with justice being done (Brown, 1993). At the end of *Jump Street* Jenko and Schmidt are successful in finding the drug suppliers and are hailed as heroes by Captain Dickson. The ending of the film fits squarely within the authority-reasserted narrative; Jenko and Schmidt retain their jobs as police officers and are given further undercover work (setting up the sequel, which takes place in a college). However, the teenage characters are not given a closing arc in the film. Molly is taken hostage as part of the car chase at the climax of the film, immediately after this she kisses Schmidt who has revealed to her that he is a police officer. She is not seen or mentioned again for the rest of the film, and does not appear in the sequel. Additionally, Eric (Dave Franco), one of the drug dealers in the school, is portrayed as a victim of child criminal exploitation, having been manipulated into selling drugs. He is clearly heavily distressed by the car chase, shootout, and revelation that people he thought to be his peers were adults who were investigating him. However, this is played for laughs, with Eric's last appearance being him sitting in a crashed limo, crying. Whilst it would be unreasonable to expect social realism from a buddy-cop action-comedy, and that many of the choices made in *Jump Street* are in keeping with film styles and trends of the 2010s, it is difficult not to see them through the lens of current knowledge about justice-involved children.

Children who are involved in drug dealing due to exploitation by adults are being increasingly highlighted by youth justice. Changing language to identify these children as victims of criminal exploitation rather than "young offenders" is a clear example of this (Goldson, 2019). These changes have largely taken place since the 2010s, which means that *21 Jump Street's* characterisation and treatment of Eric is reflective of the time in which it was created. However, the prevalence of these attitudes regarding justice-involved

"This Ain't a Girl Scout Camp!" **53**

children has been shown to be harmful, contributing to the penal populism of that time (Chaney, 2015), and influencing systems to be more punitive (Case and Bateman, 2020). Rates of imprisonment of children have generally been in decline, however, there was a spike in the use of custodial sentences in 2011, following high-profile rioting, protest, and other events that were broadly attributed to children even if that was not the case (Bateman, 2012; Lewis et al., 2011). In the UK this resulted in a real impact upon youth justice systems, as the planned Youth Justice Board reforms based upon the Charlie Taylor report (Taylor, 2016) were scrapped, and there was increasing focus on the responsibilisation of children (Muncie, 2008; Such and Walker, 2005). Whilst films like *21 Jump Street* cannot be claimed as being catalysts for these changes, their perpetuation of the idea that children are solely responsible for their behaviours and thus deserve to be punished to the fullest extent of the law, and extreme forms of practice in relation to children are permissible has allowed these changes to be viewed as acceptable within society.

Whilst changes within youth justice have been highly positive and moved towards Child First approaches (Case and Haines, 2014; Case and Hazel, 2020), the policing of children in society has not undergone the same process. More recently we have seen distrust in police increasing amongst children (Alalehto and Larsson, 2016), and it is easy to understand why this is the case. With high-profile incidents where children have died after being followed by police (Weaver et al., 2023), community concerns about the treatment of children by police have gone unheard (*Crest Advisory*, 2022), and where children are the subjects of injustice (Brunson and Pegram, 2018; McFarland et al., 2019), the police approach to children (regardless of justice-involvement) needs to change.

Children's Response to Police

As children (regardless of justice involvement) have fewer opportunities to participate freely in society and have less access to private spaces (Flacks, 2018), their over-policing in public spaces essentially sends the message that society is not accepting of children, especially those who do not conform to the image of "innocent" (by being non-white, lower class, or engaging in subculture). This societal intolerance of children justifies their punishment, reinforcing the idea that by using public space these children were doing something wrong and police action is appropriate. As a society we are seeing children becoming more politically and socially aware and active. Climate crisis movements in particular are led by children (Zamponi et al., 2022). Whilst youth has always been a site of social change (Ginwright and James, 2002), children are currently recognising the need for these changes to be engaged with by the broader systems around them, thus leading to politically targeted action such as protest. Children's protest action has frequently been

54 A Popular Criminology of Youth Justice

characterised as rioting (Lam-Knott, 2017; Miles, 2014). Whilst these incidents frequently start as peaceful, where they do become violent or hostile often in response to police actions towards the protest. Examples of this are the use of kettling during student tuition fees protests (Townsend, 2010), the lack of information given to communities following the death of Mark Duggan which contributed to the 2011 London riots, and the hostile approach and legislation towards climate change protesters more recently (Rawlinson, 2019). There seems to be a lack of reflection from police both at community and institutional levels about the impact of their approach on children.

One film that encapsulates many of these issues is *La Haine* (1995). Directed by Mathieu Kassovitz, *La Haine* follows three children throughout one day. Vinz (Vincent Cassell), Saïd (Saïd Taghmaoui), and Hubert (Hubert Koundé) all live in a Parisian banlieue (suburban housing development) and are part of marginalised groups. Vinz is Jewish, Saïd is Arabic, and Hubert is Black African. The day that the film depicts is the aftermath of a riot that occurred because a child (Abdel) from the community was hospitalised after being assaulted by police officers whilst being questioned. The banlieue is tense, with residents either siding with the rioters, or wanting them to relent to avoid further disruption and harm. Riot police, uniformed and plain-clothes police officers are a clear presence in the banlieue, the main characters have a constant sense of being observed and monitored. *La Haine* is explicitly an anti-police film, from the opening credits, story, and soundtrack, the desire for police to exit the banlieues and allow these communities to exist without oppression is clear.

> *You murderers! You can't shoot, we only have stones*
> *– opening credits of La Haine*

Within the film we see the reactions of Vinz, Saïd, and Hubert to being policed in a variety of situations. Throughout the film, Vinz is clearly radicalised against the police, having participated in the riot and being excited for further action. This firm anti-police stance is reflective of Vinz's all-or-nothing thinking about the world. He has such limited opportunities and does not see leaving the banlieue as a possible. Vinz views the riots as the start of a war against the police; this is the first opportunity in his life where change seemed tangible or possible. He views not participating in this war as siding with the police against their community, saying "we live like shit in rat holes and you do sod all to change things". Vinz views this as a zero-sum-game and is insistent that if Abdel dies from his injuries, he will kill a police officer to "even the score". However, not all the characters agree with Vinz. Saïd clearly dislikes the police; one of the opening shots of the film is of him graffiting "fuck the police" on a riot van. Saïd, despite his dislike of the police, does not share Vinz's extreme views, possibly because he has seen the impact of police involvement first hand. Saïd's brother is currently in prison, and he states at one point that his "whole family" either are or have been incarcerated. He sees prison as an inevitability for himself, but in general seems to be wary of police and authority, having only had negative experiences with them. At one point in the film the boys leave the banlieue and go into central Paris. Upon asking a police officer for directions Saïd is surprised by how he is responded to, "he called me sir!". Being in the banlieue and being viewed as a resident of the banlieue has impacted upon police's interactions with Saïd, and thus his view of police. Outside of that setting, he is able to be viewed as a citizen rather than a troublemaker. The third main character, Hubert, dislikes police but is generally against the riots. There are multiple reasons for this, one being that the rioters trashed the boxing gym he set up for children in the community. Hubert is the most pragmatic of the three, he recognises the unfairness of the police's actions, however, does not see violence as the way to create change or better his situation. At one point Vinz says Hubert "thinks too much", and it is clear that he is the most thoughtful of the three. He wants to leave the banlieue eventually and is selling drugs to get money. It also appears that Hubert is supporting his family financially, his mother asks him about household bills, he provides books for his brother (who is in prison) and is a Black African boy in France during the time where racism is becoming part of the political mainstream (Siciliano, 2007). When interacting with police, the stakes are higher for Hubert. He "thinks too much" because he has to.

The characters' perspectives on police do change somewhat throughout the film, but rather than a radical shift in views, this is more subtle. All the characters become somewhat more aware of the nuances of the relationship between themselves, their community, and the police. The plot of the film centres on Vinz finding a gun during the riot, and the question of whether or not he will use it to kill a police officer. However, the structure of the film is a series of vignettes of different interactions the three characters have with other people. Almost all of these interactions involved Vinz, Saïd, and Hubert being observed, monitored, policed, or punished in some way. Examples of this include a scene early in the film where a rooftop barbeque party is broken up by plainclothes police officers saying they have no right to that space. Later in the film Vinz, Saïd, and Hubert are prevented by police from visiting Abdel in the hospital, which leads to a confrontation. The interactions with police and authority figures almost all start with the boys trying to do something innocuous and being told this isn't permitted or they lack the status to do so. In this light, the angry responses from Vinz are not surprising.

One of the non-confrontational interactions with police in the film occurs when Vinz and Hubert go to collect Saïd from a police station after he has been arrested. A plainclothes officer that they appear to know and have had conversations with before talks to them, trying to advise them to not

56 A Popular Criminology of Youth Justice

antagonise police further. He is clearly on the side of the status quo, saying "the pigs are trying to protect you", to which Hubert replies "and who protects us from you?". This interaction is interesting, the officer clearly sees Hubert as a potential leader within the community, partially due to his running the boxing gym. Seeing Hubert as someone to influence the broader community of children is flawed, as Hubert clearly doesn't see himself as fulfilling that role or appear to want it. Hubert is supportive of the ideas that the rioters represent, even if he is not in favour of their course of action. The role of race and ethnicity in *La Haine* cannot be overlooked, as all three main characters are minorities, placing the expectation on minorities to respond "appropriately" to the racist treatment they have received from both authorities and society at large is another injustice (see Chapter 5 for further discussion of this).

Ironically, throughout the film Vinz has much less of a personal reason for hatred of the police compared to Saïd and Hubert, who are brutally assaulted by police officers whilst being questioned. The circumstances of their arrest are questionable, upon trying to visit someone who owes Saïd money, they disrupt the expectations of a middle-class apartment building. Unsure which doorbell to ring to gain entry into the building, they ring all of them, which causes one of the residents to call the police. This wariness of children and sentiment of them not belonging in specific spaces is something that is echoed in society more broadly, with children being considered as "suspicious" for simply being in public spaces, leading to middle-class residents alerting police (Dollinger, 2021; MacDonald and Shildrick, 2007). After this clash between middle-class and working-class standards of acceptable behaviour, the police arrive and search Saïd and Hubert, finding Hubert's cannabis and arresting them, whilst Vinz runs away. Not knowing the etiquette of middle-class society is essentially what leads to their arrest, and marks them out as not belonging in this environment. The contrast between the officer who called Saïd "Sir" and their treatment once they have been identified as being from the banlieue is stark. The change in how they are perceived means the three boys are suddenly labelled as troublemakers for ringing doorbells.

The notion of ownership of space runs through *La Haine*, with accessing the apartment building being an example. The visuals of *La Haine* include graffiti in the banlieue and advertisements in central Paris. The contrast between these highlights one of the film's messages, about the lack of opportunities for specific subsets of children. Adverts and public art in a graffiti style with the slogans "we are the future" and "the world is yours" are mocked by the characters, with additional graffiti saying "fuck your mother" in response. These slogans clearly do not apply to the three main characters, who have limited opportunities within the banlieue, see prison as a natural progression of their lives, and for whom leaving the banlieue seems near impossible. This suggests that the capitalist ideal of success and development is only accessible by middle and upper-class groups, and individuals like Vinz, Saïd and Hubert are part of a perpetual underclass, which is maintained through over-policing, criminalisation, and imprisonment. Linking anti-capitalism to anti-police positions has been echoed within academic literature as well, such as Wilson and O'Sullivan's (2004) notion of authority reasserted narratives. Maintaining an underclass of working-class, minority, criminalised children protects the status quo, and with it capitalist structures. This contributes to why youth protest receives such a strong response from police, as it is not only disorderly, but disruptive. All the characters in *La Haine* seem aware of the unfairness of how they are treated, but respond to this differently. Vinz is clearly focused on revenge; he desires to kill a police officer to "get even". He does not seem to consider that this will not create the change he wants on a systemic level but focuses on this as it seems to be the only tangible action he can take. Hubert seems aware of the need for broader systemic change rather than small-scale action, but is jaded by the monumentality of this task, and does not seem to want the responsibility or position as a leader. Saïd takes a slightly more absurdist approach to the situation, aware of the unfairness, he resists in childish ways such as making jokes and using graffiti to express his views. Writing "fuck the police" on a police van won't change anything but allows him a visible outlet for his feelings. Towards the end of the film Saïd graffiti's one of the adverts proclaiming, "the world is yours", changing the slogan to "the world is ours". These small acts of resistance are emblematic of the potential for a different future for children, but their locations (on police vans and advertisements) suggest the need for broader institutional buy-in for this change to happen.

La Haine is on the whole pessimistic about the future for justice-involved children. Throughout the film we see how there is resistance to change. The officers questioning Hubert and Saïd after their arrest use this opportunity to train a new recruit on how to use headlocks and chokeholds, showing that brutalising children is seen as standard practice for police. Despite the previous riots being instigated by similar forms of police brutality, the officers are undeterred, suggesting that treating arrested individuals with violence is enjoyable, and that they actively want to cause harm.

The hardest part is not going too far even though you want to.

Within *La Haine* there is a clear cycle of brutality and protest. Police actions lead to protest, which is then used to justify further harsh treatment by police. This is something that is seen outside of fictional media as well; newspapers following the London 2011 riots described those involved as "yobs", and "morons" and called for harsh punishments and more stringent policing in response (Lewis et al., 2011; Moxon, 2011). These populist narratives are almost always in favour of "law and order" approaches particularly when

58 A Popular Criminology of Youth Justice

related to children, despite evidence suggesting that this causes further harm and embeds criminal identities (Baldry et al., 2018; Crawford, 2009). The end of *La Haine* implies the cycle of brutality and protest will continue. In the closing scene of the film, Vinz gives Hubert the gun he found earlier, saying that if he keeps it, he will use it, which is something he no longer wants to do. Immediately after this, Vinz and Saïd are stopped by the same plain-clothes police officers that they encountered earlier that day. One of the officers recognises Vinz and immediately threatens to shoot him for insulting him earlier, which causes a physical confrontation. Hubert runs over to help, but the officer's gun goes off accidentally, killing Vinz. The final image of the film is Hubert and the police officer pointing guns at each other as Saïd closes his eyes, and hears a single gunshot.

The ending of *La Haine* is shocking because of the death of characters we have come to empathise with over the past 98 minutes, but also because it subverts what appeared to be a (relatively) happy ending. Vinz's change of heart was positive and seemed a fitting conclusion to the narrative that started with him finding the gun. For him to die regardless of this (and potentially because of it due to giving the gun away), does not fit with audience expectations. Some of these expectations stem from previous problem youth films; hearing of Abdel's death from a news report is the catalyst Vinz's decision to eschew violence, similar to Jim in *Rebel Without A Cause* (1955). The ending of *La Haine* further cements the notion that justice-involved children cannot change, due to either a lack of desire or external circumstances, and the result of this is death.

La Haine is explicitly an anti-police film, with writer/director Mathieu Kassovitz being inspired by incidents of children dying due to police action occurring in France at the time (Forbes, 2000). *La Haine* is one of several banlieue films (also known as *beur cinema*), which took a social realist approach to depicting these communities and the lives of those within them. *Regarde-Moi* (2007), *Banlieue 13* (2004), and *Girlhood* (2014) are all examples that have built upon the success of *La Haine* and cemented the cultural depiction of banlieues as dangerous, violent and hopeless. *La Haine* is now regarded as a modern classic of French cinema, but upon release it received a polarising response. The film was subject to controversy, and accusations of inciting violence. Shortly after its release a child was killed whilst being chased by police, leading to riots. These were discussed as being "copycats" of the film (Sharma and Sharma, 2000). *La Haine* was screened for government officials at the time of its release, with the aim being to show that additional support was needed for these communities (Vincendeau, 2012). However, *La Haine* drew criticism, Jean-Marie Le Pen used this as a call for harsher policing of children, particularly linking this to riots and tensions that were already occurring within France at the time (Siciliano, 2007). It is clear that these tensions are ongoing in France; 2023 saw riots across France after a 17-year-old from a banlieue was shot by police during a traffic stop (Otte, 2023).

The banlieue film highlights many issues that were and are present in not just French society, but representing anywhere with social, political, and economic disparities. However, regarding children, the messages of these films are broadly negative. Whilst telling the stories of these environments is valuable, the characterisation of children is often stereotypical, and this is what remains with audiences. Justice-involved children in police films are shown as being anti-authority, quick to use violence, and accepting of criminality. Whilst this is often unintentional of the filmmakers, these messages have an impact. As viewers "discount towards the middle" (Wilson and O'Sullivan, 2004), the brutality of police and conditions of poverty may be considered as sensationalism, leaving the idea that children are inherently troubled and troubling, and potentially deserving of punishment.

Imprisoning Children

Alan Clarke's 1979 film *Scum* was based upon a TV play of the same name that was banned by the BBC due to its violent and sexual content. The decision to create a film was to give the ideas and themes of *Scum* a wider audience following the ban (Cloarec, 2013). Set within a borstal, *Scum* depicts the experience of Carlin (Ray Winstone), from induction to becoming "the daddy". Borstals were youth detention centres that existed primarily in England from 1908 to 1982 and were known to be violent and abusive, contributing to their abolition. *Scum* purposefully aimed to show the negatives of borstal; the brutality and trauma it caused to children. *Scum* includes many of the hallmarks of the prison film, such as the use of violence, social hierarchies, distrust between prisoners and staff, covert power structures, racism, rape, and suicide. These features of prison films are accepted and seen as genre conventions when appearing in films about adults, and whilst still shocking, do not tend to cause outcry. *Scum* is about children though, and this contrast between the brutality of imprisonment and the innocence of children led to concerns from censors. The original TV play was banned due to looking "too much like a documentary" (Cloarec, 2013), and the film version received an X certificate due to concerns that it would incite violence amongst younger viewers. The producers of the film commented that their aim for the film was the opposite and that the X certificate was somewhat ironic as "teenage kids should see it", viewing the film's brutality as a clear deterrent against offending (*BFI*, 2019).

One of the main themes of *Scum* is distrust. The "trainees" do not trust the staff to protect them or treat them appropriately, the staff do not trust the trainees to behave or reform in any way. Archer (Mick Ford), one of the older trainees, maintains a positive attitude through civil disobedience.

60 A Popular Criminology of Youth Justice

He tries to highlight the issues inherent within the borstal system, such as the drive for unquestioning obedience over all else. However, those around him view him as cocky, stupid, or purposefully disruptive. Archer tries to reason with a guard on this point, arguing that the borstal is inhumane to both children and staff, writing them all off as unable to develop or engage with society at large. However, this is taken as an insult and leads to further punishment and ostracism for Archer.

Duke: I give you my fucking coffee, and think you can sit there and have the piss out of me?
Archer: No sir, I didn't... I, I never get the chance to express myself.
Duke: Then it's as well you don't, lad!

The violence depicted within *Scum* is unflinching and brutal. There are numerous set pieces of violence throughout the film, again mirroring the conventions of the adult prison film. Whether this violence is from staff to trainees, between trainees, self-harm, or a full-scale riot, it is portrayed as expected, with the message being that this is the norm within the borstal setting. There is evidence to support this; the poor conditions and violence being one of the contributing factors to the closure of borstals (Gibbens, 1984; Warder and Wilson, 1973) and the development of Young Offender Institutions (YOIs) as a replacement. However, this does not mean that violence and harm resulting from custody are no longer an issue within youth justice. Research highlights that YOIs, and their private counterparts, Secure Training Centres, are still dangerous places for children (Simpson, 2021; Stone, 2012). Whilst the levels of violence are much lower when compared to borstals, violence does still occur, including from staff. This takes both unsanctioned and sanctioned forms, particularly linked to the practice of secure restraint and the use of physical force (Peterson-Badali and Koegl, 2002; Puffett, 2016).

Writer Roy Minton has said that audiences and censors may have responded better to the film version of *Scum* than the TV play because the cast was older, all being over 20. Audiences did not appreciate a critique of borstals being acted out by those young enough to actually be detained in them. This shows the need for youth justice films to appear fictional enough to be palatable to audiences. *Scum* received a polarised response from the public. Some were appalled by the depiction of violence, seeing the film as sensationalist and glorifying criminality. Others viewed it as a damning indictment of the borstal system, highlighting the harms it caused to children (Cloarec, 2013). The film remained controversial for years following its release; Channel 4 was prosecuted for showing it in 1982, and despite the video and DVD releases of the film never being banned, it is commonly listed as a "video nasty". *Scum* was followed by similar films, such as *Scrubbers* (1982), which is often considered as a companion piece to *Scum*. However, few have had the same cultural impact, or dared to show the same level of violence. *The Loneliness of the Long Distance Runner* (1962) is set in a borstal, however focuses on one boy's personal reflections on his life and what has led to his institutionalisation. *Borstal Boy* (2000), focuses on the romance between two trainees. There are generally few other prison films about children. The British social realist trend of filmmaking was too difficult to apply to imprisoned children. Other filmmakers developed their own approach, such as depicting prison camps. Children's prison camp films are interesting to consider because many of them utilise conventions of adult prison films, but also conventions of adult prisons. Borstal films such as *Scum* did emphasise that the characters were children, even if this was to highlight their "dangerousness". However, prison camp films take a different approach; adultifiying their young characters.

The prison camp film is a uniquely American type of media, featuring in both film and documentary/reality television. Few countries use prison camps as sites of punishment, and fewer for children. The prison camp film is also unique in that it shows punishment, but avoids the context of a formal prison, meaning that it doesn't instantly appear as restrictive or harsh as the classic prison film, and doesn't conjure the same stereotypes in the minds of the audience. *Holes* (2003) is one of the most popular examples of the juvenile prison camp film and is interesting in that it is one of the few films depicting punishment of justice-involved children that is intended for and marketed to children. *Holes* was produced by Disney, which creates certain expectations; such as not featuring death, swearing, and being appropriate for a wide audience (the BBFC awarded the film a PG certificate, with a content note for "mild violence"). In considering *Holes*, we can develop an understanding of how the narratives of punishment of justice-involved children are addressed in more child-friendly stories, opposed to the social realism of *Scum*.

Holes is the story of Stanley Yelnats (Shia LeBeouf), who is arrested for theft and sentenced to 18 months at a prison camp; Camp Greenlake, where the punishment is to dig a 5ft deep hole every day. At the beginning of the film, the hole digging is framed by the staff of Camp Greenlake as "character building". Both this and the language used by the staff towards the children at the camp (they are frequently referred to as "girl scouts") sets out the idea that justice-involved children are too "soft" and need to learn the harsh lessons of reality, which can be achieved through manual labour. This echoes the messages from *Blackboard Jungle* (1955); that justice-involved children's purpose is manual labour and to become accustomed to (and compliant with) this early in life.

As Stanley enters Camp Greenlake he is shown around by Mr Sir (Jon Voight), who points out the lack of fences or guard towers at Camp Greenlake; there is no need for security measures as the desert setting of the camp is so inhospitable that escape is essentially impossible. This device

62 A Popular Criminology of Youth Justice

means that the film does not have to show "guards" in the traditional mould of prison films, and both Mr Sir and the counsellor Dr Pendanski (Tim Blake Nelson) treat the children in their charge (who are referred to as campers rather than prisoners) reasonably well. Whilst their language towards them is derisory, their actions are relatively passive. Some of this may be due to being a Disney film, meaning adults behaving violently towards children would be inappropriate. The setting of the film being a prison camp is made clear through common tropes of prison films; the boys wear orange jumpsuits, they eat in a canteen from trays and the food is essentially slop, and sunflower seeds are equivalent to currency (a child appropriate proxy for cigarettes). However, the architecture of Camp Greenlake is distinctly different from that of a prison; it more resembles a summer camp. When being sentenced the Judge even gives Stanley the option of Camp Greenlake or a juvenile detention centre. This contrast of setting and situation means the audience is clear that this is a proxy for a prison, priming them to expect certain things, without the film having to portray them. This means *Holes* can avoid a lot of the concerns and issues that come with presenting children in prison, whilst still drawing upon the cultural narratives of the prison film.

The boys at Camp Greenlake have clearly developed into a prison culture. They all have nicknames and use these exclusively, to the point that even the staff at the camp don't use their given names. There is a clear social hierarchy, with in-groups and out-groups, and social exclusion and violence are clear consequences of violating this hierarchy. This can be seen in things like when the boys queue up for water, there is a clear order to the queue, with boys being told by others to "get in their place". This can also be seen in relation to the reward system in the camp. The holes that are dug are namely to "build character" however, the governor is clearly looking for something valuable buried in the desert and is using child labour to find it, only running the camp for this purpose. If during the course of digging anything deemed suitably interesting is found, that boy will receive the rest of the day off. When Stanley finds an engraved lipstick tube (which is mistaken for a bullet casing), X-Ray (Brenden Jefferson), who is the leader of their group, demands to be given it as he's been there longer and is therefore more deserving of a day off. The social hierarchy of the camp uses exclusion as a way of showing who is favoured. Zero (Khleo Thomas) has very little status with the other campers, he is resented because he is good at digging and finishes his hole quicker than everyone else, and excluded socially because he doesn't speak. Making fun of Zero becomes such an in-group activity that even the staff engage in this with camp counsellor Dr Pendanski (Tim Blake Nelson) saying he received that nickname because he "has zero in his head".

Camp Greenlake has made some concessions to appear inclusive and supportive of children's development. However, these are clearly only cosmetic. The "library" is full of spades rather than books, the "mentor" Stanley is

"This Ain't a Girl Scout Camp!" **63**

assigned only shows him the prison culture rather than genuine mentoring, and staff encourage violence between campers. When Stanley is punched by another camper, Dr Pendanski tells him to "teach him a lesson, hit him back". The idea of a prison camp as a "softer" form of punishment when compared to a prison is not born out at Camp Greenlake. The philosophy of Camp Greenlake is made explicit by the characters.

> *You take a bad boy, make him dig holes all day in the hot sun, and it turns him into a good boy*

The adult characters in the film mirror the narratives of individual responsibility that have pervaded punitive aspects of youth justice (Kelly, 2001). They are told that they have "screwed up" their lives in group counselling and that it is their responsibility to "fix it". Additionally, any form of cooperation is frowned upon or actively punished by the camp. Stanley begins to teach Zero to read, in exchange for help digging his holes each day. Rather than viewing this as developing a pro-social bond and a genuine opportunity for mentoring, this is prohibited, with Dr Pendanski saying "If Zero digs your hole, you're not learning your lesson". The ethos of the staff is that the boys need toughening up to be able to cope with the adult world they are entering, that their criminal behaviour is a sign that they have not yet adjusted to the rules and restrictions of the world around them, but they will over time, much like they will adjust to the arduousness of digging ("Everything turns to callous eventually"). The idea that life is a Sisyphean endeavour and the transition to adulthood is where children come to terms with the challenges of life is an interesting one, that has been echoed throughout history and philosophy. However, the idea that for children struggling with this transition, the appropriate support is to make things harder to speed up this process is flawed. Justice-involved children have often already missed out on cultural cues or informal teaching on how to "become" an adult, due to social exclusion, low socio-economic status, and cycles of offending in families (Barry, 2017; MacDonald, 2006). Therefore assuming they will pick up these implicit lessons through being required to carry out manual labour is a foolhardy endeavour, and means that these children are more likely to become embedded in criminal pathways.

The overall message of *Holes* is not one of prison abolition, or youth justice reform. It very clearly conforms to the "justice restored" and "authority reasserted" narratives. Despite the conditions and attitudes of those at Camp Greenlake, the film portrays change in the young characters, implying that this type of punishment is effective. Both Stanley and Zero agree that being at the camp has changed them in positive ways, through allowing them to meet each other, and encouraging them to do new things. The adversity they have faced at the camp has allowed them to "build character". Stanley would

64 A Popular Criminology of Youth Justice

still be a loser with bad luck had he not been sent to Camp Greenlake. The other young characters are also subtly telegraphed as having been positively changed by their experience. When Stanley is released at the end of the film, the other campers crowd around him, asking him to pass on messages to their families. One camper says "Tell my momma I'm sorry. Tell her Theodore says sorry". This use of a given name (a name "society will recognise") as opposed to a nickname, alongside the repentant message, indicates the campers do recognise the harms of their criminal identities and see the need for change. The film challenges the idea of punishment being used as a means for private profit, however, it does not challenge the need for punishment or harsh treatment of justice-involved children at all. At the end of *Holes*, Camp Greenlake is taken over by the government, to end the corrupt child labour practices currently occurring. One of the state agents even says, "lets show these boys a different side to the criminal justice system". With the state taking control of Camp Greenlake, "real justice" can be done; the authority has been reasserted and the punishment of children can happen in the "right" way. However, it is not clear what this means and given that it will Camp Greenlake will become state run, it is more likely to be in the mould of a "traditional" prison institution, which is no guarantee of "justice".

Holes is different to the other films discussed in this chapter. *Scum* and *La Haine* are explicitly anti-authority, anti-police, and anti-prison. *Holes'* implicit message is pro-prison and pro-punishment. That this is the message from a Disney film is not necessarily surprising, however, that this film is aimed at young audiences is somewhat troubling. Clearly children receive societal messages about what "justice" is from an early age, and that these messages essentially responsiblise justice-involved children and promote harsh treatment as a mechanism for change shows the extent to which the demonisation of children has become mainstream. That films depicting the policing and imprisonment of children only emphasise that what is expected of them is conformity is problematic. Works like *Scum* and *La Haine*, whilst criticising criminal justice's treatment of children, do not depict justice-involved children differently to the problem youth films that reinforced the social construction of children as delinquent and deserving harsh treatment. This emphasises the need for a differing approach to portraying justice-involved children in film, one that depicts them as children.

Film List

21 Jump Street (2012)
Banlieue 13 (2004)
Blackboard Jungle (1955)
Borstal Boy (2000)
Cop and A Half (1993)

Dixon of Dock Green (1955-1976, TV Series)
Girlhood (2014)
Hot Fuzz (2007)
Kindergarden Cop (1990)
La Haine (1995)
Life on Mars (2006-2007, TV Series)
Mid90s (2018)
Paddington 2 (2017)
Porridge (1974-1977, TV Series)
Rebel Without A Cause (1955)
Regarde-Moi (2007)
Scrubbers (1982)
Scum (1979)
The Green Mile (1999)
The Loneliness of the Long Distance Runner (1962)
The Shawshank Redemption (1994)

References

Abrams LS (2005) Listening to juvenile offenders: Can residential treatment prevent recidivism? *Child and Adolescent Social Work Journal* 23(1): 61–85.

Ahlin EM (2019) Moving beyond prison rape: Assessing sexual victimization among youth in custody. *Aggression and Violent Behavior* 47: 160–168.

Alalehto T and Larsson D (2016) Measuring trust in the police by contextual and individual factors. *International Journal of Law, Crime and Justice* 46: 31–42. Academic Press.

Alliance for Youth Justice (2022) The neglected realities of child stop and search - StopWatch. Available at: https://www.ayj.org.uk/news-content/stopwatch-child-stop-and-search (accessed 27 June 2023).

Baldry E, Briggs DB, Goldson B, et al. (2018) 'Cruel and unusual punishment': An inter-jurisdictional study of the criminalisation of young people with complex support needs. *Journal of Youth Studies* 21(5): 636–652. Routledge.

Bandes SA (2021) From Dragnet to Brooklyn 99: How Cop Shows Excuse, Exalt and Erase Police Brutality. 3835444, SSRN Scholarly Paper. Rochester, NY. Available at: https://papers.ssrn.com/abstract=3835444 (accessed 11 July 2023).

Barry M (2017) '*Youth Offending, Youth Transitions and Social Recognition*': *Rethinking Youth Justice Policy and Practice*. In: Direção-Geral de Reinserção e Serviços Prisionais (ed.). Lisbon: Ministry of Justice [Portugal]. Available at: https://strathprints.strath.ac.uk/62694/ (accessed 21 July 2022).

Bateman T (2010) Reoffending as a measure of effectiveness of youth justice intervention: A critical note. *Safer Communities* 9(3): 28–35.

Bateman T (2011) 'We now breach more kids in a week than we used to in a whole year': The punitive turn, enforcement and custody. *Youth Justice* 11(2): 115–133.

Bateman T (2012) Who pulled the plug? Towards an explanation of the fall in child imprisonment in England and Wales. *Youth Justice* 12(1): 36–52. SAGE Publications.

Bennett J (2006) The good, the bad and the ugly: The media in prison films. *The Howard Journal of Criminal Justice* 45(2): 97–115.

BFI (2019) Scum at 40: Still the daddy. Available at: https://www.bfi.org.uk/features/scum-40 (accessed 17 May 2023).

Blagg H (2012) Re-imagining youth justice: Cultural contestation in the Kimberley region of Australia since the 1991 Royal Commission into Aboriginal Deaths in Custody. *Theoretical Criminology* 16(4): 481–498. SAGE Publications Ltd.

Bowling B and Phillips C (2007) Disproportionate and discriminatory: Reviewing the evidence on police stop and search. *Modern Law Review* 70(6): 936–961. Wiley/Blackwell (10.1111).

Brown JA (1993) Bullets, buddies, and bad guys: The "action-cop" genre. *Journal of Popular Film and Television* 21(2): 79–87. Routledge.

Brunson RK and Pegram K (2018) "Kids do not so much make trouble, they are trouble": Police-youth relations. *Future of Children* 28(1): 83–102. Center for the Future of Children.

Case S and Bateman T (2020) The punitive transition in youth justice: Reconstructing the child as offender. *Children and Society* 34(6): 475–491.

Case S and Haines K (2014) Children first, offenders second positive promotion: Reframing the prevention debate. *Youth Justice* 15(3): 226–239. SAGE Publications.

Case S and Hazel N (2020) Child first, offender second – A progressive model for education in custody. *International Journal of Educational Development* 77: 102244.

Chaney P (2015) Popularism and punishment or rights and rehabilitation? Electoral discourse and structural policy narratives on youth justice: Westminster Elections, 1964-2010. *Youth Justice* 15(1): 23–41. SAGE Publications Inc.

Cloarec N (2013) From the Banned Telefilm to the Feature Film: The Two Versions of Alan Clarke's Scum (1977-1979). *Revue LISA/LISA e-journal. Littératures, Histoire des Idées, Images, Sociétés du Monde Anglophone – Literature, History of Ideas, Images and Societies of the English-speaking World* (Vol. XI-n°3). Vol. XI-n°3. Presses Universitaires de Rennes. Epub ahead of print 26 November 2013. https://doi.org/10.4000/lisa.5549

Crawford A (2009) Crieminalizing sociability through anti-social behaviour legislation: Dispersal powers, young people and the police. *Youth Justice* 9(1): 5–26. SAGE Publications.

Crest Advisory (2022) Forgotten voices: Policing, stop and search and the perspectives of Black children. Available at: https://www.crestadvisory.com/post/forgotten-voices-policing-stop-and-search-and-the-perspectives-of-black-children (accessed 27 June 2023).

Davies S (2022) Strip search of children by the Metropolitan Police Service - new analysis by the Children's Commissioner for England. Available at: https://www.childrenscommissioner.gov.uk/blog/strip-search-of-children-by-the-metropolitan-police-service-new-analysis-by-the-childrens-commissioner-for-england/ (accessed 27 June 2023).

Dollinger B (2021) *Changing Narratives of Youth Crime: From Social Causes to Threats to the Social.* S.l.: Routledge.

Dowler K;, Fleming T; and Muzzatti SL (2006) Constructing crime: Media, crime, and popular culture. *Canadian Journal of Criminology and Criminal Justice* 48: 837–850.

Ellem K and Richards K (2018) Police contact with young people with cognitive disabilities: Perceptions of procedural (in)justice. *Youth Justice* 18(3): 230–247. SAGE Publications Inc.

Flacks S (2018) The stop and search of minors: A 'vital police tool'? *Criminology & Criminal Justice* 18(3): 364–384. SAGE Publications.

Forbes J (2000) La haine. In: Forbes J and Street S (eds) *European Cinema: An Introduction*. London: Macmillan Education UK, pp. 170–180. Available at: https://doi.org/10.1007/978-1-137-08034-9_12 (accessed 3 May 2023).

Garland J and Bilby C (2011) 'What next, dwarves?': Images of police culture in life on Mars. *Crime, Media, Culture* 7(2): 115–132. SAGE Publications.

Gibbens TCN (1984) Borstal boys after 25 years. *The British Journal of Criminology* 24(1): 49–62. Oxford University Press.

Ginwright S and James T (2002) From assets to agents of change: Social justice, organizing, and youth development. *New Directions for Youth Development* (96): 27–46.

Goldson B (2005) Child imprisonment: A case for abolition. *Youth Justice* 21(1): 77–90.

Goldson B (2019) *Youth Justice: Contemporary Policy and Practice*. Routledge, Taylor & Francis Group. Available at: https://www.routledge.com/Youth-Justice-Contemporary-Policy-and-Practice/Goldson/p/book/9781138360044 (accessed 11 July 2023).

Gooch K and von Berg P (2019) What happens in the beginning, matters in the end: Achieving best evidence with child suspects in the police station. *Youth Justice* 19(2): 85–101. SAGE Publications Inc.

Griffiths A, Milne B and Cherryman J (2011) A question of control? The formulation of suspect and witness interview question strategies by advanced interviewers. *International Journal of Police Science and Management* 13(3): 255–267.

Haydon D (2020) Detained children: Vulnerability, violence and violation of rights. *International Journal for Crime, Justice and Social Democracy* 9(4): 16–30. Queensland University of Technology.

Hedges I (2014) Prison films: An overview. *Socialism and Democracy* 28(3): 203–207. Routledge.

Independent Police Complaints Commission (2014) Deaths in or following police custody continue to fall but mental health remains an issue. Available at: https://www.ipcc.gov.uk/news/deaths-or-following-police-custody-continue-fall-mental-health-remains-issue (accessed 26 February 2015).

Jackson DB, Fahmy C, Vaughn MG, et al. (2019) Police stops among at-risk youth: Repercussions for mental health. *Journal of Adolescent Health* 65(5): 627–632. Elsevier USA.

Jewkes Y (2005) Creating a stir? Prisons, popular media and the power to reform. In: Paul Mason (ed) *Captured by the Media*. Oxon: Willan, pp. 137–153.

Kelly P (2001) Youth at risk: Processes of individualisation and responsibilisation in the risk society. *Discourse: Studies in the Cultural Politics of Education* 22(1): 23–33. Routledge.

Lam-Knott S (2017) Understanding protest "violence" in Hong Kong from the youth perspective. *Asian Anthropology* 16(4): 279–298. Routledge.

Levan K, Polzer K and Downing S (2011) Media and prison sexual assault: How we got to the "don't drop the soap" culture. *International Journal of Criminology and Sociological Theory* 4(2). 2.

Lewis P, Newburn T, Taylor M, et al. (2011) Reading the riots. Available at: https://www.theguardian.com/uk/series/reading-the-riots (accessed 1 October 2017).

Linnemann T (2019) Bad cops and true detectives: The horror of police and the unthinkable world. *Theoretical Criminology* 23(3): 355–374. SAGE Publications Ltd.

MacDonald R (2006) Social exclusion, youth transitions and criminal careers: Five critical reflections on 'risk'. *Australian & New Zealand Journal of Criminology* 39(3): 371–383. SAGE Publications Ltd.

MacDonald R and Shildrick T (2007) Street corner society: Leisure careers, youth (sub)culture and social exclusion. *Leisure Studies* 26(3): 339–355. Routledge.

Martin T (2023) The genre of police. *Crime, Media, Culture* 20(1): 17416590231168523. SAGE Publications.

Mason P (2003) The screen machine: Cinematic representations of prison. In: Paul Mason (ed) *Criminal Visions*. Oxon: Willan, pp. 278–297.

McFarland MJ, Geller A and McFarland C (2019) Police contact and health among urban adolescents: The role of perceived injustice. *Social Science and Medicine* 238: 112487. Elsevier Ltd.

Miles S (2014) Young people, 'flawed protestors' and the commodification of resistance. *Critical Arts* 28(1): 76–87. Routledge.

Moxon D (2011) Consumer culture and the 2011 'riots'. *Sociological Research Online* 16(4): 1–5.

Muncie J (2008) The `punitive turn' in juvenile justice: Cultures of control and rights compliance in Western Europe and the USA. *Youth Justice* 8(2): 107–121.

O'Sullivan S (2001) Representations of prison in nineties hollywood cinema: From con air to the Shawshank redemption. *The Howard Journal of Criminal Justice* 40(4): 317–334.

Otte J (2023) 'French people are angry': Communities react after protests. *The Guardian*, 10 July. Available at: https://www.theguardian.com/world/2023/jul/10/french-people-are-angry-communities-react-after-protests (accessed 13 July 2023).

Payne B, Hobson J and Lynch K (2020) 'We just want to be treated with respect!': Using restorative approaches and the dramatic arts to build positive relationships between the police and young people. *Youth Justice* 21(3): 255–274. SAGE Publications Inc.

Peterson-Badali M and Koegl CJ (2002) Juveniles' experiences of incarceration: The role of correctional staff in peer violence. *Journal of Criminal Justice* 30(1): 41–49.

Puffett N (2016) Urgent call for staffing overhaul to make youth custody safer. *Children and Young People Now* 2016(2): 8–9. Mark Allen Group.

Rafter NH (2000) *Shots in the Mirror: Crime Films and Society*. Oxford Berlin: Oxford University Press.

Rawlinson K (2019) Scotland Yard defends response to climate change protests. *The Guardian*, 18 April. Available at: https://www.theguardian.com/environment/2019/apr/18/scotland-yard-defends-response-to-climate-change-protests (accessed 13 July 2023).

Reiner R (2010) The dialectics of dixon: The changing image of the TV Cop (1994). In: Chris Greer (ed) *Crime and Media*. Oxon: Routledge, pp. 302–310.

Sharma S and Sharma A (2000) `So Far So Good…': La Haine and the poetics of the everyday. *Theory, Culture and Society* 17(3): 103–116. SAGE Publications Ltd.

Siciliano A (2007) La Haine: Framing the 'urban outcasts'. *ACME: An International Journal for Critical Geographies* 6(2): 211–230.

Simpson F (2021) Custody rethink needed, say critics. *Children and Young People Now* 2021(12): 11–11. Mark Allen Group.

Stephens Griffin N (2021) 'Everyone was questioning everything': Understanding the derailing impact of undercover policing on the lives of UK environmentalists. *Social Movement Studies* 20(4): 459–477. Routledge.

Stone N (2012) Legal commentary 'A Sorry Tale': Forcible physical restraint of children in custody. *Youth Justice* 12(3): 245–257. SAGE Publications.

Such E and Walker R (2005) Young citizens or policy objects? Children in the 'rights and responsibilities' debate. *Journal of Social Policy* 34(1): 39–57.

Taflan P and Jalil R (2020) Children in Custody 2019-19. HM Inspectorate of Prisons. Available at: http://www.justiceinspectorates.gov.uk/hmiprisons/about-our-inspections/ (accessed 12 August 2020).

Taylor C (2016) *Review of the Youth justice System in England and Wales*. Ministry of Justice London: The Stationery Office. Epub ahead of print 2016.

Townsend M (2010) Metropolitan Police face legal action for kettling children during tuition fees protest. *The Observer*, 26 December. Available at: https://www.theguardian.com/uk/2010/dec/26/metropolitan-police-lawsuit-student-protest (accessed 13 July 2023).

Vincendeau G (2012) La haine and after: Arts, Politics, and the Banlieue. Available at: https://www.criterion.com/current/posts/642-la-haine-and-after-arts-politics-and-the-banlieue (accessed 14 June 2023).

Waid-Lindberg CA, Dobbs RR and O' Connor Shelley T (2011) Blame the media? The influence of primary news source , frequency of usage, and perceived media credibility on punitive attitudes. *Western Criminology Review* 12(3): 41–59.

Warder J and Wilson R (1973) British Borstal training system, *The Journal of Criminal Law and Criminology* 64: 118.

Weaver M, Morris S and Grierson J (2023) Police admit following e-bike before crash that killed Cardiff teenagers. *The Guardian*, 23 May. Available at: https://www.theguardian.com/uk-news/2023/may/23/south-wales-police-van-was-pursuing-teenagers-in-cardiff-force-admits (accessed 13 July 2023).

Whyte WF (1993) *Street Corner Society: The Social Structure of an Italian Slum*. Chicago: University of Chicago Press.

Wilson D and O'Sullivan S (2004) *Images of Incarceration: Representations of Prison in Film and Television Drama*. Winchester, U.K: Waterside Press.

Wilson D and O'Sullivan S (2005) Re-theorizing the penal reform functions of the prison film: Revelation, humanization, empathy and benchmarking. *Theoretical Criminology* 9(4): 471–491. SAGE Publications Ltd.

Young B and Turanovic JJ (2022) Spatial distance as a barrier to visitation for incarcerated youth and why families overcome it. *Justice Quarterly* 39(2): 354–378. Routledge.

Youth Justice Board (2023) Youth Justice Statistics: 2021 to 2022 (accessible version). Available at: https://www.gov.uk/government/statistics/youth-justice-statistics-2021-to-2022/youth-justice-statistics-2021-to-2022-accessible-version (accessed 27 June 2023).

Zamponi L, Baukloh AC, Bertuzzi N, et al. (2022) (Water) bottles and (street) barricades: The politicisation of lifestyle-centred action in youth climate strike participation. *Journal of Youth Studies* 25(6): 854–875. Routledge.

4

"I KILLED THE TEEN DREAM! DEAL WITH IT!"

Gender, Violence, and Crime

The way in which criminal justice treats girls and women as perpetrators of crime is a growing, but still under-explored area. Whilst the majority of criminal behaviour is carried out by men and boys (Austin, 1993), girls' and women's criminal behaviour has long been a subject of societal and criminological interest. Gender and crime is a broad subject and has focused on women's victimisation, criminalisation, and demonisation (Heidensohn, 1989). From bio-essentialist theories (Gatti and Verde, 2012) to more recent feminist work (Chesney-Lind, 1989) and the development of intersectional criminologies (Calleja, 2022), the how and why of women's justice involvement is an ever-evolving area. This development is an interesting contrast with youth justice, as both areas have emerged over similar timeframes, and have been subject to overlapping societal concerns. Just as the innocent-dangerous dichotomy has shaped youth justice responses on both social and legal levels, women involved in crime are also often subject to a similar binary. Due to broader stereotypes and (patriarchal) social expectations of women, those who become involved in criminal justice tend to be categorised as either "ideal victims" (Christie, 1986), or as doubly deviant (Heidensohn, 1989). For justice-involved girls, this poses an additional layer of complexity. Justice-involved girls are perceived as transgressing multiple social boundaries (Flores et al., 2018), which often means they are considered as dangerous rather than as victims (Modrowski et al., 2021). Firstly, by breaking the law, and thus behaving inappropriately. Secondly, by going against the expected behaviour for a child, and becoming deviant. Thirdly, by acting outside the social expectations of femininity. It is this third dimension that this chapter will explore in more detail; how the expectation of children and young women to be "good girls" has played out in

DOI: 10.4324/9781003403159-4

society, and how those who defy these expectations through criminalised behaviours are portrayed in media.

The social perception of justice-involved girls has a profound impact upon their experiences with criminal justice. Research has suggested that girls are treated differently at almost all stages of criminal justice processes, from arrest through to sentencing (Baidawi et al., 2023). Feminist scholars have questioned these differences, arguing that this often arises from misogynistic and patriarchal perceptions of women (Sharpe, 2016). For justice-involved girls there is also a clear intersection of these issues with class, as those who meet the expectations of middle-class standards are often treated differently within criminal justice systems than working-class girls, of whom crime is expected behaviour (Hollingworth, 2015; Modrowski et al., 2021), and thus are responsibilised for it (Kelly, 2001). This is compounded when intersecting with race, and the expectations for minority ethnicity girls are even more difficult to uphold (Drew et al., 2022; Farinde-Wu et al., 2022) The expectations of femininity are complex and for girls, these are also bound up in expectations of "childhood". This means that "girlhood" has a unique set of pressures and requirements that other childhood experiences do not. Currie *et al.* (2007) point out the specific contradictions of "girlhood", arguing that it is a falsity that is placed upon girls through adults, media and their own expectations, creating an impossible standard.

> girls must be pretty but not "self-absorbed" about their appearance; they must be attractive to boys but not seen to be too sexually "forward"; they must be noticed and liked by the "right people" but not a social climber; independent but not a "loner"; and so on.
>
> *Currie et al. (2007: 24)*

For girls in the transitional stages between childhood and adult, the expectations of girlhood place a focus on their own agency, meaning the ability to make choices about their own lives and act on them. However, there are clear limits on what is a socially acceptable use of this agency. Being empowered means building social networks and relationships (including expectations of heteronormative relationships), developing self-confidence and bodily acceptance (through engaging with fashion and makeup in traditionally feminine ways) and taking advantage of the opportunities offered to them (through engaging with formal education and/or work). This requires girls to be constantly aware of themselves and their surroundings and to be active in seeing positive opportunities. However, there are social imposed limits on this use of agency; taking too much pride or being empowered in the wrong way, such as by questioning authority, deviating from social norms, being queer, or using agency in ways perceived as selfish, means that a girl has become deviant, difficult, and/or "mean" (Chesney-Lind and Irwin, 2008). Girlhood is in

72 A Popular Criminology of Youth Justice

essence an impossible state to achieve or maintain, as is the expectation of adult femininity in a patriarchal system.

The expectations of girlhood impact upon justice-involved girls in particular. The results of this are that girls in criminal justice who appear to meet the standards of girlhood often receive more lenient sentences than not only their male counterparts (Bath, 2017), but also girls who do not necessarily conform to these expectations (Baidawi et al., 2023). Girls who do not meet these standards are often those who are from working-class backgrounds, of a minority ethnicity, are more likely to have experienced poverty, neglect, abuse, and have unsupported physical health, mental health, and educational needs (Sharpe, 2012, 2016; Sharpe and Gelsthorpe, 2009) shows the problematic nature of these assumptions within criminal justice. For justice-involved girls, the deck was stacked against them from the beginning, and their lack of social agency or power is perceived as yet another failing. Given their social exclusion, it is not surprising that some girls' responses to these pressures are alternative, or criminal actions.

The discrepancies in the treatment of justice-involved girls intersects with social concerns and moral panics, meaning some justice-involved girls are perceived as being "doubly deviant" (Heidensohn, 1989). Sexualisation is a key example of this. During the late 1990s and early 2000s there was a focus on girls' sexual behaviour, and concern that this was a "ruination" of children (Gelsthorpe and Worrall, 2009; Sharpe, 2009). This in particular was tied to adolescence and the idea that sexual behaviour is an example of teenage girls' uncontrollability (Chesney-Lind and Irwin, 2008), with many perceiving this as deviant behaviour and associating it with criminality (Sharpe and Gelsthorpe, 2009). This association created a larger social focus on justice-involved girls, and thus increased the reporting of crime statistics relating to them. Following this change in reporting, societal concerns shifted to violent behaviours. The panic around girls' sexuality and uncontrollability contributed to the concern regarding girls' violence (Sharpe and Gelsthorpe, 2009), with commentators asking why girls were behaving "like boys" (Chesney-Lind and Irwin, 2008). This mirrored cultural changes at the time, with the desire for gender parity leading to gender-blind approaches within criminal justice institutions. These approaches often led to theories, ideas, and evidence for "what works" with boys, being applied to girls (Hodgson, 2022), further contributing to changes in statistical reporting on girls' criminal behaviours. What appeared as a sudden increase in violent crimes by girls, was really a result of increased attention (Sharpe and Gelsthorpe, 2009). However, this ignited social fears about girls' propensity for violence, in a similar way to concerns about teenage boys and delinquency in the 1950s. The portrayal of girls' violence within society was viewed through the lens of femininity; boys' violence is viewed as being due to aggression and taking a physical form, whereas girls' violence is seen as relational, and involving psychological manipulation (Currie et al., 2007; Peguero and Popp, 2012).

The idea that a "good girl" could suddenly transform into a violent, sexually active, uncontrollable monster was respectable society's "worst nightmare", playing on existing fears, stereotypes, and tropes, further embedded by films like *The Bad Seed* (1956) and *Reform School Girls* (1986). Predictably, this played out in fictional films, however, this was not given the serious treatment of boys offending. Whereas boys' violence on film became ultraviolence, girls' violence became comedy. Representations of justice-involved children on film are not always aiming for accuracy, whilst some filmmakers explicitly try to create social realism in their works, others explicitly veer away from this, using the tropes of genre film. But the choice of genre appears to be gendered in a way that emphasises fear in relation to boys' crimes and dismissal of girls. Reflecting the social horror expressed at teenage delinquency, some films use the trappings of horror films to represent justice-involved children, and often these are violent boys, bent on destruction for the pleasure it gives them. *A Clockwork Orange* (1971) is a prime example of this. *A Clockwork Orange* revels in the violence of the main character Alex and his friends, confronting audiences with heavily stylised versions of their social fears. However, this violence is not presented uncritically. Alex receives clear consequences for his actions, being sentenced to prison and participating in a trial for a form of aversion therapy, where Alex is forced to view violence in an effort to become desensitised to it, paralleling the position of the audience. Many films about violent boys utilise the idea of media influence and the cultural fascination with violence. *Benny's Video* (1992), *Funny Games* (1997), and *The Big Finish* (2000) all play with the relationship between media and crime to create social commentary, whilst also showing violence committed by children. The tone of these films is serious, they are presented as high culture, and have resulted in debate, scholarship, and critical consideration (Frey, 2006; Grundmann, 2010; Jackson, 2000). Boys' violence has become "serious cinema". However, depictions of girls' violence differ greatly, often using comedy rather than horror or drama, sending the message that girl's violence is an entertaining diversion, not to be taken seriously. These films tend to be set within high schools, and the violence depicted is generally a way for the characters to protect their lifestyles, gain social power, or remove competitors. The violence portrayed in these films is a reflection of the social perception of girlhood, and how girls are characterised. Just as girls in society are not taken seriously, neither are films about girls' violence. These films may reference *A Clockwork Orange but* are likely to immediately satirise it. Girls' violence on film is played as a joke, but this allows genuine critiques of the pressures of girlhood to avoid the gaze of academic film discourse and speak directly to those it impacts, girls. To truly understand the impact of media upon

74 A Popular Criminology of Youth Justice

perceptions of justice-involved girls, the relationship between media and girlhood must be considered. We need to enter girl world.

Girl World as a Site of Violence

The lives and behaviours (criminal or otherwise) of girls are difficult to discuss without considering cultural conceptions of girlhood. These ideas not only impact upon how girls are perceived by those around them but also what girls expect of and how they interpret their own experiences. Much as the teenage years have been given their own iconography through film (with much credit to James Dean), girlhood has also received its own narratives, language, and visual markers from film, with a (un)healthy dose of patriarchy, misogyny, and gender role expectations from the broader culture. Whereas the expectations of "monstrous youth" are behavioural, the expectations of girl world are largely relational. At a time of life when peer relationships become increasingly central in a child's life (Chui et al., 2021), media and culture tells girls that their relationships have additional dimensions and are of the utmost importance. Boys have friends, girls have frenemies. How girls navigate their relationships in "girl world" is a fundamental part of how they are perceived by others and the social status they receive. And in "girl world", social status is power. This power affords opportunities for violence, which is paradoxically perceived as unacceptable and mean, but also essential to maintaining the social hierarchy (Cecil, 2008; Currie et al., 2007).

Girl world is characterised as a violent place. This violence may not always be physical, psychological and social violence are not only something to be aware of in girl world, but something to be used and leveraged. For girls, one of the few opportunities they have to freely use agency is in their peer relationships. Parents and teachers try to exert control over their choices, their bodies, and their behaviours (Sharpe, 2009), boys try to exert control over their sexuality (Chesney-Lind and Irwin, 2008), and society exerts control over their femininity (Heidensohn, 1989). In girl world, the only true opportunity to express agency and gain power is within peer relationships and social hierarchies. This has become a frequent topic within society, media, and research. Parental concerns regarding their children's behaviour have focused on girls being "nice" (often meaning compliant), research has given relational aggression a platform it would not otherwise have had (Cecil, 2008), and film has capitalised on both of these things by incorporating these fears and findings into the teen comedy. *Mean Girls* (2004) has become the archetype of the genre, being based upon the book *Queen Bees and Wannabes* by Wiseman (2002). Whilst teen films had reflected upon relational aggression prior to this, *Mean Girls* did so in a way that appealed to both adults and teenagers and conformed to the problem youth convention of having the issues resolved by the end of the film,

"I Killed the Teen Dream! Deal with It!" **75**

meaning audiences could revel in the violence of girl world, whilst believing that the problems inherent in this would be resolved through "growing up". However, *Mean Girls* would not exist if not for a group of films that came before it. The violence in *Mean Girls* is subtle, and social rather than physical. Giving someone foot cream instead of face cream is *mean* but not *harmful*. Prior to *Mean Girls* there were a group of films featuring teenage girls that were meaner, darker, and bloodier.

Heathers (1989) is the prototype of bad girl films. Featuring dazzling costumes, sardonic writing, and death, it became a cult classic inspiring future teen comedies regardless of whether or not they feature crime. The film's tagline, "Best friends, social trends and occasional murder", makes clear that this is not only different from the John Hughes-style teen comedies of the time but is a reaction to their presentation of teenagerhood (Markovitz, 2014). *Heathers* is the story of Veronica Sawyer (Winona Ryder), a teenage girl struggling with the social dynamics of her high school. She is part of the popular clique the "Heathers", so-called because its three other members all share the same first name. However, Veronica doesn't feel comfortable with her place in the clique, using her diary as a way to express her feelings; "Tomorrow, I'll be kissing her aerobicized ass, but tonight, let me dream of a world without Heather, a world where I am free". Veronica seems to be the lowest in the pecking order of the group and used by leader Heather Chandler (Kim Walker) to do homework, forge signatures, and host the groups croquet games. Veronica is keenly aware of the social hierarchy of high school and the power within this; however, she doesn't necessarily want to be part of it, refusing to accept her place and the power and agency this brings. When she meets and falls for new student JD (Christian Slater), Veronica is faced with an opportunity to change the social hierarchy through radical means and grapples with the morality and consequences of this throughout the film.

In *Heathers* the relational aggression used by Heather Chandler is a way to gain and maintain power within the social hierarchy of the school. She is keenly aware of how she is perceived and doesn't care that she is feared rather than liked, as at least she has agency and control over the situation. By buying-in to the warped social dynamics of high school, Heather Chandler doesn't experience the same angst about it as her peers. By submitting to her social role, the existential questions of who she is and what she should be are resolved, allowing her to act (Long, 1990). When asked why she behaves this way Heather's pithy response is emblematic of her desire to take control of her life by engaging with social structures even if she knows they are harmful and "mean".

> *Heather, why can't you just be a friend? Why do you have to be such a mega-bitch?*
> *Because I can be.*

76 A Popular Criminology of Youth Justice

Veronicas distaste for the relational aggression displayed by her "friends" leads to genuine violence. Veronica's rejection of the Heathers acceptance and submission to the hierarchy means she is much more receptive to the ideas of JD than others would be. JD's radical ideas about creating change rely on violence in its more traditional form: murder. JD wants to kill the power players in the school and stage the deaths to look like suicides, and he and Veronica are successful in removing Heather C and two of the school's best football players in this way. JD's stated motive is to expose the hollow nature of social hierarchies in schools and societies more broadly. However, a closer reading of the work suggests that JD wants power of his own, power over Veronica specifically. Veronica goes along with JD's plans until she realises that this would be swapping a secondary place in one hierarchy (under the Heathers) for another (under JD). Throughout the film Veronica resists and denies her own agency and ability to create change. She's clearly perceived as the "nice one" of the Heathers, which has a power of its own, but Veronica cannot perceive how to use this power without losing part of herself and becoming corrupted in the way that Heather Chandler has.

Heathers cultural impact can't be understated. By placing teen girls at the centre of violence, and characterising them as smart, funny, and stylish, Heathers created an archetype for a new type of teen film, the bad girl comedy. Femme fatales in customised school uniforms began to take over cinema, fuelling parental concerns about their daughters' "meanness" and adding to broader societal concerns about teen "super-predators" (Pizarro et al., 2007). The idea that boys could be violent, and imagery associated with this was well established, but girls killing girls as an extension of relational aggression and doing it in enviable outfits whilst spouting pop-culture-ready quips became a phenomenon beloved by both teenagers and adults. These girls were not just committing crimes, they were killers and loved it.

Commodification of Girls Violence

Heathers was not an immediate hit but developed a cult following. With this came cultural status, particularly through influencing other media. Much as James Dean's appearance in Rebel Without A Cause (1955) impacted upon the presentation of justice-involved children in films, the appearance of the Heathers has become a visual grammar of "mean girl" dress. Plaid skirts, preppy styling, scrunchies and colour co-ordination have all become markers of popular mean girls in media. The visual styling of Heathers is reflected in Clueless (1995), Mean Girls (2004), and Do Revenge (2022) all of which use fashion as a way of symbolising power over peers, and implying the relational aggression that frequently goes with this (Cecil, 2008). One mean girl film takes Heathers ideas about power, death, social status, and fashion iconography to the extreme, creating a candy-coloured world in which being a

"I Killed the Teen Dream! Deal with It!" **77**

teen girl is deadly. *Jawbreaker* (1999) leans into the hyperrealism of teen films (Long, 1990), to showcase the cruelty of high school.

Jawbreaker, directed by Darren Stein, is another cult favourite teen film. The film focuses on a high school clique of four beautiful, popular, and cruel girls. Courtney, Foxy, Julie and Liz. This "flawless four", as they are referred to by peers, rule their school with the standards hallmarks of relational aggression; meanness, social repercussions, and "bitchy" comments (Crick et al., 2007; Gentile et al., 2011). On Liz's birthday her friends play a prank of "kidnapping" her before taking her out for breakfast. Courtney uses a jawbreaker candy to gag Liz, which results in her choking to death. Rather than admitting to what appears to be an accidental death, Courtney convinces the others to cover up Liz's death by staging a rough sex murder (Bows and Herring, 2020). Coutney is characterised as Machiavellian, witty, and ruthless. There is a question as to whether or not she planned to kill Liz, her biggest rival for prom queen, or if it truly was an accident. Courtney is very aware of the social concerns regarding young women and girls and uses this to her advantage to both create a convincing false narrative regarding Liz's death and to position herself as innocent and benevolent in the eyes of the adults around her.

> *They'll believe it because it's their worst nightmare: Elizabeth Purr, the very picture of teenage perfection, obliterated by perversion.*

Courtney's manipulation of the existing societal pressures on girls to achieve their goals pokes fun at these expectations. Whilst Courtney behaves in unacceptable ways, her presentation as clever, beautiful, and self-aware has made her a cult icon (Sunderland, 2016). *Jawbreaker* plays on the idea that the teenage years are a period of transformation; that the path to becoming an adult must involve a difficult interim period which is characterised by stress, anxiety and violence. It also echoes the non-conformity as death narrative of 1950s problem youth films (as discussed in Chapter 2) but subverts this; those who conform and accept the social order are killed at the hands of extremist social reformers seeking power for themselves. In these films transformation into deviance means becoming a femme fatal, which is still perceived as socially desirable. The underlying message is that violence may seem an appropriate response to the traumas of girl world and whilst transforming into a bad girl may give power in the short term, it doesn't necessarily make a successful adult. *Jawbreaker* shows transformation through a teen film standard: the makeover (Smith, 2017). As part of the coverup, Courtney, Foxy and Julie need to convince Fern, a witness to them staging the crime scene, to keep quiet. Fern is not popular and bears the visual hallmarks associated with this, frizzy hair, clunky shoes, and shyness. In exchange for her silence, Fern is transformed and takes Liz's place as one of the flawless four,

78 A Popular Criminology of Youth Justice

including being given a new name: Vylette. The trading of power and popularity in girl world is antithetical to conceptions of justice, painting girls and young women as selfish. A murder is excusable if it leads to an increase in social standing.

Jawbreaker presents a hyperrealist view of girls' high school experiences (Smith, 2017) and has to some extent become aspirational. The characters are stylish, pretty, funny and live enviable lives. Just as Fern wants to be part of the "flawless four", many girls would also like to have aspects of these lifestyles (Chesney-Lind and Irwin, 2008). They have large houses, cars, and education does not seem to be difficult for them. *Jawbreaker* and many of these subgenres of films are not representative of most girls' actual high school experiences, let alone the experiences of justice-involved girls. Justice-involved girls often lack power and agency in their lives, unlike the characters in these films. Justice-involved girls are more likely to be perceived and assessed as being vulnerable than justice-involved boys (Gelsthorpe and Worrall, 2009), having higher levels of care experience (Fitzpatrick, 2017; Flores et al., 2018), sexual exploitation (Bath, 2017), and mental health needs (Modrowski et al., 2021). Within education, justice-involved girls more frequently do not have expected levels of English and maths ability in comparison to their peers, which increases further for those who have received custodial sentences (Office for National Statistics, 2022). Justice-involved children are also more likely to have been "persistently absent" from school and received an exclusion or suspension (Arnez and Condry, 2021). This means that for justice-involved girls, the characters in *Jawbreaker* and *Heathers* who revel in school politics seem to be an entirely different world to their own. Many justice-involved children report feeling socially excluded from school by teachers and other staff, as well as peers (Day, 2022; Moylan et al., 2020). It seems that the bad girls portrayed in these films have a level of social and/or cultural cachet that allows them to remain in educational spaces whilst behaving in transgressive ways. For real girls who transgress, even if their transgressions are minor compared to murdering classmates, the repercussions are clear, that school is not a place for them. This contrast between the media presentation of justice-involved girls and the realities of their lives has a negative impact upon children, as the expectations of the adults around them have been framed by these films and their broader narratives. The bad girl film is not attempting to portray social realism, however, by skewering aspects of girls' realities such as sexism and relational aggression (Currie et al., 2007) through black comedy, viewers receive the implicit message that whilst these films are exaggerated, they are based on real phenomena, creating expectations of how real girls should behave and affecting the lens through which their behaviour is perceived.

The bad girl teen film became something of a cultural phenomenon, with studios rushing to cash in on their popularity, and have a hit with their own

"I Killed the Teen Dream! Deal with It!" **79**

version. A key aspect of these films' marketability is that their intended audiences were teen girls, this was selling a hyperbolic version of their own lives back to them. Not all dealt with crime, however almost all displayed relational aggression in some way. *Clueless* (1995), *10 Things I Hate About You* (1999), *She's All That* (1999), *Teaching Mrs. Tingle* (1999), *American Pie* (1999), *Get Over It* (2001), *Drop Dead Gorgeous* (1999), and *Dick* (1999) are just a small selection. Teen girls had become a viable market, and so their lives and concerns were a commodity not only for their own entertainment, but a spectacle for those around them to consume and enjoy, these films made watching violence fun. However, not all these films reached the same level of status. Of those that feature crime, murder led to popularity whereas more humanising depictions showing crime as a response to social exclusion were overlooked.

Sugar & Spice (2001) follows the black-comedy template and high-school setting but doesn't conform to the murder and relational aggression tropes. In *Sugar & Spice* a group of teenaged cheerleaders plan and carry out an armed bank robbery. The instigation for the plan is head cheerleader Diane (Marley Shelton) and her boyfriend Jack (James Marsden) being disowned by their parents due to Diane becoming pregnant. Both Diane and Jack find jobs to support themselves and their growing family, whilst finishing high school, and keeping-up their extra curriculars! However, Diane is concerned that this will not be enough in the long term, and that without additional resources they will always live a life of financial hardship. Diane is inspired to rob a bank whilst watching *Point Break* (1991) at a cheer-squad sleepover, and the squad is tasked with watching heist films as homework to develop a plan that won't get them caught. *Sugar & Spice* is actively aware of the mediatisation and spectacle of crime (Presdee, 2000), and jokes about this throughout.

> If the O.J. trial taught us anything, it's that in America you can cut someone's head off and get away with it as long as you have enough money

The cheerleaders in *Sugar & Spice* are not the bad girls seen in *Heathers* and *Jawbreaker*. They are not mean to those around them, care about others, and do not display the typical relational aggression. Whereas *Heathers* and *Jawbreaker* are coded as aspirational, *Sugar & Spice* is the more empowering tale, of girls realising their own agency and finding resources to achieve their goals (albeit through criminal means), whilst maintaining strong and supportive social connections. In *Sugar & Spice* the social aggression towards the girls mainly comes from adults who underestimate them. The squad is repeatedly dismissed by the adults around them, particularly because of their gender and due to being cheerleaders. However, the characters are aware of and in some situations are able to use this to their advantage. When trying to buy guns, the arms dealer dismisses them and threatens to report them to the

80 A Popular Criminology of Youth Justice

authorities. To which Diane replies "what kind of deal would we get if I tell the police that you're selling guns illegally? To minors! To *girl* minors!". They are aware of the way in which society underestimates girls and women and try to use this to their advantage, similarly to Courtney in *Jawbreaker*. The cheerleaders do take inspiration for their plan from adult role models; however, these are not the typical examples of adult success. Kansas (Mena Suvari) asks her mother, who is in prison, for advice. The whole squad then begins to repeatedly visit the women's prison and talks to a variety of prisoners to gain help, support, and feedback on their ideas. It is telling that these are the only adult characters who treat the girls and their ideas as credible and with respect. Strain theory (Agnew, 1992) suggests that when acceptable means to achieve goals are denied to individuals, they will find alternatives, and this narrative is clearly present in *Sugar & Spice*. The characters' goals are typical of their age, they want to pay for college, to live comfortably, and have access to the futures they were told by society that they should want. Diane recognises that being a teenage mother is not ideal but is also aware that this is still broadly in line with the expectations of young women.

> *I always planned on getting married and having kids, I'm just going a little out of order.*

These bright, funny, colourful films with iconic fashion and cool soundtracks make girls crime seem fun and almost empowering. Kill your frenemies and rule your school, rob a bank and achieve your dreams. These films depict a highly simplified version of women's empowerment, suggesting that being able to break the rules in the way that boys do is equivalent to gender equality, but this equality is only accessible to white, middle-class, Western girls and women. That these films are commercial products and have inspired future commercialism (particularly related to fashion), is reflective of the societal responses to girls offending; it is something to be exploited and sold, much like other aspects of girlhood. This belittles and overlooks the realities of justice-involved girls, who are often victims themselves (Modrowski et al., 2021), are discriminated against by both society and criminal justice systems, and whose offending can often be attributed to a lack of opportunity, agency, or safety (Sharpe, 2012; Sharpe and Gelsthorpe, 2009).

Class and Consequences

Of the films discussed so far there is a commonality; all the characters are middle class, white, and wealthy. This is not representative of actual justice-involved girls, who tend to be from lower-class backgrounds (Modrowski et al., 2021), have histories of neglect or abuse (Fox et al., 2015), and have experienced poverty or a lack of resources (Sharpe, 2012). Some films do

"I Killed the Teen Dream! Deal with It!" **81**

depict the experiences of these girls; however, their tone is different. *Thirteen* (2003) is a gritty drama that some criticised for its realism (Bell, 2023) whilst others decried its glamourisation of criminality (Bell, 2023; Conway and Vermette, 2006). *Thirteen* depicts the developing friendship between Tracy (Evan Rachel Wood) and Evie (Nikki Reed), as Tracy reconsiders her social status and how she wants to be perceived by others. Both girls are from working-class families, and Tracy's mother frequently mentions a lack of money when Tracy asks why she can't have or do certain things. Tracy becomes engaged in shoplifting, drug taking, and sexual activity due to the influence of Evie. This is far more reflective of the actual types of crime justice-involved girls engage in, as opposed to the rarity of murder (Feld, 2009). However, both Tracy and Evie are portrayed as somewhat tragic figures. They do not get to be funny or clever in the same ways as their counterparts in *Heathers* and *Jawbreaker*. *Thirteen* engages in the adultification of its characters, we are encouraged to be shocked by the contrast between the characters' ages and their behaviour. This contrast was heightened by the main actresses being close to the ages of their characters, which was somewhat unusual for teen films (Doherty, 2002). This serious tone was not the original intention of *Thirteen*, which began as a comedy in the style of *Heathers* or *Jawbreaker*, co-written by Nikki Reed and director Catherine Harwicke. But this developed into a more serious drama as Reed began to reflect upon her own family life (Bell, 2023). The tone of *Thirteen* is much closer in terms of genre and style to films showcasing boys' violence than the bad girl films discussed in this chapter. The class dimensions placed limits on how Tracy and Evie could be portrayed and perceived. Girls who live in cities rather than suburbs, whose parents hold low-status professions and are not privileged do not get to be portrayed as happy, fun, or admirable. *Thirteen* is dramatic, serious, and tense; lit with blues and greys. Despite being set in the same state as *Heathers, Jawbreaker* and *Sugar and Spice*, *Thirteen* clearly displays a different world.

The class-differences in film portrayals of justice-involved girls are reflective of how class impacts upon societal perception of individuals and criminalisation. Lower-class individuals are often assumed to engage in or be more susceptible to criminality than their middle-and-upper-class counterparts, to the point where class markers are frequently used as risk factors in assessing potential for criminal behaviours (Briggs, 2013; Modrowski et al., 2021). For girls, this intersects with the innocent-dangerous dichotomy in a way that leads to additional stigmatisation. Girls are often assumed by society to be "innocent" and are often portrayed as potential victims (Sharpe, 2009). However, when girls hold little class status, this is seen through the lens of potential criminality. For lower-class girls, there is the assumption that they are either victims of their situation and will be subject to abuse, neglect and sexual exploitation, or that they are active criminals and will thus be violent,

82 A Popular Criminology of Youth Justice

uncontrollable, and sexually promiscuous (Chesney-Lind and Irwin, 2008). That these two categorisations heavily overlap has not gone unnoticed by those working in the field, and the negative impacts of the stigma associated with being labelled as criminal are well documented (Creaney, 2012; Feld, 2009; Fraser and Atkinson, 2014). This has contributed to calls for Child First approaches to be used both within and beyond youth justice (Case and Haines, 2015). However, more work is needed to ensure this recognises the intersecting complexities of class, gender, and justice-involvement.

The consequences of criminal behaviour are impacted by privilege and the intersections of various demographic factors. Middle- and upper-class children are more likely to receive less severe sentences than their lower-class counterparts (Malloch and McIvor, 2011). This might be due to having greater resources to provide support and advice during legal processes, or having access to adults who will advocate on their behalf; however, the impact of societal bias clearly has an effect. Similarly, minority ethnicity (particularly Black) children also tend to receive more punitive sentences (Mallett et al., 2011), which when coupled with higher rates of arrest and overall criminalisation (Peguero and Popp, 2012) reflects the unfairness within criminal justice systems. These aspects are not explicitly considered in the films discussed throughout this chapter, but the same biases are clearly reflected in their stories. For justice-involved girls, class and race mediate questions of responsibility and culpability, thus impacting upon the consequences they face from criminal justice systems.

In *Heathers* Veronica is not necessarily responsible for any of the murders but views herself as such. She was definitely involved, but her culpability is questionable. She took the cup of drain cleaner to Heather C without necessarily knowing its contents, and she initially believed that the bullets used to kill the football players were tranquilisers rather than live rounds. The film leaves enough ambiguity as to whether or not Veronica is genuinely unaware of the realities of the situation or if she is knowingly feigning ignorance as JD suggests.

You believed it because you wanted to believe it. Your true feelings were too gross and icky to face

The responsibility for the crimes in these films varies, but throughout all of them, the girls blame themselves. Veronica views herself as a murderer, Courtney, Julie, and Foxy in *Jawbreaker* quickly change their view of Liz's death as an accident to viewing themselves as killers, and in *Thirteen* Tracy views herself as an active participant despite the complex factors that have influenced her behaviour. Only in *Sugar & Spice* is the responsibility for the crime unquestionable; the group planned the robbery explicitly, sought out guns to use, and planned disguises.

The consequences the characters face in all of the films are not through criminal justice. They are social and relational. Veronica is never attached to or blamed for the deaths of Heather C, the football players, or JD. The consequences she faces are taking over the social hierarchy of the school and changing it. By replacing the Heathers, Veronica sees herself as responsible for maintaining this new balance and protecting it from radicalist ideals such as JD's. This is an idealised and sanitised ending of the film, where Veronica has saved herself and her school (representing all teenagerhood). The scripted ending of the film was changed due to being viewed as "too dark" (Markovitz, 2014). In this version JD is shot by Veronica, but his overall plan is successful, as Veronica then straps the bomb to herself and blows up the school. True to JDs quip that "the only place different social types can genuinely get along with each other is in heaven", the script ends with an angelic prom where all the students finally get along without being in cliques.

The consequences in *Jawbreaker* are similarly social. Upon finding evidence to prove that Courtney was involved in Liz's death, Julie doesn't go to the police, but to the prom. In girl world justice isn't being tried and punished through criminal justice, but not getting to be prom queen (Smith, 2017). Courtney's downfall is facing the hatred of one's peers and knowing that the power you have cultivated through shaping yourself to a predefined mould is lost. Whereas *Carrie* (1976) is drenched in pigs' blood as a sign of disdain from her peers, *Jawbreaker* maintains glamour; Courtney is pelted with corsages whilst mascara runs artfully down her face. There is no question of involving authorities, having seen adults buy in to the fake story of Liz's death through deviant sexual behaviour, they know that adults are not necessarily concerned with the truth of the situation or justice. Therefore, taking matters into their own hands becomes necessary, and social downfall is the only punishment they can actually administer.

In *Sugar & Spice*, because the girls' crime is not against a peer, but a bank, the spectre of criminal justice consequences looms large. Their planning is not necessarily about the logistics of how to access the bank, but about how to avoid being identified and caught. Disguises, masks, and codenames are all borrowed from films, but aren't effective. The squad is almost caught, but saved by making a bargain with a witness who happens to want to be a cheerleader. They use their social status as leverage to avoid consequences, and the closing scene of the film shows them celebrating as they "launder" the money (by literally washing it). For the girls in these films, going to prison is not seen as a genuine possibility, they are convinced that they will get away with their criminal behaviours, or will be able to outwit the authorities to cast themselves as innocent victims. The idea that women are not treated equally by justice systems is one that has pervaded criminological and cultural discourse (Heidensohn, 1989; Sharpe and Gelsthorpe, 2009), and media

84 A Popular Criminology of Youth Justice

not only maintains this, but also suggests that justice-involved girls actively manipulate this to avoid consequences.

The popularity of films like *Heathers* and *Jawbreaker* portraying murder creates the assumption that justice-involved girls are violent, malevolent, and unrepentant. However, in reality girls' crimes are very different. Girls offending is a minority of youth crime, accounting for only 14% of all recorded offences (Youth Justice Board, 2023). The types of crimes for which girls are cautioned, sentenced, and detained are reflective of their gender as well. 94% of girls' crimes are considered as "less serious", meaning they did not involve violence, sexual abuse, weapons etc. This also reflects the custody rates for girls, who only make up 3% of the custodial population (Youth Justice Board, 2023), as custodial offences are only used as a last resort for justice-involved children. This suggests that *Thirteen* may be the most accurate of these films' presentations of justice-involved girls, however, this is not necessarily something to celebrate. Whilst *Thirteen* is accurate regarding crime types and severity, it also clearly engages with narratives of responsibilisation and adultification, which have been found to be harmful to justice-involved children (Chesney-Lind and Irwin, 2008; Creaney, 2012; Holt, 2009; Kelly, 2001). The contrast between *Thirteen* and *Jawbreaker* shows the clear need for Child First presentations of justice-involved girls.

The media presentation of girls' crimes as being born of social jockeying, and for the girls themselves to be conniving and mean in their presentation is a contrast with how boys' offending is presented. In films portraying boys' violence, it is done to gain a specific outcome or purely for the thrill of the experience. Boys offending may be about power, but it isn't personal. However, for girls, violence is a way of creating social change, boosting themselves up the social hierarchy or removing inconveniences from their lives. That these bad girl films are the main depiction of justice-involved girls in film creates an expectation of who justice-involved girls are; white, wealthy, and violent. This minimises the experiences of real justice-involved girls whilst also casting them as "unfeminine". The bad girl film highlights the impossible standards expected of young women, whilst creating an additional layer: if you're going to be a criminal then you'd better look fabulous whilst you do it. This further intersects with class and race, meaning that justice-involved girls are unlikely to ever to be able to meet the societal standards of acceptable femininity.

Film List

10 Things I Hate About You (1999)
A Clockwork Orange (1971)
American Pie (1999)
Bennys Video (1992)
Carrie (1976)

Clueless (1995)
Dick (1999)
Do Revenge (2022)
Drop Dead Gorgeous (1999)
Funny Games (1997)
Get Over In (2001)
Heathers (1989)
Jawbreaker (1999)
Mean Girls (2004)
Natural Born Killers (1994)
Point Break (1991)
Rebel Without a Cause (1955)
Reform School Girls (1986)
She's All That (1999)
Sugar and Spice (2001)
Teaching Mrs Tingle (1999)
The Bad Seed (1956)
The Big Finish (2000)
Thirteen (2003)

References

Agnew R (1992) Foundation for a general strain theory of crime and delinquency. *Criminology* 30: 47–88.

Arnez J and Condry R (2021) Criminological perspectives on school exclusion and youth offending. *Emotional and Behavioural Difficulties* 26(1): 87–100. Routledge.

Austin RL (1993) Recent trends in official male and female crime rates: The convergence controversy. *Journal of Criminal Justice* 21(5): 447–466.

Baidawi S, Papalia N and Featherston R (2023) Gender differences in the maltreatment-youth offending relationship: A scoping review. *Trauma, Violence, & Abuse* 24(2): 1140–1156. SAGE Publications.

Bath E (2017) 50.2 Girls and the juvenile justice system: Specialty courts and approaches to work with commercially sexually exploited youth in the Los Angeles County Juvenile Court System. *Journal of the American Academy of Child & Adolescent Psychiatry* 56(10, Supplement): S74. AACAP's 64th Annual Meeting.

Bell S (2023) 20 years on, Thirteen is still a raw representation of teenhood. Available at: https://i-d.vice.com/en/article/9kmvw3/thirteen-film-teenage-coming-of-age (accessed 22 September 2023).

Bows H and Herring J (2020) Getting away with murder? A review of the 'rough sex defence'. *The Journal of Criminal Law* 84(6): 525–538. SAGE Publications Ltd.

Briggs DB (2013) Conceptualising risk and need: The rise of actuarialism and the death of welfare? Practitioner assessment and intervention in the youth offending service. *Youth Justice* 13(1): 17–30. SAGE Publications Sage UK: London, England.

Calleja N (2022) Intersectionality and processes of belonging: Thinking critically about sociomaterial entanglements with the voices of upper-primary school-aged young people in youth research. *Journal of Applied Youth Studies* 5(4): 317–334.

86 A Popular Criminology of Youth Justice

Case S and Haines K (2015) *Positive Youth Justice: Children First, Offenders Second*. London: Policy Press.

Cecil D (2008) From Heathers to mean girls: An examination of relational aggression in film. Journal of Criminal Justice and Popular Culture 15(3): 262–276. Epub ahead of print 1 January 2008.

Chesney-Lind M (1989) Girls' crime and woman's place: Toward a feminist model of female delinquency. *Crime & Delinquency* 35(1): 5–29.

Chesney-Lind M and Irwin K (2008) *Beyond Bad Girls: Gender, Violence and Hype*. Oxon: Routledge.

Christie N (1986) The ideal victim. In: Fattah EA (ed) *From Crime Policy to Victim Policy*. London: Palgrave Macmillan UK, pp. 17–30.

Chui H, Li X and Luk S (2021) Does peer relationship matter? A multilevel investigation of the effects of peer and supervisory relationships on group supervision outcomes. *Journal of Counseling Psychology* 68(4): 457–466. American Psychological Association.

Conway MB and Vermette P (2006) Lessons for middle school teachers from the film thirteen. *Middle School Journal* 38(2): 37–42. Routledge.

Creaney S (2012) Targeting, labelling and stigma: Challenging the criminalisation of children and young people. *Criminal Justice Matters* 89(1): 16–17.

Crick NR, Ostrov JM and Kawabata Y (2007) Relational aggression and gender: An overview. In: Daniel J Flannery, Alexander T Vazsonyi, and Irwin D Waldman (eds) *The Cambridge Handbook of Violent Behavior and Aggression*. New York, NY, US: Cambridge University Press, pp. 245–259.

Currie DH, Kelly DM and Pomerantz S (2007) 'The power to squash people': Understanding girls' relational aggression. *British Journal of Sociology of Education* 28(1): 23–37. Routledge.

Day A-M (2022) Disabling and criminalising systems? Understanding the experiences and challenges facing incarcerated, neurodivergent children in the education and youth justice systems in England. *Forensic Science International: Mind and Law* 3: 100102.

Doherty TP (2002) *Teenagers and Teenpics: The Juvenilization of American Movies in the 1950s*. Rev. and expanded ed. Philadelphia: Temple University Press.

Drew V, Wilson ML and McCarter SA (2022) The overcriminalisation of Black girls: Using an intersectional lens to examine the school-to-prison pipeline. *Critical and Radical Social Work* 10(2): 242–259. Policy Press.

Farinde-Wu A, Butler BR and Allen-Handy A (2022) Policing Black femininity: The hypercriminalization of black girls in an urban school. *Gender and Education* 34(7): 804–820 Routledge. Epub ahead of print 3 October 2022.

Feld BC (2009) Violent girls or relabeled status offenders?: An alternative interpretation of the data. *Crime & Delinquency* 55(2): 241–265. SAGE Publications Inc.

Fitzpatrick C (2017) What do we know about girls in the care and criminal justice systems? *Safer Communities* 16(3): 134–143. Emerald Group Publishing Ltd.

Flores J, Hawes J, Westbrooks A, et al. (2018) Crossover youth and gender: What are the challenges of girls involved in both the foster care and juvenile justice systems? *Children and Youth Services Review* 91: 149–155.

Fox BH, Perez N, Cass E, et al. (2015) Trauma changes everything: Examining the relationship between adverse childhood experiences and serious, violent and chronic juvenile offenders. *Child Abuse & Neglect* 46: 163–173.

Fraser A and Atkinson C (2014) Making up gangs: Looping, labelling and the new politics of intelligence-led policing. *Youth Justice* 14(2): 154–170. SAGE Publications Inc.

Frey M (2006) Benny's video, caché, and the desubstantiated image. *Framework: The Journal of Cinema and Media* 47(2): 30–36. Wayne State University Press.

Gatti U and Verde A (2012) Cesare Lombroso: Methodological ambiguities and brilliant intuitions. *International Journal of Law and Psychiatry* 35(1): 19–26.

Gelsthorpe L and Worrall A (2009) Looking for trouble: A recent history of girls, young women and youth justice. *Youth Justice* 9(3): 209–223. SAGE Publications.

Gentile DA, Coyne S and Walsh DA (2011) Media violence, physical aggression, and relational aggression in school age children: A short-term longitudinal study. *Aggressive Behavior* 37(2): 193–206.

Grundmann R (ed.) (2010) *A Companion to Michael Haneke*. Wiley-Blackwell Companions to Film Directors. Malden, MA: Wiley-Blackwell.

Heidensohn F (1989) Gender and crime. In: Heidensohn F (ed.) *Crime and Society*. Sociology for a Changing World. London: Macmillan Education UK, pp. 85–111. Available at: https://doi.org/10.1007/978-1-349-19763-7_5 (accessed 3 October 2023).

Hodgson J (2022) An anti-carceral feminist response to youth justice involved girls. In: Monk H, Tucker K, Atkinson K, et al. (eds) *Feminist Responses to Injustices of the State and Its Institutions: Politics, Intervention, Resistance*. Bristol University Press, pp. 235–255. Available at: https://www.cambridge.org/core/books/feminist-responses-to-injustices-of-the-state-and-its-institutions/an-anticarceral-feminist-response-to-youth-justice-involved-girls/34CF566DBBFE4B9C27114A4C5A617BCE (accessed 3 October 2023).

Hollingworth S (2015) Performances of social class, race and gender through youth subculture: Putting structure back in to youth subcultural studies. *Journal of Youth Studies* 18(10): 1237–1256.

Holt A (2009) (En)Gendering responsibilities: Experiences of parenting a 'young offender'. *The Howard Journal of Criminal Justice* 48(4): 344–356.

Jackson C (2000) Little, violent, white: The bad seed and the matter of children. *Journal of Popular Film and Television* 28(2): 64–73. Routledge.

Kelly P (2001) Youth at risk: Processes of individualisation and responsibilisation in the risk society. *Discourse: Studies in the Cultural Politics of Education* 22(1): 23–33. Routledge.

Long S (1990) Nightmare in the mirror: Adolescence and the death of difference. *Social Text* (24): 156–166. Duke University Press.

Mallett CA, Stoddard-Dare P and Seck MM (2011) Explicating correlates of juvenile offender detention length: The impact of race, mental health difficulties, maltreatment, offense type, and court dispositions. *Youth Justice* 11(2): 134–149.

Malloch M and McIvor G (2011) Women and community sentences. *Criminology and Criminal Justice* 11(4): 325–344.

Markovitz A (2014) 'Heathers': An oral history. Available at: https://ew.com/article/2014/04/04/heathers-oral-history/ (accessed 25 July 2023).

Modrowski CA, Rizzo CJ, Collibee C, et al. (2021) Victimization profiles in girls involved in the juvenile justice system: A latent class analysis. *Child Abuse & Neglect* 111: 104774.

Moylan P, White J, Corcoran T, et al. (2020) Youth justice, educational exclusion and moral panic. In: *Inclusive Education Is a Right, Right?* Brill, pp. 51–63. Available at: https://brill.com/display/book/9789004434783/BP000012.xml (accessed 9 May 2023).

Office for National Statistics (2022) The education and social care background of young people who interact with the criminal justice system. Available at: https://www.ons.gov.uk/peoplepopulationandcommunity/educationandchildcare/articles/theeducationandsocialcarebackgroundofyoungpeoplewhointeractwiththecriminaljusticesystem/may2022 (accessed 17 October 2023).

Peguero AA and Popp AM (2012) Youth violence at school and the intersection of gender, race, and ethnicity. *Journal of Criminal Justice* 40(1): 1–9.

Pizarro J, Chermak S and Grunewald J (2007) Juvenile "super-predators" in the news: A comparison of adult and juvenile homicides. *Journal of Criminal Justice and Popular Culture* 14(1): 84–111.

Presdee M (2000) *Cultural Criminology and the Carnival of Crime*. London; New York: Routledge.

Sharpe G (2009) The trouble with girls today: Professional perspectives on young women's offending. *Youth Justice* 9(3): 254–269.

Sharpe G (2012) *Offending Girls: Young Women and Youth Justice*. Abingdon, Oxon; New York: Routledge.

Sharpe G (2016) Re-imagining justice for girls: A new agenda for research. *Youth Justice* 16(1). SAGE Publications Inc.: 3–17.

Sharpe G and Gelsthorpe L (2009) Engendering the agenda: Girls, young women and youth justice. *Youth Justice* 9(3): 195–208.

Smith F (2017) *Rethinking the Hollywood Teen Movie: Gender, Genre and Identity*. Edinburgh: Edinburgh University Press.

Sunderland M (2016) 'Perverting the youth of America': The oral history of teen classic 'Jawbreaker'. In: *Vice*. Available at: https://www.vice.com/en/article/paeyk9/perverting-the-youth-of-america-the-oral-history-of-teen-classic-jawbreaker (accessed 14 August 2023).

Wiseman R (2002) *Queen Bees & Wannabes: Helping Your Daughter Survive Cliques, Gossip, Boyfriends, and Other Realities of Adolescence*. 1st ed. New York: Crown Publishers.

Youth Justice Board (2023) Youth Justice Statistics: 2021 to 2022 (accessible version). Available at: https://www.gov.uk/government/statistics/youth-justice-statistics-2021-to-2022/youth-justice-statistics-2021-to-2022-accessible-version (accessed 27 June 2023).

5

"I'M NOT A GHETTO BOY, I JUST LIVE IN DEPTFORD"

Urban 'Realities', Ethnicity, and Cities

As discussed in the previous chapter, justice-involved girls are depicted differently from their male counterparts. Similarly, ethnic minority justice-involved children are depicted differently from their white counterparts. However, where girls' violence is viewed through the lens of comedy, ethnic minority children's stories are treated with the utmost seriousness, whether violent or not. Films depicting the lives of ethnic minority children involved with crime are predominantly dramas set in cities, that combine social realism with stylistic elements of other film traditions such as banlieue films (Schroeder, 2001; Vincendeau, 2012). This in particular can be seen in British films from the early-mid 2000s. Many of these films have contributed to rectifying the dearth of ethnic minority perspectives in media, and by telling the stories of these children were viewed as modern counterparts to classic films, such as *Rebel Without A Cause* (1955). However, despite these films fulfilling a positive need regarding representation, they raise questions regarding how they are representing the lives of justice-involved ethnic minority children. Many of these films conform to the existing stereotypes that persist within society regarding race, ethnicity, crime, and "urbanness". This chapter explores these issues through examining *Bullet Boy* (2004), *Kidulthood* (2006), and *Blue Story* (2019) amongst others.

Urban films were a particular trend in the early 2000s and were seen by some as a response to the banlieue films of France (see Chapter 3 for further discussion of this) or the "hood" films of America, such as *Boyz "n" The Hood* (1991) (Berghahn, 2010). The urban film was a distinctly British take on this trend, with many focusing on London. This led to a unique type of media, that utilised aspects of underground youth culture such as fashion, music, and language and showcased this through the "issue focused"

DOI: 10.4324/9781003403159-5

90 A Popular Criminology of Youth Justice

approach of the "hood" films, whilst combining this with the social realist traditions in British filmmaking (Halper, 2014). The influence of Ken Loach in particular cannot be overlooked, to the point where the pitch for *Bullet Boy* (2004) described it as "Kes with guns" (Sen, 2005). The association with Ken Loach's work gave urban films credibility, but also the expectation that the depiction of social problems was realistic and paired with an active call for change. The rise of urban films was viewed as a positive, as this increased representation in media, gave young Black filmmakers opportunities that were previously inaccessible, and launched the careers of a number of prominent actors, filmmakers, and musicians (Nwonka and Malik, 2018). However, the narratives that these films present about not only cities, but the young (often Black) people who live within them were often regressive, upheld stereotypes, and conformed to the risk-based and punitive frameworks used within youth justice at the time (Blyth et al., 2007; Briggs, 2013).

Cities as Places of Fear

Narratives of the city as a place of danger, criminality, and struggle have long been embedded into society. The city is a place where the industrious go to work or study, to access entertainment and culture, but do not live. City-dwellers are poor, dirty, savage. As seen in *The Young Savages* (1961), the city is a place to be feared, with escape only possible for those who are hardworking and morally robust. London in particular has a mythos which is intertwined with crime. From Jack the Ripper to current gang concerns, London has always been perceived as a place of danger, but this is posed in both factual and fictional media in a way that is thrilling (Forshaw, 2012). This gives audiences the message that crime is an exciting form of entertainment, but also that it is contained in specific places, allowing a sense of safety. This trend means that London is a frequent setting for crime films, as the audience is primed to expect disorder and violence. London is not homogenous though; any city of a similar size, scale and population density encompasses different areas with different purposes (Fuhg, 2021). There is a clear distinction in London between the places where tourists come to sightsee, engage in culture, and spend money, and the suburbs and estates where people live (MacLeod, 2018). For crime films, many take place in the suburbs and estates of London, and feature characters from these areas. The only reason for these films to venture into tourist or commercial spaces is for heists, police chases, or dramatic standoffs on public landmarks. For audiences, this boundary work means they can both enjoy the spectacle (and spectre) of a criminal London, whilst feeling safe engaging in tourism or leisure activity in the city. Much of the visual language of the London crime film was cemented in culture by Guy Ritchie's work: *Lock, Stock and Two Smoking Barrels* (1998) and *Snatch* (2000) (Forshaw, 2012). The idea of a seedy underbelly in the city was now linked to people's homes and communities, creating a sense of fear of these places. For London in particular, this negative association impacted ethnic minority, impoverished, and working-class communities more than others. Films about these areas are pitched and marketed as crime films, but they could also be considered as underclass films (Halper, 2014). In the case of London, separating the imagery and activity of different areas of the city is something of a falsity (Fuhg, 2021). Areas of poverty and wealth co-exist, often in close proximity, as was highlighted following the Grenfell Tower Fire (MacLeod, 2018). However, the label of urban is only applied to specific types of areas in cities, and the term is often used in a disparaging way. Urban no longer means from or within a city, no longer means the opposite of rural, but has cultural connotations of class, race/ethnicity, wealth and criminality (Hutchison, 2010). This can be seen through the classification of "urban music", which often refers to Black underground or sub-cultural artists (Ilan, 2012), urban fashion coming from Black culture being taken in to the mainstream (Hutchison, 2010), and urban spaces often referring to minority ethnicity communities (Benz, 2014). However, this reclassification of Black culture as urban is separated from the social, political, and economic factors that mean these communities are often limited in terms of housing access (Shihadeh and Steffensmeier, 1994; Wacquant, 1993), and occupation of urban spaces is not necessarily a choice. Urban has come to mean Black (Hutchison, 2010; Wacquant, 1993) and this linguistic change has allowed broader society to reignite historical "concerns" about Black communities in a more implicit manner. It is through this construction of urban that film, news, cultural commentators and society can discuss the problems of "urban culture" or "urban crime" without having to consider and confront the racist, classist, and harmful implications of these narratives.

The association between urban spaces and crime has now reached a point where environment design is being considered through the lens of crime prevention (Benz, 2014). Increased use of street lamps, CCTV cameras, and planting new trees are all suggested as crime prevention measures (Piroozfar et al., 2019). These ideas are heavily steeped in theories of crime such as social disorganisation theory (Shaw and McKay, 1942) and broken windows theory (Kelling and Wilson, 1982). However both of these theories have been largely discarded by mainstream criminology in favour of more complex, nuanced approaches (O'Brien et al., 2019; Sampson and Groves, 1989). These theories all frame the environment through the lens of risk, which has also been one of the main practice approaches within youth justice (Armstrong et al., 2005; Case, 2006). However, this sets out the narrative that some environments are inherently "risky" in that they will cause or lead to crime. For those who live in these environments, there is the suggestion that they will be the ones committing these crimes. This in essence others and criminalises those living in urban environments, which given these communities are

92 A Popular Criminology of Youth Justice

frequently predominantly ethnic minorities, has troubling associations with racist cultural narratives (Sealey-Ruiz and Greene, 2015; Shihadeh and Steffensmeier, 1994).

During the early 2000s there was a raft of films that focused on justice-involved children in cities, in particular London. Many of these films were supported by public funding, as part of schemes to diversify film and television production and bring new stories to light, which at the time was dubbed part of "Cool Britannia". However, Nwonka and Malik (2018) have suggested that this image of inclusivity was simply surface level, and the support for these films was largely tokenistic and wavered if they were not financially successful. The imperative to "get something Black made" (Nwonka and Malik, 2018) led to these films being greenlit but did not extend to allowing full creative control or support. It is telling that the urban films of the 2000s tend to follow a similar pattern; a naïve or well-meaning character becomes embroiled with a local gang and has to engage in deviant, criminal, and/or violent activity to protect themselves and/or their loved ones and survive the harsh realities of city life. Many of these films have bleak endings, particularly for the central character (whom the audience is encouraged to empathise with). The overriding message of this is that cities are to be feared, and the people who live within them (who are portrayed within these films as being ethnic minorities) should be feared too. Whilst these films were heralded as beacons of diversity and inclusivity, the messages they present are steeped in the cultural and systemic racism of the society they depict (King, 2003; Nwonka, 2023; Sealey-Ruiz and Greene, 2015).

The cultural standard of urban films was exemplified in *Bullet Boy* (2004), directed by Saul Dibb. This film centres on the relationship between Ricky (Ashley Walters), an 18-year-old who has just been released from a Young Offenders Institution, and his 12-year-old brother Curtis (Luke Fraser). Curtis idolises his older brother but does not seem to be fully aware of his criminal activities. The brothers live in a tower block on an estate with their mother (Clare Perkins), who is trying her best to ensure her children have opportunities for a good life. She encourages Curtis to try in school and whilst she loves and supports Ricky, she is wary of the influence he has over Curtis. There is an implicit concern regarding poverty in the film; the brothers share a room with bunk beds, and their mother works long hours to support the family. There are clear positive influences in their lives, Curtis has friends at school, teachers seem to like him, and the family is part of the local community through their church. These would all be considered as protective factors within youth justice (Armstrong et al., 2005; Briggs, 2013; Case, 2006), however, the risk of having an older brother who has been in custody would be significant enough to counteract this, meaning Curtis would be considered as being at risk of offending within the practice frameworks of the time (Armstrong et al., 2005; Case, 2006).

"I'm Not a Ghetto Boy, I Just Live in Deptford" **93**

Ricky is clearly struggling to adapt to his release from custody, he is eager to see his girlfriend and happy to see his brother but is struggling to reconcile his relationships with both his mother and friend group. Ricky wants to change and avoid criminality, but the lack of situational change upon his release means he is within the same pressures, strains, and context that led to his offending initially. As many of the factors linked to criminal behaviour are situational (Kinsey, 2019), for change and desistance to be effective, there needs to be post-release support for individuals (Barry, 2010; McAra and McVie, 2007). Being released to an area where crime is prevalent and Ricky is known as being criminal means that the work of maintaining change is made harder by having to overcome the expectations and assumptions of those around him as well. Ricky's best friend, Wisdom (Leon Black), assumes Ricky won't have changed at all whilst in custody and does not understand his reticence to engage in the same activities they had before, even returning to Ricky the gun that led to his incarceration.

The backdrop to *Bullet Boy* is East London, and this context gives viewers a lot of unspoken information about the lives of the characters. Because Ricky and Curtis live in a tower block and the neighbourhood is populated by groups of young Black men who wear hoodies and own pitbull dogs it is suggested that there is gang activity in the area. The main conflict of the film starts when Wisdom accidentally breaks the wing mirror on someone's car. That small, accidental damage can lead to shootings and death is indicative of the expectations of these areas, and the perception of danger associated with cities. *Bullet Boy* showcases Curtis's descent into criminal behaviour, even if this is not necessarily purposeful on his part. The underlying message of the film is that circumstances such as those Ricky and Curtis have grown up in are inescapable. Ricky actively tries to leave the city at one point in the film, having been asked to move out of the family home by his mother, lost his friend to violence, and is being pursued by members of the gang. He feels he cannot have a clean start in East London, and that Curtis is being harmed by his presence as well.

> *The whole point of me going is to help you [...] this room's too small for the both of us now. You're a big boy, you can represent on your own.*

However, Ricky is ambushed by members of the gang whilst he is waiting on the train station platform and is killed. There is no escape from his deviance, even though he had changed and was genuinely trying. Ricky is the cautionary tale to allow Curtis to have a good life, mirroring Plato and Jim in *Rebel Without A Cause* (1955) (see Chapter 2). *Bullet Boy* was critically acclaimed at the time and hailed as a sensitive portrait of inner-city life (Sen, 2005). Ashley Walter's portrayal of Ricky was also lauded, with the character's complexity being a key talking point. In this way *Bullet Boy* set the standard for urban films, having a sympathetic central character who wants to change but is frustrated by their circumstances. This heavily mirrors the cultural narratives of the time about crime and risk; the individual is not necessarily at fault, but the risk level surrounding them contributes to criminality in a way that is unavoidable (Axford et al., 2023; Blyth et al., 2007). Moving away from individualised frameworks of offending to more generalised ones allowed youth justice systems to focus on broader factors such as education, housing, peer groups, parenting, and health (Arnez and Condry, 2021; Durant et al., 1995; Jeong et al., 2021; Kroll et al., 2002) opposed to individual factors such as ethnicity. But the impact of this was that those identified as being "high risk" were often ethnic minorities (Farmer, 2010; Pitts, 2020). The risk-based framework itself was not considered critically by those who created and applied it (Briggs, 2013; Case, 2006), meaning that it perpetuated White middle-class ideals of what is appropriate, often with the result being that ethnic minority youth were still targeted by criminal justice systems (Toro et al., 2019). The narrative was no longer that Black youth are criminal, but that inner-city youth are criminal. Films like *Bullet Boy* genuinely tried to deconstruct these narratives, but due to the limitations imposed by funders, producers, and censors, this was hampered.

The funding behind many of these films emphasised diversity (Nwonka and Malik, 2018), however, these films maintain the notion that cities are also dangerous spaces (Forshaw, 2012), thus associating ethnic minorities and particularly Black people with dangerousness. There is a long history of activism, theory, and research that discusses the relationship between structural racism, poverty, housing, and how this has constructed the "hood" phenomenon (Berghahn, 2010; Childress, 2004). The children depicted in these films could be considered as examples of Wacquant's (1993) "urban outcasts". Wacquant's work discussed the impact of "ghettoisation" in cities and the ways in which systemic neglect of certain areas, demographics, and lifestyles creates a sense of isolation within communities. Whereas the concept of urban outcasts was actively critical of the ways in which city management, resourcing, and financial constraints contribute to and impact upon these communities, urban films are less analytical in their messaging, showing individuals in cities as outcasts, but not necessarily recognising or addressing the structural factors that led to this marginalisation. This means that audiences are left with the message that young Black people are on the outskirts of society, but it is not explained why, leaving the pervasive biases of society to fill in this gap. Many urban films were created under the banner of representation and inclusivity. This means that in depicting the lives of those in urban environments, these films are participating in the myth-making about these communities separate from in-depth consideration of how and why these behaviours emerged.

Like many of the urban films of the time, *Ill Manors* (2012), written and directed by Ben Drew (aka rapper Plan B), explicitly places itself as a "slice of life" film, representing the urban outsiders of London. This depiction is a far cry from other London-centric films, such as *Notting Hill* (1999), or *Passport to Pimlico* (1949) which depict the city as charming, elegant and a place where dreams come true. *Ill Manors* built explicitly upon the legacy of *Bullet Boy*, allowing it to be louder, brasher, and more explicit. It also partially aimed to show the lie inherent in the romantic comedy presentation of London. Cities are only a place of joy and charm for the well off, whilst within half a mile there are estates home to individuals living very different lives. *Ill Manors* showcases the interconnected stories of eight characters over the course of a week. Drug dealing, violence, abuse and gang activity are not only present, but prevalent in all the character's lives, whether this is through participation or victimisation. The opening of the film, set to a song by Plan B sets the tone, and tells the audience to expect the worst.

Are you sittin' comfortably? Well put your seatbelts on, cause you're in for a harrowing ride Cause this is Ill Manors, where dark shit goes on at night

One of the stories in *Ill Manors* centres on 12-year-old Jake (Ryan De La Cruz) who through the course of the film becomes involved with a gang through trying to buy drugs. He is quickly seen as useful by one of the gang leaders and is exploited into participating in a violent crime. The film presents this as a highly possible scenario, due to children wanting the respect and attention of their older peers who are perceived as having power or influence on the estate. This is reflective of research findings on why children join gangs, with the desire for belonging and group participation being one factor (Densley and Stevens, 2015; Frisby-Osman and Wood, 2020). In *Ill Manors* Jake's entry into the gang is highly simplified though; Jake and a friend try to buy drugs from Marcell (Nick Sagar), a gang member, who says he will only sell them drugs if Jake punches his friend. Jake very quickly succumbs to this peer pressure and not only punches his friend, but gives him a heavy beating, egged on by the gang. Marcell sees this as an opportunity to involve Jake in the gang and lets him join them for the rest of the day, going shopping and to a party, promising him fun, drugs, and girls. These are all hallmarks of child criminal exploitation and grooming and are commonplace methods of recruitment for county lines gangs (Maxwell et al., 2019; Robinson et al., 2019). In *Ill Manors* Jake is not asked to transport drugs, but to shoot someone for Marcell. He is hesitant and visibly distressed by the request, saying he can't. But Marcell threatens to kill him if he doesn't. Child criminal exploitation mirrors other cycles of abuse, in that victims are often "love bombed" or showered with affection, gifts, and attention, which are used as leverage to

96 A Popular Criminology of Youth Justice

justify more overtly abusive behaviours or gain compliance (Hargreaves et al., 2023; Stone, 2018).

> *You think you can roll round with me all day and then when shit gets deep pussy out?*

Ill Manors sensationalises the grooming and exploitation of Jake, suggesting it can happen all in a single day, that a child can go from trying to buy cannabis to murdering someone in a matter of hours. Additionally, in *Ill Manors* the consequences depicted for engaging in gang life are extreme. When Jake goes to carry out the murder requested by Marcell, he shoots a bystander in the process, who happens to be the sister of another gang leader in the area. This leads to a revenge subplot, which ends with both Marcell and Jake being killed as an act of retribution. Showing this story as taking place over the course of a single day normalises the idea that violence is an inherent part of life for children in cities, and also plays upon the idea of transformation into a criminal that was emphasized by the problem youth films of the 1950s (see Chapter 2 for further discussion). Jake's descent into criminality happens so quickly and so severely that the film is clearly suggesting that any engagement with gangs or drugs is a "slippery slope". Ben Drew has discussed wanting the film to be a warning to both children and parents against gang involvement and drug taking. However, Jake's story is a subplot of the film, with the focus being on adult characters trying to make drug deals, pay money to those they owe, and managing the complexities of their social groups. Jake's character is the one that could have a potential impact on children as a cautionary tale, but it is given so little time that it appears to audiences that Jake's criminality was inevitable rather than avoidable.

The emphasis that many urban films place upon the cities in which they are set and created creates an association between the behaviour and the setting. Fear has long been associated with cities (and often with race also (Benz, 2014; Chiricos et al., 1997). The intersectional nature of place, class, means, and race has been well established (Benz, 2014; *British Film Institute*, 2016; Calleja, 2022; Chummel, 2010). However, in "Cool Britannia" the idea that Britain had moved beyond racism was prevalent (Nwonka and Malik, 2018), with diversity in media and the urban films created in response to this being touted as evidence. This meant that discussions of race were often not explicit, if talked about at all. The conversation moved on to various risk factors being indicative of offending, such as poverty, educational engagement, and individual attitudes. This was encapsulated in David Cameron's "hug a hoodie" speech (Cameron, 2006). Whilst the aim of this speech was to encourage third-sector organisations to work with the government in supporting children and responding to various types of needs, the response to it emphasized Cameron's discussion of "hoodies" (Boldison, 2006; Featherstone, 2013;

"I'm Not a Ghetto Boy, I Just Live in Deptford" **97**

Pearson, 2006). Rather than referring specifically to hooded sweatshirts that were rising in popularity at the time, the term had become to mean children who were often impoverished, neglected, and criminal. "Hoodie" almost became synonymous with "chav", and the negative labelling that came along with this (Hayward and Yar, 2006). By characterising justice-involved children as "hoodies" and "chavs" this meant the cultural conversation could still clearly have an "other" to demonise, sensationalise, and fear, without having to engage with difficult conversations about race and ethnicity. This cultural conversation was also deeply enmeshed with the urban films of the time, David Cameron even specifically talked about *Kidulthood* in his speech. This idea that cities had become overrun with "hoodies" had become part of the mainstream conversation, reinforcing the narrative of justice-involved children as dangerous and uncontrollable. Except this was framed through the lens of risk.

Blackness as a Risk Factor

The risk-based framework was a key innovation of youth justice in the 2000s (Maurutto and Hannah-Moffat, 2007; Paylor, 2011). Also referred to as the scaled approach (Haines and Case, 2012), this assessed a child's life in terms of the risks it posed. The Asset form used by Youth Justice Teams to complete this assessment shows starkly how this approached viewed children not as being "at risk" but risky in and of themselves (Almond, 2012). This notion of risk made its way into the cultural consciousness through political rhetoric, reporting and broader media. When members of the cabinet are openly saying that "it's frightening for a man in a suit to walk down certain streets at night" (Cameron, 2006), even if the next sentence is about the fear children experience, the overall message is that respectable, law-abiding adults are and should be afraid of children in the streets. One film that encapsulated and became an emblem for these concerns at the time was *Kidulthood* (2006). Set over the course of a single day, *Kidulthood* depicts how a group of teenagers in London spend a day off school. The film shows their lives as violent, dangerous, and devoid of adult supervision.

Using similar stylistic and cinematic traits as *Bullet Boy* and building on the commercial and cultural desire for stories of inner cities, *Kidulthood* emphasised the ways in which children's lives are filled with risk. Whereas *Bullet Boy's* Curtis was influenced by his older sibling, *Kidulthood* focuses on the lives of 15- and 16-year-olds as a peer group, using this as a way to shock the audience into wondering what their own children are up to. Similar to *Bullet Boy* being based on the experiences of teenagers in Hackney (Halper, 2014), *Kidulthood* reflects the teenage experience of its writer, Noel Clarke (Jones, 2016). Clarke wanted to create opportunity for himself as a Black actor, having been dissatisfied with the parts he received previously,

98 A Popular Criminology of Youth Justice

and seeking work that was interesting, nuanced, and reflected reality. *Kidulthood* was noted for its realism in shooting scenes in London, using young actors to portray the characters, the use of slang and language used by children at the time, and the costuming and soundtrack being reflective of underground youth culture (Gooch, 2019). *Kidulthood* was highly successful, both commercially and culturally, and paved the way for a string of films imitating its style and approach. However, this often took the form of sensationalising the violence, sex, and drug taking present in *Kidulthood*, meaning that this became the dominant perception of children in cities, and particularly ethnic minority children. Without the success of *Kidulthood* there would not be *Shank* (2010), *Sket* (2011), *Anuvahood* (2011), *Ill Manors* (2012), or *Blue Story* (2019).

Many urban films are ensemble pieces, with large and diverse casts of young actors. Many of these individuals have since gone on to greater levels of fame, with these urban criminality films acting as a springboard or breakthrough performance. Interestingly, a number of these actors (e.g. Ashley Walters, Riz Ahmed, John Boyega) have gone on to criticise the opportunities available to ethnic minorities in film, saying that they should be considered for stories other than those of urban violence and crime (Ahmed, 2016). The use of ensemble casts within these films means that the underlying suggestion is that urban children are part of a group or gang, rather than individuals whose stories deserve attention on their own. This also subtly reinforces cultural narratives about groups of children being dangerous or that any group of children could transform in to a "gang" (Fraser and Atkinson, 2014). The notion of a "criminal gang" is highly contested and cannot be discussed in isolation from the approach to policing gangs (Densley and Pyrooz, 2020). There is no clear definition of a "gang" and no clear distinction between a group of friends, other than the implicit assumption of criminality or violence. Whereas "organised crime groups" would be the terminology applied to a group of adults actively engaging in crime, when children do it, they are termed a "gang" (Densley and Stevens, 2015). This linguistic difference can be attributed to fearmongering on the part of the media, and the demonisation of children more generally (Densley and Stevens, 2015; Esbensen and Tusinski, 2007).

Within *Kidulthood* the spectre of gang crime looms large. However, the gang is not lead by children, but adults. Trife (Aml Ameen), one of the central characters of the film is recruited into the gang by his uncle, Curtis. Curtis gives Trife affection and the sense of belonging he was not finding elsewhere, and a role model that respects him as an individual. Gradually, Trife is asked to "prove himself" through a series of tasks, one of which includes intending to commit an assault. With this, Trife gains access to the social aspects of the gang, being able to hang out in nice spaces, with alcohol, drugs and girls all available to him. With the hindsight of the 2020s,

"I'm Not a Ghetto Boy, I Just Live in Deptford"   **99**

this is a clear case of child criminal exploitation (CCE), however, this was not the terminology or perspective of the time. These tactics of giving children attention and gifts, access to money, and asking them to carry out increasingly deviant tasks, is a standard approach of CCE (Maxwell et al., 2019), and is how many children initially become involved in gangs or other criminal enterprises (Wroe, 2021).

Urban films' use of ensemble casts impacts upon their pacing, with quick changes between different characters or perspectives. Within these films many of these changes are signalled by shots of the city or transport in particular, the roar of a passing train, the blaring of traffic, and the glare of streetlights. Visually this marks a change in the narrative, moving to a different location or a different character. However, this also signifies what the lives of children in cities are like; loud, frantic, and unstable. Many of these films present a single day or unfold over a short time period. Whilst this is a frequent filmmaking device to build tension or focus on the interesting or exciting parts of a story whilst skipping over the dull aspects (eating, sleeping, schoolwork), the "sin of commission" (Wilson and O'Sullivan, 2004) created by this is that viewers feel this is reflective of children's lives, that their day-to-day existence is frantic, dangerous, and constantly shifting. *Kidulthood* takes place over a single day, *Bullet Boy* over 5 days, and *Ill Manors* over 7 days. Within all of these films, the short period sees violence, theft, arrests and deaths. However, the films present these as not unusual events in the character's lives. The characters themselves do not seem particularly shocked or surprised at the events that take place. There is a sense of inevitability, that someone was always going to get killed, it was simply a question of who.

Having large, ensemble casts portraying intersecting stories with differing scenes or sections of films focusing on different characters suggests that urban children's lives are transitory, chaotic, and unstable. They do not have consistent relationships, they do not stay in consistent locations, and they themselves are not worth focused attention. Perhaps the choice to use this framing and approach within these films is specifically to highlight that this is how society treats children in these environments and that these aspects of their lives are a result of circumstance rather than choice. However, this commentary is not explicit enough, and the message that audiences are left with is that urban children are uncontrolled and uncontrollable.

During the 2000s, youth justice in England and Wales was undergoing a transformation. This period saw heavy criticism from researchers and campaigners, as it was perceived as a "punitive turn" (Case and Bateman, 2020), focusing on risk and viewing justice-involved children as inherently risky (Paylor, 2011). The move towards risk-based frameworks was prompted by the Crime and Disorder Act 1998 and has been described as the "zombification" of youth justice (Pitts, 2001). Prior to this period, youth justice in England and Wales had been heavily focused on diversion and avoiding the impact of labelling children as "offenders" (Smith, 2005). However, the New Labour agenda focused heavily on crime and justice, with children being a focal point. The idea that children were committing crimes and "getting away with it" was prevalent within society, being driven by media and politicians. A moral panic around media influence on children spurred by both the Columbine shootings and the James Bulger murder only heightened this concern (Altheide, 2009). This was a key factor in the impetus for a change in the structure and organisation of youth justice, which included changing the ideology of practice from one of child protection and diversion to that of risk assessment and management (Muncie, 1999; Pitts, 2001). Justice-involved children became perceived as a collection of risk factors, many of which were (and are) beyond the control of the individual. Housing, family histories, the quality of education and more were all indicative factors of a child's propensity to offend (Burton, 2007; Dionne and Altamirano, 2012; Durant et al., 1995; McAra and McVie, 2016), as was their location. Those living in "high-crime environments" were classed as more likely to offend themselves (McAra and McVie, 2016), which means that all children living in cities are instantly perceived as more "risky" than their peers in towns or rural environments.

Many of the films depicting justice-involved children during this time showcased high levels of violence, drug use, and sex, presenting this as a normal part of children's lives. This is an exaggeration for the dramatic purposes of film, however, this played into narratives of adultification. Adultification is the process through which a child is perceived as an adult due to their behaviour (Burton, 2007), or is required to behave in more "adult" ways due to the social, cultural, and emotional expectations of the world around them (Davis, 2022). The concept of adultification cannot be separated from the cultural construction of children and childhood, as this implicitly forms the basis on which an individual can be labelled as "not a child". For ethnic minority children, the notion of "childness" is complicated by the stereotypes and prejudices attached to cultural constructions of "Blackness" (Davis and Marsh, 2020). For ethnic minority children (and particularly Black children), being perceived as a child is more difficult, as the associations of Blackness conflict with the associations of childhood. This is one of many ways in which racism is intersectional. Urban films primarily show Black children engaging in risk-taking and use a social realist approach acts as a form of validation for the adultification of these children. The impacts of this go beyond how audiences may perceive ethnic minority children. It has been shown that the adultification of ethnic minority children changes how they are treated by police, magistrates, and the custodial estate (Farmer, 2010; Fekete, 2018; Francis et al., 2020). The impact of

"I'm Not a Ghetto Boy, I Just Live in Deptford" **101**

adultification is almost always negative and further marginalises ethnic minority children, compounding their exclusion from society.

The films discussed in this chapter do not present central London as a solely Black space, urban spaces are heterogeneous. However, these films often subtly nod at the intersection of factors that make the experience of living in cities very different for certain groups of children. Class is the clearest example of this, and the way in which these films depict class is very much in keeping with the British social realism tradition (Malik, 2010; Quinn, 2005). The white characters in these films are often from the same neighbourhoods as the Black characters, or go to the same schools, but do not live in the same types of housing. The tower block flats of the Black characters are contrasted with the semi-detached or detached houses of the white characters. In those homes Black parents are seen as trying hard to provide the best for their children in difficult circumstances, and not having the level of resources they would like. Conversely, white parents in these films are able to provide material needs and comforts but are portrayed as indifferent and unobservant of their children. This is not necessarily unrealistic but could be considered as a simplistic view of the intersection of race and class and plays upon some of the pre-existing tropes that have emerged within a framework of structural racism.

The construction of ethnic minority children in these films can be clearly contrasted with similar work featuring a white protagonist. *Sweet Sixteen* (2002) directed by Ken Loach is set in Greenock, Scotland. Despite having many similarities to the urban films frequently set in London, *Sweet Sixteen* was responded to very differently. *Sweet Sixteen* focuses on Liam (Martin Compston) who is trying to develop his sense of identity and make decisions about his future as he approaches his 16th birthday. Liam's Mum (Michelle Coulter) is in prison, and he lives with his Grandfather and mother's boyfriend, both of whom are involved with drug selling. Liam is very against his family's criminal behaviours and wants to leave Greenock with his mother and live elsewhere. To raise money for this, he begins selling drugs and becomes involved in a gang. *Sweet Sixteen* features many of the hallmarks of urban films, such as being set in an impoverished or run-down area, where crime is prevalent, gangs are a common concern, children are groomed into joining gangs, drug use and sale is rife, violence is expected, and police are viewed as the enemy. However, being set outside of London, and featuring white protagonists, *Sweet Sixteen* was not marketed, reviewed, or culturally contextualised in the same way as *Kidulthood, Bullet Boy* or other contemporaries. Being directed by Ken Loach immediately gave *Sweet Sixteen* a level of prestige and cultural significance that the work of Ben Drew and Rapman etc. do not receive. The similarities in story, tone, and visuals are overlooked, meaning these films are not considered as equivalent. The race and

102 A Popular Criminology of Youth Justice

ethnicity of the characters in the London-set films clearly influenced how their stories were perceived by audiences (Davis, 2008; Nwonka and Saha, 2021). This difference meant that *Sweet Sixteen* was considered as serious art (Djurasovic and Djurasovic, 2019), whilst *Kidulthood* was the basis for a moral panic (Gooch, 2019). Whilst the London-set films draw more from mainstream cinema to create visually striking and spectacular set pieces, in contrast to Ken Loach's clear references to *The 400 Blows* (1959), it is clear that the difference in reception to these films is not purely based on taste or stylistic merits. The setting of these stories, and who they portray cannot be overlooked.

The Perpetuation of Fear

The endings of these films are often either ambiguous or gloomy. The characters do not transform into law-abiding young adults with future options. They are often left facing difficult choices, difficult situations, and difficult futures. At the end of *Kidulthood*, Trife's girlfriend Alisa (Red Madrell) is pregnant, her closest friendship has been broken, her peer group have excluded her for perceived "sluttyness", and the father of her child has been killed in a violent incident to which she was a witness. There is no implication that this will act as a catalyst for change in her life, as would be expected in the problem youth films of the 1950s. As the credits begin, the expectation is that Alisa will have a difficult life, having been indelibly stained by the association with criminality. In *Bullet Boy* Curtis is also bereaved, having lost a role model in his older brother. Whilst this is a catalyst for him to throw away his brother's gun, implying his rejection of gangs and violence, he is still in the same circumstances that led to both his and his brother's involvement initially. He is more isolated than previously, and lacking social support it is unclear if his resolution to change the cycle of violence will be successful. In *Ill Manors* (2012) the young characters all are killed in response to their deviance, with Jake being shot as vengeance for shooting Chanel (Sasha Gabmle), whose death occurs immediately after trying crack cocaine for the first time. The only survivor of the child characters in *Ill Manors* is Jody (Eloise Smyth), who refused drugs, was wary of the person who appeared to be trying to sexually exploit her and Chanel and was helpful to others. However, even she succumbs to the deviant nature of city life. As the film ends she is brutally beating up a girl who bullies her. These films have taken on the legacy of the Hays code, where deviant and criminal behaviours cannot be perceived as being a pathway to success or happiness in any way (Pavés, 2023). However, whereas the problem youth films all had a central character survive and reform, the urban films of the 2000s do not. The message to those watching these films is that becoming involved with a gang leads to death.

"I'm Not a Ghetto Boy, I Just Live in Deptford" **103**

This negative message regarding gang involvement and criminal behaviours was an explicit aim of many of the filmmakers. Many of the writers and directors of these films have spoken openly about wanting to make a social issue film that appealed to children that actively discouraged gang involvement, knife carrying, drug use, and violence (Nwonka, 2023). Rapman (director of *Blue Story*), Ben Drew (director of *Ill Manors*) and Noel Clarke (writer of *Kidulthood*) have all said that their work was influenced by their own childhood experiences, and they wanted to serve as an inspiration to other children in deprived areas of cities (particularly London), to show that there is another path or a way out of gang life (Nwonka and Saha, 2021). This position can be compared to that of Assistant District Attorney Hank Bell (Burt Lancaster) from *The Young Savages* (1961), who also wanted to show the young gang members in his former neighbourhood that there were other options. However, whilst the rhetoric of *The Young Savages* was that work and dedication were the way out of poverty and difficult circumstances, urban films suggest creative endeavours may be the answer.

> *Don't listen to people they chat shit. And I don't mind if you wanna call yourself tiny madder but be your own man, you don't have to be like me. Just stick to your music and you could be the next Stormzy or something*

However, despite the filmmakers themselves being examples of this, they are clearly exceptions. The disparity in society means that many children will not "make it big" like their heroes in the music scene. For children who are perennially excluded from society, this compounds the sense of isolation, meaning they turn to alternative means to find connection and community, which for many children was one of the reasons they joined or stayed part of a gang (Densley and Stevens, 2015; Frisby-Osman and Wood, 2020; Pitts, 2020). In the films themselves, the characters who appear to have options, the prospect of social mobility, and a way out of their current situation don't achieve this. In *Blue Story*, Leah (Karla-Simone Spence) had ambitions of becoming a singer but is killed whilst she is trying to break up a fight. Timmy (Stephen Odubola) is so traumatised by her death that he vows revenge, cementing his own future as a criminal. The overriding message of these films is that there is no escaping London estates, and this then impacts upon how audiences perceive those who live there.

These films showcase the difficulties of life for ethnic minority children in cities, and whilst there might be minor acknowledgements of some systemic factors such as police racism, there is little consideration of the broader social issues that lead or contribute to these situations. Whilst some narratives of these films consider the role of families, and cycles of violence, this is not placed into the context of broader social exclusion or lack of social opportunity. This means that the films present these narratives as an individual

104 A Popular Criminology of Youth Justice

circumstance, essentially leaving audiences to blame the characters for their choices. As these films are inherently framed, marketed and presented as being based upon real experiences and issues, this impacts how the broader public perceives real people impacted by gang violence. Whilst these films aimed to avoid glamourisation of violence and send the message that gang involvement is harmful and should be avoided, due to the lack of deeper examination of the structural issues, the underlying message is that the transition into criminality is permanent, and that the social circumstances that have contributed to this are inescapable. This negative message only further stigmatises ethnic minority communities and children, perpetuating the assumption that all children in cities are involved in gangs, carry knives or take drugs. For the audience, this only further embeds the racist stereotypes of society into their thinking.

Many of these films have been discussed as being representative of reality, as something parents should be concerned about, and that caution should be taken in allowing children to watch them. Given that the majority of these films received a 15 or 18 certificate from the BBFC suggests that they are not intended for very young audiences, however, the concerns occurred anyway. *Blue Story* in particular has received a lot of media attention due to a high-profile incident that took place at a cinema showing the film in Birmingham. Two large groups fought in the cinema lobby, with reports of machetes being used (BBC News, 2019). This led to two major cinema chains (Vue and Cineworld) removing the film from their programme. This has given *Blue Story* a reputation of being much more graphically violent, explicit and dangerous than the film actually is. Whilst there is graphic violence within the film, it was only significant enough to warrant a 15 rating from the BBFC, despite also including frequent swearing, drug references and sexual scenes. The film itself is moralising, using a narrator (played by Rapman) to explicitly condone the violence depicted, and urging others to reconsider joining a gang or carrying a weapon.

RIP for all these innocent lives. I hope these youngers wake up and start seeing the light

The broader social concerns regarding children and weapon carrying (in particular knives) have informed what is acceptable in relation to films and media presenting Black stories. The initial imperative to "get something Black made" (Nwonka and Malik, 2018) was done in such a way that film producers, funders, and film-makers struggle to perceive the stories of young Black people outside of the lens of crime. Only showing Black stories through the lens of violence is not true representation. These films teach white people to be afraid of cities and the (non-white) people who live within them. They also teach Black children that the only way they will receive recognition is through the spectacle of violence, even in the context of the arts. The characters in *Blue Story* hold up John Boyega as an example of someone like them who "made it", and director Rapman has explicitly said that he wants to act as a similar example. But the only way these examples gain visibility is through recreating and performing the spectacle of violence that is expected by a structurally racist culture. Even John Boyega has commented (Famurewa, 2020) on the lack of opportunities available to him prior to *Star Wars: Episode VII - The Force Awakens* (2015), with many of his roles being young delinquents, such as in *Attack the Block* (2011), *My Murder* (2012), and *Imperial Dreams* (2014). Similarly, Riz Ahmed has spoken on the lack of opportunity for actors of colour (Ahmed, 2016), and the need for representation to go beyond simply telling stories that engage with harmful cultural attitudes. The urban films of the 2000s show that whilst there was growing awareness of the need for stories about justice-involved children to go beyond idealism, and to incorporate layers of truth, this still was not truly representative and viewed justice-involved children as offenders first.

Film List

Anuvahood (2011)
Attack The Block (2011)
Blue Story (2019)
Boyz N The Hood (1991)
Bullet Boy (2004)
Ill Manors (2012)
Imperial Dreams (2014)
Kes (1969)
Kids (1995)
Kidulthood (2006)
La Haine (1995)
Lock, Stock and Two Smoking Barrels
Menace II Society (1993)
My Murder (2012)
Notting Hill (1999)
Passport to Pimlico (1949)
Rebel Without A Cause (1955)
Shank (2010)
Sket (2011)
Snatch (2000)
Star Wars: Episode VII - The Force Awakens (2015)
Sweet Sixteen (2002)
The Young Savages (1961)

References

Ahmed R (2016) Typecast as a terrorist. *The Guardian*, 15 September. Available at: https://www.theguardian.com/world/2016/sep/15/riz-ahmed-typecast-as-a-terrorist (accessed 23 April 2024).

Almond T (2012) Asset: An assessment tool that safeguards or stigmatizes young offenders? *Probation Journal* 59(2): 138–150.

Altheide DL (2009) Moral panic: From sociological concept to public discourse. *Crime, Media, Culture* 5(1): 79–99. SAGE Publications.

Armstrong D, Hine J, Hacking S, et al. (2005) *Children, Risk and Crime: The On Track Youth Lifestyles Surveys*. Home Office Research, Development and Statistics Directorate (ed.). London: Home Office, Development and Statistics Directorate.

Arnez J and Condry R (2021) Criminological perspectives on school exclusion and youth offending. *Emotional and Behavioural Difficulties* 26(1): 87–100. Routledge.

Axford N, Tredinnick-Rowe J, Rybcyznska-Bunt S, et al. (2023) Engaging youth at risk of violence in services: Messages from research. *Children and Youth Services Review* 144: 106713.

Barry M (2010) Youth transitions: From offending to desistance. *Journal of Youth Studies* 13(1): 121–136.

BBC News (2019) Blue Story: UK cinema ban called 'institutionally racist'. *BBC News*, 26 November. Available at: https://www.bbc.com/news/newsbeat-50543213 (accessed 4 July 2022).

Benz TA (2014) At the intersection of urban sociology and criminology: Fear of crime and the postindustrial city. *Sociology Compass* 8(1): 10–19.

Berghahn D (2010) Coming of age in 'the hood': The diasporic youth film and questions of genre. In: Berghahn D and Sternberg C (eds) *European Cinema in Motion: Migrant and Diasporic Film in Contemporary Europe*. Palgrave European Film and Media Studies. London: Palgrave Macmillan UK, pp. 235–255. Available at: https://doi.org/10.1057/9780230295070_12 (accessed 13 November 2023).

Blyth M, Solomon E and Baker K (2007) *Young People and 'Risk'*. Bristol: Policy Press.

Boldison L (2006) *'Hoodies': A New Moral Panic?: An Examination of Media Representations of Crime, Youth Subcultures, Moral Panics and the Application of the Moral Panic Theory to Media Reporting of 'Hoodies' in Britain's National Newspapers*. Leicester: University of Leicester.

Briggs DB (2013) Conceptualising risk and need: The rise of actuarialism and the death of welfare? Practitioner assessment and intervention in the youth offending service. *Youth Justice* 13(1): 17–30. SAGE Publications Sage UK: London, England.

British Film Institute (2016) Strife and the city: Urban space in the essay film | Sight & Sound. Available at: https://www2.bfi.org.uk/news-opinion/sight-sound-magazine/features/strife-city-urban-space-essay-film (accessed 17 October 2023).

Burton L (2007) Childhood adultification in economically disadvantaged families: A conceptual model. *Family Relations* 56(4): 329–345. [National Council on Family Relations, Wiley].

Calleja N (2022) Intersectionality and processes of belonging: Thinking critically about sociomaterial entanglements with the voices of upper-primary school-aged young people in youth research. *Journal of Applied Youth Studies* 5(4): 317–334.

"I'm Not a Ghetto Boy, I Just Live in Deptford" **107**

Cameron D (2006) Speech to the Centre for Social Justice, London 2006. Available at: http://www.britishpoliticalspeech.org/speech-archive.htm?speech=318 (accessed 6 February 2024).

Case S (2006) Young people 'at risk' of what? Challenging risk-focused early intervention as crime prevention. *Youth Justice* 6(3): 171–179.

Case S and Bateman T (2020) The punitive transition in youth justice: Reconstructing the child as offender. *Children and Society* 34(6): 475–491.

Childress H (2004) Teenagers, territory and the appropriation of space. *Childhood* 11(2): 195–205.

Chiricos T, Eschholz S and Gertz M (1997) Crime, news and fear of crime: Toward an identification of audience effects. *Social Problems* 44(3): 342–357.

Chummel (2010) Race and place: Hollywood's vision of urban youth in Los Angeles Film. In: *American Studies Journal*. Available at: http://www.asjournal.org/54-2010/race-and-place-hollywoods-vision-of-urban-youth-in-los-angeles-film/ (accessed 17 October 2023).

Davis J (2022) Adultification bias within child protection and safeguarding. *Academic Insights* 6: 1–14. Her Majesty's Inspectorate of Probation.

Davis J and Marsh N (2020) Boys to men: The cost of 'adultification' in safeguarding responses to Black boys. *Critical and Radical Social Work* 8(2): 255–259. Policy Press.

Davis JM (2008) Living black, living white: Cultural choices in crime films. *World Literature Today* 82(3): 9–12. University of Oklahoma.

Densley JA and Pyrooz DC (2020) The matrix in context: Taking stock of police gang databases in London and beyond. *Youth Justice* 20(1–2): 11–30. SAGE Publications Inc.

Densley JA and Stevens A (2015) 'We'll show you gang': The subterranean structuration of gang life in London. *Criminology & Criminal Justice* 15(1): 102–120. SAGE PublicationsSage UK: London, England.

Dionne J and Altamirano C (2012) The challenges of a real youth justice system: A psychoeducational perspective. *Universitas Psychologica* 11(4): 1055–1064.

Djurasovic A and Djurasovic M (2019) Cities that degrade: Ken Loach on social ills. In: Anne Wagner and Le Cheng (eds) *Law, Cinema, and the Ill City*. Oxon: Routledge.

Durant RH, Getts AG, Cadenhead C, et al. (1995) The association between weapon carrying and the use of violence among adolescents living in and around public housing. *The Journal of Adolescent Health: Official Publication of the Society for Adolescent Medicine* 17(6): 376–380.

Esbensen FA and Tusinski K (2007) Youth gangs in the print media. *Journal of Criminal Justice and Popular Culture* 14(1): 21–38.

Famurewa J (2020) John Boyega: 'I'm the only cast member whose experience of Star Wars was based on their race'. Available at: https://www.gq-magazine.co.uk/culture/article/john-boyega-interview-2020 (accessed 23 April 2024).

Farmer S (2010) Criminality of Black youth in inner-city schools: 'Moral panic', moral imagination, and moral formation. *Race Ethnicity and Education* 13(3): 367–381. Routledge: .

Featherstone M (2013) "Hoodie horror": The capitalist other in postmodern society. *Review of Education, Pedagogy, and Cultural Studies* 35(3): 178–196. Routledge.

Fekete L (2018) Lammy review: Without racial justice, can there be trust? *Race & Class* 59(3): 75–79. SAGE PublicationsSage UK: London, England.

Forshaw B (2012) The age of acquisition: New crime. In: Forshaw B (ed.) *British Crime Film: Subverting the Social Order*. Crime Files Series. London: Palgrave Macmillan UK, pp. 157–166. Available at: https://doi.org/10.1057/9781137274595_14 (accessed 17 October 2023).

Francis S, Welsh T and Adesina Z (2020) Met Police 'four times more likely' to use force on black people – BBC News. Available at: https://www.bbc.co.uk/news/uk-england-london-53407560?intlink_from_url=https://www.bbc.co.uk/news/topics/c48yrnxgd7rt/black-lives-matter&link_location=live-reporting-story (accessed 11 August 2020).

Fraser A and Atkinson C (2014) Making up gangs: Looping, labelling and the new politics of intelligence-led policing. *Youth Justice* 14(2): 154–170. SAGE Publications Inc.

Frisby-Osman S and Wood JL (2020) Rethinking how we view gang members: An examination into affective, behavioral, and mental health predictors of UK gang-involved youth. *Youth Justice* 20(1–2): 93–112. SAGE Publications.

Fuhg F (2021) Working-class youth and the social transformation of Post-war London. In: Fuhg F (ed.) *London's Working-Class Youth and the Making of Post-Victorian Britain, 1958–1971*. Palgrave Studies in the History of Subcultures and Popular Music. Cham: Springer International Publishing, pp. 151–204. Available at: https://doi.org/10.1007/978-3-030-68968-1_5 (accessed 4 April 2023).

Gooch K (2019) 'Kidulthood': Ethnography, juvenile prison violence and the transition from 'boys' to 'men'. *Criminology & Criminal Justice* 19(1): 80–97.

Haines K and Case S (2012) Is the scaled approach a failed approach? *Youth Justice* 12(3): 212–228.

Halper T (2014) Trainspotters and bullet boys: Race and class in British underclass movies, 1980–the present☆. *City, Culture and Society* 5(4): 11–20.

Hargreaves F, Carroll P, Robinson G, et al. (2023) County Lines and the power of the badge: The LFC Foundation's approach to youth intervention. *Safer Communities* 22(2): 91–105. Emerald Publishing Limited.

Hayward K and Yar M (2006) The 'chav' phenomenon: Consumption, media and the construction of a new underclass. *Crime, Media, Culture* 2(1): 9–28. SAGE Publications.

Hutchison R (2010) Urban culture. In: *Encyclopedia of Urban Studies*. Thousand Oaks: SAGE Publications, Inc., pp. 857–859. Available at: https://sk.sagepub.com/reference/urbanstudies/n301.xml (accessed 24 January 2024).

Ilan J (2012) 'The industry's the new road': Crime, commodification and street cultural tropes in UK urban music. *Crime, Media, Culture* 8(1): 39–55. SAGE Publications.

Jeong J, Bhatia A, Skeen S, et al. (2021) From fathers to peers: Association between paternal violence victimization and peer violence perpetration among youth in Malawi, Nigeria, and Zambia. *Social Science & Medicine* 278: 113943.

Jones W (2016) 10 years on, we speak to Noel Clarke about the making of 'kidulthood'. *Complex*. Available at: https://www.complex.com/pop-culture/2016/03/noel-clarke-kidulthood-ten-years-on (accessed 28 July 2022).

Kelling GL and Wilson JQ (1982) Broken windows. *The Atlantic*, 1 March. Available at: https://www.theatlantic.com/magazine/archive/1982/03/broken-windows/304465/ (accessed 23 April 2024).

King L (2003) Review of Black City Cinema: African American urban experiences in film. *African American Review* 37(2/3): 445–447. [Indiana State University, Saint Louis University, African American Review, African American Review (St. Louis University)].

Kinsey L (2019) *'Youth Knife Crime' in Context. Adolescents Beyond Objects of Concern.* Cambridge: National Association for Youth Justice.

Kroll L, Rothwell J, Bradley D, et al. (2002) Mental health needs of boys in secure care for serious or persistent offending: A prospective, longitudinal study. *The Lancet* 359(9322): 1975–1979.

MacLeod G (2018) The Grenfell Tower atrocity. *City* 22(4): 460–489. Routledge.

Malik S (2010) The dark side of hybridity: Contemporary Black and Asian British cinema. In: Berghahn D and Sternberg C (eds) *European Cinema in Motion: Migrant and Diasporic Film in Contemporary Europe.* Palgrave European Film and Media Studies. London: Palgrave Macmillan UK, pp. 132–151. Available at: https://doi.org/10.1057/9780230295070_7 (accessed 17 October 2023).

Maurutto P and Hannah-Moffat K (2007) Understanding risk in the context of the Youth Criminal Justice Act. *Canadian Journal of Criminology and Criminal Justice* 49(4): 465–491. University of Toronto Press.

Maxwell N, Wallace C and Bayfield H (2019) A systematic map and synthesis review of Child Criminal Exploitation October 2019. Cascade Children's Social Care Research and Development Service: Cardiff University. Available at: https://orca.cardiff.ac.uk/id/eprint/131950/1/Child%20Criminal%20Exploitation%20Report%20Final.pdf

McAra L and McVie S (2007) Youth justice?: The impact of system contact on patterns of desistance from offending. *European Journal of Criminology* 4(3): 315–345.

McAra L and McVie S (2016) Understanding youth violence: The mediating effects of gender, poverty and vulnerability. *Journal of Criminal Justice* 45: 71–77. 'Protective Factors against Youth Offending and Violence: Results from Prospective Longitudinal Studies'.

Muncie J (1999) Institutionalized intolerance: Youth justice and the 1998 Crime and Disorder Act. *Critical Social Policy* 19(2): 147–175.

Nwonka C and Saha A (2021) *Black Film British Cinema II.* London: MIT Press.

Nwonka CC (2023) *Black Boys: The Social Aesthetics of British Urban Film.* USA: Bloomsbury Publishing.

Nwonka CJ and Malik S (2018) Cultural discourses and practices of institutionalised diversity in the UK film sector: 'Just get something black made'. *The Sociological Review* 66(6): 1111–1127. SAGE Publications Ltd.

O'Brien DT, Farrell C and Welsh BC (2019) Broken (Windows) theory: A meta-analysis of the evidence for the pathways from neighborhood disorder to resident health outcomes and behaviors. *Social Science & Medicine* 228: 272–292.

Pavés GM (2023) Unacceptable matters: The Hays code, family, film noir and RKO radio pictures. *Historical Journal of Film, Radio and Television* 43(2): 359–379. Routledge.

Paylor I (2011) Youth justice in England and Wales: A risky business. *Journal of Offender Rehabilitation* 50(4): 221–233. Routledge.

Pearson G (2006) Disturbing continuities: Peaky blinders to hoodies. *Criminal Justice Matters* 65(August 2013): 6–7.

Piroozfar P, Farr ERP, Aboagye-Nimo E, et al. (2019) Crime prevention in urban spaces through environmental design: A critical UK perspective. *Cities* 95: 102411.

Pitts J (2001) Korrectional karaoke: New labour and the zombification of youth justice. *Youth Justice* 1(2): 3–16.

Pitts J (2020) Black young people and gang involvement in London. *Youth Justice* 20(1–2): 146–158. SAGE Publications.

Quinn L (2005) Review of migrating to the movies: Cinema and Black urban modernity. *Film Criticism* 29(3): 73–78. Allegheny College.

Robinson G, McLean R and Densley J (2019) Working county lines: Child criminal exploitation and illicit drug dealing in Glasgow and Merseyside. *International Journal of Offender Therapy and Comparative Criminology* 63(5): 694–711. SAGE Publications Inc.

Sampson RJ and Groves WB (1989) Community structure and crime: Testing social-disorganization theory. *American Journal of Sociology* 94(4): 774–802. The University of Chicago Press.

Schroeder E (2001) A multicultural conversation: La Haine, Raï, and Menace II Society. *Camera Obscura* 16(1): iv–179. Duke University Press.

Sealey-Ruiz Y and Greene P (2015) Popular visual Images and the (mis)reading of Black Male Youth: A case for racial literacy in urban preservice teacher education. *Teaching Education* 26(1): 55–76. Routledge.

Sen P (2005) Bullet boy. *BMJ* 330(7496): 910. British Medical Journal Publishing Group.

Shaw CR and McKay HD (1942) *Juvenile Delinquency and Urban Areas.* Juvenile delinquency and urban areas. Chicago, IL, US: University of Chicago Press.

Shihadeh ES and Steffensmeier DJ (1994) Economic inequality, family disruption, and urban Black violence: Cities as Units of stratification and social control*. *Social Forces* 73(2): 729–751.

Smith R (2005) Welfare versus justice- again! *Youth Justice* 5(2): 3–16.

Stone N (2018) Child criminal exploitation: 'County lines', trafficking and cuckooing. *Youth Justice* 18(3): 285–293. SAGE Publications.

Toro JD, Lloyd T, Buchanan KS, et al. (2019) The criminogenic and psychological effects of police stops on adolescent black and Latino boys. *Proceedings of the National Academy of Sciences of the United States of America* 116(17): 8261–8268. National Academy of Sciences.

Vincendeau G (2012) La haine and after: Arts, politics, and the banlieue. Available at: https://www.criterion.com/current/posts/642-la-haine-and-after-arts-politics-and-the-banlieue (accessed 14 June 2023).

Wacquant LJD (1993) Urban outcasts: Stigma and division in the Black American Ghetto and the French Urban Periphery*. *International Journal of Urban and Regional Research* 17(3): 366–383.

Wilson D and O'Sullivan S (2004) *Images of Incarceration: Representations of Prison in Film and Television Drama.* Winchester, U.K: Waterside Press.

Wroe LE (2021) Young people and "county lines": A contextual and social account. *Journal of Children's Services* 16(1): 39–55. Emerald Publishing Limited.

6

"THANK YOU FOR RESPECTING ME AND MY FAMILY'S PRIVACY"

True Youth Crime, Sensationalism, and Fictionalisation

True crime is one of the most enduring genres of all media and has recently seen a resurgence through documentary series (Bruzzi, 2016). It has been described as "the little black dress of filmmaking" (Ringer, 2012) due to its perennial popularity. The ability to believe that media is representative of reality is an attractive quality for audiences, making the phrase "based on a true story" a commonplace feature of many films. This has become a trope to the point where clearly fictional films such as *Fargo* (1996) claim that "this is a true story" in the opening credits. The idea that the films we consume are true or speak to broader truths about our world is appealing, making media engagement feel like a worthy endeavour that goes beyond pure entertainment. For the crime film, this is a boon because there are plenty of cases, stories, and incidents that lend themselves to film adaptation. Criminal investigations have a clear narrative arc, stories of victims getting justice provide uplifting and happy endings, and stories of criminals allow us to vicariously participate in violence, immoral behaviour, and to revel in the complexity of the anti-hero. Many crime stories follow the narrative structure of popular film, with a set-up, exciting incident, and clear resolution (Seger, 2011), making this a popular choice of subject matter for writers and producers. It has been commented that true crime stories have to seem like fiction, otherwise they would strain audiences' suspension of disbelief (Seltzer, 2007). The true crime film also benefits producers as there is something of a grey area regarding the intellectual property rights of stories about true events (Klenk, 2018), particularly if the story is changed enough to be "inspired by" or "based upon" true events rather than claiming to be an accurate portrayal (Ringer, 2012). This means that for some crime films, the costs of accessing the rights to the material are reduced. Crime films work well in cinema and true crime

DOI: 10.4324/9781003403159-6

112 A Popular Criminology of Youth Justice

films in particular have developed a lasting popularity, where audiences then want to know more, leading to books, documentaries and podcasts discussing the same cases. True crime is inseparable from capitalism and the commodification of crime (Ilan, 2012; Wiltenburg, 2004). But it is also a self-sustaining industry, because it is selling to the public understanding and insight into an unanswerable question that has confounded society since its beginning: why do people do bad things?

True crime films do not cover all types of crime. There is a particular style to this media; they discuss violence with an emphasis on murder or serial killings; for example, *Zodiac* (2007), *My Friend Dahmer* (2017), and *Extremely Wicked, Shockingly Evil and Vile* (2019). Where true crime films do not portray murder they tend to be about gang crime, such as *The Irishman* (2019) and *Donnie Brasco* (1997); or fraud/financial crimes such as *Catch Me If You Can* (2002) and *Molly's Game* (2017). Whether murder-centric or not, true crime films always emphasise harm, a visual representation of "wound culture" in society (Seltzer, 2017). Wound culture refers to the public's fascination with atrocity and harm, and the apparent need of the public to see visceral and bodily damage in order to believe in its existence. True crime is one example of wound culture's prominence in society (Seltzer, 2007); its focus on murder and/or violence, and its emphasis that it is portraying "truth" allows the private wounds of victims and their families to become public. True crime films in particular suggest that these traumas are not only appropriate for consumption by the general public, but entertaining and fun.

Regardless of the subject matter, true crime films centre the lead up to crime, and often try to give some explanation of why this happened, with the perpetrator often being the focal character. This focus on perpetrators means that these films are often criticised for glamourising these individuals, or portraying them as sympathetic, attractive and worthy of attention, at the expense of victims, their families, and those involved in delivering justice (Klenk, 2018). The focus on violence means that these films are frequently violent themselves and are aimed at adult audiences rather than children. True crime stories don't tend to focus on children as criminals. Where children do feature in these films it is as victims, witnesses or family members of criminals, with these categories overlapping. Some true crime films may show the childhood of the central character (frequently a murderer) to create some context as to "what went wrong" in their lives to lead to such violence. This lack of child-centred stories may be because of the pattern of true crime films; of allowing the audience understanding of and empathy for people who commit crimes is incompatible with the culturally constructed image of "juvenile offender". This means that the true youth crime film is almost a genre of its own, combining the tropes of the adult crime film, with the features of the youth crime film that have been discussed in the previous chapters. This makes the true youth crime film unique. Focusing almost exclusively on violence,

"Thank You for Respecting Me and My Family's Privacy" 113

and utilising genre conventions from coming-of-age stories, crime stories, and thriller/horror films, audiences can revel in the vicarious enjoyment of violent crime whilst also engaging in moralising judgement about the behaviour of younger generations. The true youth crime film also maintains the convention of trying to explain why these events occurred, with many films defaulting to the corruption of innocence due to drugs, sexuality, or the downfall of modern society. This makes the true youth crime film highly attractive to audiences because they can consume the things they are afraid of, whilst also feeling secure that it will not happen to their own children.

Many true youth crime films depict cases that are already well-known or within the public's consciousness. This notoriety shows producers that there is already an audience willing to consume media about this specific story, making these films seem potentially more profitable. Of course, the cases that are well known are those that have been publicised and likely sensationalised through news media. The Starkweather murder spree, the murder of Bobby Kent, and the Hollywood Hills Burglars were all brought to the public's attention via the news, then subsequently turned into books and or articles, and later feature films. The Starkweather murder spree in particular has inspired multiple films, including *Badlands* (1973) and *Natural Born Killers* (1994); the latter of which caused controversy due to accusations of causing copycat killings (Boyle, 2001), the veracity of which has been questioned (Harbord, 1997; Schmid, 2008). True youth crime films play on the dichotomised image of justice-involved children throughout society, highlighting the childlike immaturity of the characters at the same time as their adult features such as sexuality, propensity for violence, and emotional responses (or lack thereof). By heightening the "adult" aspects of their behaviour and showing emotional immaturity or a lack of intellectual development, these films benefit from the effect of both tropes, showing children as innocent victims and dangerous criminals simultaneously.

Sensationalised Truth

The true youth crime film tends to fall into one of two categories: fictionalised truth, or sensationalised truth. Fictionalised truth films may not be depicting a specific case or incident but speak to the realities of lived experiences of children's justice involvement. An example of this is *County Lines* (2019), which shows a highly realistic account of what can happen to a child who is exploited into trafficking drugs. Fictionalised truth is based on a generalised reality rather than a specific true story, and whilst it has potentially more freedom to take liberties with how events play out, doesn't tend to. These are largely social issue films, created to not only show the experience of these children, but also as a form of activism and/or campaigning for change (Hernandez, 2019; Rowen, 2017). *Boy A* (2007) also uses this

114 A Popular Criminology of Youth Justice

approach, portraying a fictionalised story with high levels of similarity to the James Bulger case. *Boy A* shows the negative impact of media sensationalism and the lack of support for upon leaving custody for incarcerated children. Fictionalised truth wants audiences to perceive the often negative realities of criminal justice for children, and in their awareness of the potential harms of media exposure (Dowler, 2020; Klenk, 2018), many creators of these works turn to fictionalised stories to avoid putting further spotlight and scrutiny on real individuals.

Sensationalised truth films draw the "truth" aspects from being explicitly based upon a "true story". However, having this basis means that the filmmakers have the flexibility to use style, cinematography, and scripting as a way of creating a specific slant or perspective. The sensationalism in these films is highly evident; violence is graphic and a central feature, as is sexuality. *Bully* (2001) is a clear example of this, as is *Natural Born Killers*, or *Badlands*. These films focus on the violence of the cases, skirting but not falling into the horror film genre. Conversely, *The Bling Ring* (2013) focuses on consumption and theft opposed to violence, but still sensationalises this, appealing to the grotesque nature of overconsumption (Pesce, 2015), showcasing this in a similar way to violence in other films. Maintaining status as dramas or thrillers allows these films to still be perceived as believable, as opposed to shlock (Brien, 2009; Valsesia et al., 2017). The question that sensationalised truth films ask is why did these crimes happen? Whilst not explicitly moralising in the vein of problem youth films, true youth crime films do give audiences explanations for the offending behaviours of the characters. These explanations are surprisingly similar to those of the problem youth films though, desire. Whether this is desire for sex, drugs, alcohol, or consumer goods, the desirous nature of youth is cast as the driving factor behind criminal behaviour in these cases. This reinforces the cultural narrative of the need to control children, to contain and quell their desires, lest they topple the societal order. In a way, sensationalised truth films are carrying the torch of the problem youth film, but free from the restrictions of the Hays code (Maltby, 1995; Pavés, 2023), they can also show the gore, the skin, the excesses of youth in a way that titillates audiences whilst also allowing them to feel superior to the characters because they didn't make those choices.

The sensationalised sexualisation of justice-involved children is no clearer than in *Bully*. *Bully* is a fictionalised version of the murder of Bobby Kent, which was carried out by a group of his friends. In this film director Larry Clark featured numerous scenes of sex and nudity, similarity to his previous work in *Kids* (1995). Whilst the argument has been made (by Clark amongst others) that to remove or reduce the level of sexuality in the film would be doing a disservice to the truth of the story (Willing, 2022), there was a clear choice to feature sex and nudity so heavily in the film. A good example of this

"Thank You for Respecting Me and My Family's Privacy" **115**

choice is the use of nudity in scenes where it wasn't necessarily warranted. For example, in one scene Lisa (Rachel Miner) telephones the home of one of her accomplices upon finding out he has been arrested. The conversation is about her fear of being arrested and the unconcerned response of others. Throughout this scene Lisa is naked, looking at herself in a mirror, with the audience also clearly being encouraged to observe her body. Whilst nudity in films is not necessarily problematic in and of itself, the choice of when and how to use nudity in *Bully* appears to have been purely to view children as sex objects. The camera frequently lingers on the actors' bodies both male and female, showing full frontal nudity often. Larry Clark's work has been praised for showing children as active in their own sexuality, recognising the agency of children (Giroux, 1996). However, the way this is portrayed in *Bully*, particularly for the female characters, is entangled with abuse. One shot slowly highlights the bruises on Lisa's body as she lies in bed, with the implication that she was sexually assaulted by Bobby (Nick Stahl). Her assault by Marty (Brad Renfro) is also shown in detail after she tells him she is pregnant. The character of Aly (Bijou Phillips) is not only shown graphically being raped in the film but is subsequently asked to have sex with her rapist on multiple occasions, to act as "bait" for the murder. Whilst this is true to the story that inspired *Bully*, the choice to use graphic nudity and framing similar to conventional sex scenes in portraying an underage victim being coerced into having sex with her abuser is uncomfortable, particularly for modern audiences. Some would argue that this discomfort is the point the film is trying to make, that this is another sign of the controlling of children's agency. However, comments from Larry Clark and the casting choices suggest that this criticism of societal moralising isn't the main aim of the film. In a podcast discussion about the film, Clark stated;

> She [Kelli Garner] had the most beautiful breasts in the whole world and she's only 16–17 years old or something. And I actually have her naked in a naked scene with Michael Pitt lying in bed naked in the film and that was a big coup to be able to do that scene.
>
> *(Ellis, 2016)*

Garner was the youngest of the cast, who were of similar ages to the teenage characters they portray (ranging from 21 to 17 at the time of the film's release). The choice to use nudity heavily in this film doesn't necessarily reflect a desire to portray "truth", but a sensationalised use of children's bodies to draw in audiences, create discussion (both good and bad), and use the "true crime" framing to commodify and sexualise children.

The spectre of sexuality lingers over sensationalised truth films even when they do not portray graphic nudity. In *Badlands*, the relationship between Holly and Kit is clearly a sexual one, in *Let Him Have It* (1991), Derek is

116 A Popular Criminology of Youth Justice

clearly looking to engage in a romantic relationship, and Chloe and Sam in *The Bling Ring* are both engaged in sexual relationships with adults. Because these films rarely try to give an explicit answer as to why criminal behaviour occurred, the implication is that these children were corrupted or lead astray by the drinking, drugs, and/or sex that seem omnipresent in their worlds. Children's consumption is to be concerned about and moderated. The sensationalised truth film hints at children's sexuality, drug use, and engagement with consumer culture as corrupting, whilst also showing it in vivid, graphic detail. The audience gets to be titillated and appalled simultaneously, which makes these films an attractive proposition to funders and producers. The moralising tone of the problem youth films has become unfashionable though, and the explicitness of films like *Bully* has become questioned as societal awareness of child exploitation increases (Steinberg, 2018). This means that the true youth crime film has had to change in response. The moralising and exhibition of sex and drug use seems overdone and is no longer shocking to audiences. One of the most successful true youth crime films of recent years takes a different approach. Rather than attributing the blame to the consumption of sex or drugs, it instead takes aim at consumerist society.

The Bling Ring, directed by Sophia Coppola, loudly proclaims that it is "based on true events" in both marketing materials and at the start of the film. There is a clear drive to emphasise the realness of the story, as otherwise it would seem somewhat unbelievable. As Seltzer (2007: 2) has argued, "true crime is crime fact that looks like crime fiction", therefore it is necessary to emphasise the true underpinnings of the story. The fantastical nature of *The Bling Ring* comes from both the audacity of the children involved, and the celebrity of the victims. Telling the tale of the Hollywood Hills Heists (Pesce, 2015), the film depicts a group of children who enter celebrities' homes and take money, clothes, drugs and the cultural status associated with the star. Consumerism is a large part of the film, with the characters even describing their criminal activities as "going shopping". The group feel a sense of ownership over the celebrities they steal from, as they are given access to so much of their lives through both traditional and social media, and gossip blogs. The excessive consumption of these stars themselves is also used by the group as a way of justifying their behaviour, whilst also positioning themselves in a similar sphere to their idols. Because Paris Hilton has an "has so much stuff" it is ok for them to take some; because Mischa Barton "got another DUI" it is ok for them to drink and drive, because Lindsay Lohan went to jail it is not only survivable, but a publicity opportunity for them.

she was in orange like all of us

The Bling Ring is interesting in that it fits more with conventional teen films than youth justice films. The characters go nightclubbing, try on clothes in

"Thank You for Respecting Me and My Family's Privacy" 117

their bedrooms, go to school, interact with peers (Doherty, 2002). It is more like *Mean Girls* (2004) than *Natural Born Killers* (1994). The lack of violence in their crimes may have facilitated this, however, Sophia Coppola's choices as a director are a feature in this as well. Her work often focuses on the experiences of young women, and the listlessness of teenage girlhood (Wilkinson, 2017). Whereas other true youth crime films have centred the lack of opportunity for the young characters, the need to escape their situation, the characters in *The Bling Ring* have relatively stable, secure lives, where their desires to be actors, stylists, and celebrities seem possible without having to engage in criminal behaviour. The teenage years are frequently characterised (particularly in film) as being the site of a Proustian battle, in which struggling is necessary to developing one's adult character. Analysis of *The Bling Ring* has commented on the profound lack of struggle for these privileged children living in Hollywood, the children of producers and business owners (Henderson, 2020). There have been suggestions that this lack of struggle in a late-stage capitalist society may have been a fuelling factor in the criminal behaviour, trying to create excitement and struggle artificially (Stapleton, 2015). Coppola's work does seem to centre the opportunity as a reason, compounded by the influence and desire for consumption and cultural status. That gossip blogs highlighted not only where these celebrities lived, but also when they wouldn't be home, and what was in their homes, made this crime seem feasible. And the potential payoff, of not just having expensive things, but culturally relevant expensive things makes it all the more attractive (Henderson, 2020). Through the lens of anti-social potential theories (Farrington, 2020), it is easy to see how the culture made this crime seem not only possible, but inevitable.

Fictionalised Truth

Whilst sensationalised truth is trying to titillate, fictionalised truth is more sensitive as it is trying to gain empathy for children. Fictionalised truth films do not use the "based on a true story" tag in the same way as sensationalised truth films; this isn't a key part of the marketing but is a key part of the social discussion around the film. Fictionalised truth films are still based on true stories but may not use the names of individuals that the stories centre, may have changed certain details to maintain privacy or avoid sensationalism, and tend to focus on the emotional journey of the individual rather than the experiential aspects of the crime. These films are not necessarily as "true" as sensationalised truth films in terms of details, however, they actively speak to a larger truth about youth crime. In this regard fictionalised truth films are more similar to social issue films, such as the work of Ken Loach, whereas sensationalised truth films draw from horror or suspense films. Fictionalised truth films are explicit in their messaging and are often seen as a form of

118 A Popular Criminology of Youth Justice

activism or campaigning, as they are trying to raise public awareness of a particular issue. *Let Him Have it* (1991) is a clear example of this, using the Derek Bentley case as a way of campaigning for the death penalty to remain out of use and for children with additional needs to be given specific consideration by criminal justice systems.

Let Him Have It, directed by Peter Medak, reenacts the life of Derek Bentley, who was executed at 19 years old for murder by shooting of a police officer. The case garnered much attention because Bentley was accused under joint enterprise principles, having not fired the gun, and having been under the custody of police at the scene of the crime at the time it was committed. Bentley's guilt was based upon the title phrase of the film; he yelled "let him have it" to co-accused Chris Craig. The 16-year-old Craig took this as meaning to shoot the police officer, whereas Bentley argued it meant to give up the gun. Medak's film is centred on the aftermath of the guilty verdict, and the appeal process to try and gain clemency for Bentley, based not only on the tenuous nature of his guilt, but also the fact that he had health and neurodevelopmental needs. Bentley was epileptic and assessed as having a "sub-normal" IQ (Watson, 2020). *Let Him Have It* shows the difficulties in both Derek (Christopher Eccleston) and Chris's (Paul Reynolds) lives, emphasising their childlike nature and the level of need both boys have. Whilst Derek is the main character of the story, we also see that Chris is essentially raised by his brother Niven (Mark McGann) and is deeply affected by his arrest. Chris clearly blames authority figures and police for his brother's arrest and sentence, furthering his association with anti-social pathways (Gray et al., 2019; McAra and McVie, 2012). Chris does not feel able to access society through conventional norms, and his love of gangster movies is commented on frequently by characters in the film. Chris sees the criminal underworld as the place that will accept him and feels that this is the only option available to him. The lack of social mobility in society and the lack of opportunity for children has frequently been commented on as a factor influencing criminal behaviour (Boudon, 1973; Goldman and Rodriguez, 2022; Kashani et al., 1999). From strain (Agnew, 1992), to criminal pathways (McAra and McVie, 2012), to anti-social potential (Farrington, 2020), theorists have long considered the lack of opportunity within society to be a factor associated with criminality. Being aware of this lack of opportunity at a young age can allow feelings of hopelessness to develop in children (Burnside and Gaylord-Harden, 2019), making them more susceptible to exploitation, but also the potential excitement and sense of belonging in criminal enterprises (Calleja, 2022). This is clearly the implication of what has led Chris to identify with and idolise gangsters in *Let Him Have It*. During the shootout, when it is clear Chris will not escape he appears to prefer to die rather than be arrested. He taunts the police officers hoping they will shoot at him, yelling "come on you fuckers, I'm only 16", and when he is about to be arrested

"Thank You for Respecting Me and My Family's Privacy" **119**

Chris attempts to shoot himself. The implication is that this child doesn't see a future available to him if he is arrested, he lacks hope that his life will be better in any way outside of the criminal underworld.

Let Him Have It is clearly trying to gain sympathy for both Derek and Chris by showing them as vulnerable. Derek particularly so, as his story is the main feature of the film. There is an emphasis on the positive nature of the Bentley family, and that Derek could have had a different life if he had been given the opportunity. Prior to meeting Chris and Niven, Derek has left approved school (a residential school for children who were criminal or uncontrollable), he has a good relationship with his parents and his sister, has hobbies, and finds a job as a street cleaner. Whilst Derek has limited options due to his inability to read and low IQ, the film sets out that he was unlikely to have entered into crime if he had not met and befriended Chris. Derek even states at one point that he doesn't "ever want to go back to approved school", making clear his intention to live a law-abiding life. Whilst Chris is shown sympathetically and as a victim of his situation, there is a clear narrative that Derek was led astray by him, and their friendship was the key factor that led to Derek's arrest and death. This somewhat undermines the overall message of the film; *Let Him Have It* has been described as "outrage towards a system hell bend on vengeance" (Wiener, 2002: 369), however, seems to place blame on a 16-year-old and implies that he should have received a harsher sentence.

The justice system in *Let Him Have It* is portrayed as cynical, uncaring, and rigid. The judge during the trial negates both Derek and Chris's ages and encourages the jury to consider them as adults.

> *These youths are not children, one is 16, the other 19. It would be idle to suggest that they didn't know what they were doing*

The speed of the processes is also framed as a source of injustice; there was a gap of two months between Derek's arrest and execution, and much of the film places emphasis on the family's struggle to submit appeals within set deadlines, and their attempts to gain political support for Derek's appeal. This sets the justice and political systems at high levels as uncaring, whilst showing the individuals working within those systems positively. Prison staff support Derek, writing letters to his family for him, playing draughts, and reading him the paper. The critique within the film is clearly for the system as a whole and the lack of opportunities for compensation, reconsideration, or flexibility. This criticism is the main purpose of *Let Him Have It*, and the main reason for using a true case as its basis. Whilst the film is ostensibly about Derek Bentley, it is also about injustice and the need for systemic reform. However, fictional stories or other cases would not display this message as well as *Let Him Have It*. A fictionalised version of the truth was necessary to put this message across to audiences.

120 A Popular Criminology of Youth Justice

Another example of fictionalised truth, which shows a greater use of fictionalisation is *County Lines* (2019). This film is not based upon one specific case, but the current concerns regarding a type of crime. County lines refers to a specific type of drug trafficking, which often exploits children (Stone, 2018). Gangs based in cities and other metropolitan areas recruit children to transport drugs to rural locations to be sold. This allows the gang to control a larger area and develop larger profits (Wroe, 2021). Having the drugs be transported by exploited children allows the higher-up members of the gang to avoid the risk of detection and arrest and place this upon individuals who do not have information that could damage them or their operation and are viewed as expendable within the gang structure (O'Hagan and Edmundson, 2021; Robinson et al., 2019). County lines crime has increasingly become an issue of safeguarding as much as it is an issue of crime prevention (Koch et al., 2024).

In the film *County Lines* we see a child being systematically recruited, groomed, and exploited by an adult. Tyler (Conrad Khan) is 14, has difficulty in school, frequently is responsible for the care of his younger sister, and has a difficult relationship with his mother. He meets Simon (Harris Dickinson) who tells him of having similar problems when he was Tyler's age. Tyler is clearly enchanted by Simon, as this is one of the first times an adult has not only listened to him but treated him with respect. Tyler's life is full of adults who tell him what to do and how to be, but don't provide solutions to the situation that prevents him from meeting their demands, which is largely one of poverty. Tyler's teacher encourages him to get into sport or other hobbies, but don't recognise that the practices are during times when he picks up his little sister from school or has care responsibility for her. Their mother works irregular shifts, including nights, to be able to afford food and housing for the family. Poverty is the main barrier facing them, and no one offers a solution, except for Simon. But this solution is for Tyler to transport drugs to a seaside town where they will be sold by other gang members, taking on not only risk, but the burden of secrecy. As the film progresses, we see not the usual "gangster" narrative of Tyler rising through the ranks of the organisation, but him becoming increasingly excluded from those around him, whilst simultaneously being expendable to the gang. Tyler's admiration of Simon is what maintains his involvement, with the idea of being a "boss" and a "man" appealing to him. For children like Tyler, the idea of independence is alluring, and someone not only acting as a model for this, but also offering a possibility of achieving it, can easily become a role model, even if their methods are criminal (Windle et al., 2020).

County Lines shows in shocking detail the realities of child criminal exploitation. We see Tyler transporting drugs, including hiding and retrieving them from a bodily cavity. We see the cuckooed house where Tyler delivers drugs for them to be sold on, and the home's owner being exploited by a

"Thank You for Respecting Me and My Family's Privacy" **121**

member of the operation. As Tyler leaves the seaside town to return home, we see another child being picked up, implying that this is a continuing cycle and Tyler's story is not unusual. The film makes clear the unpleasantness of these situations and Tyler's disgust at both himself and his situation. The film also includes violence, on a later trip, Tyler is stabbed and attacked with a corrosive substance by children who have been recruited by another gang. But *County Lines* cannot be accused of glamourisation; the violence is brutal emotionally, as we see another clearly exploited child being urged to stab Tyler as a display of loyalty and the distress this causes both boys. The details of drug transportation are shown only once, and differently to how sensationalised truth films would portray this. *County Lines* alludes to the situation, showing a jar of Vaseline, Tylers disgusted and saddened expression, and his faeces-covered hand. The film centres Tylers emotional experience of the situation rather than sensationalising the physical aspects. If Larry Clark had directed *County Lines* it is likely that this would have been treated much more graphically using nudity and showing more explicit detail. There was a clear choice in *County Lines* to make clear the negative realities of these experiences, but to not sensationalise this as shocking or extreme for the audience's enjoyment. We only see the details of drug runs once in the film, with Tyler's relationships, feelings, and experiences being the main focus instead.

> *After that first trip away you get it. You think: "Okay, this is fucked up." He is in way over his head. You don't need to see that again.*
> *—Henry Blake (in France 2020)*

Director Henry Blake made *County Lines* to highlight the realities of this type of crime for general audiences (*BFI*, 2020). However, there is also a clear message in the film supporting the role of youth workers. Blake is a former youth worker and drew from his experiences directly in making *County Lines* (France, 2020). At the end of the film Tyler meets with a youth worker who wants to listen to and support him, but also makes explicit their priority of safeguarding him. This is the only adult character who explicitly does both of these things. One of the messages of the film is the importance of youth workers in reducing and responding to county lines crime and child criminal exploitation (*BFI*, 2020). Given the ongoing impact of austerity on youth work and the continued reduction of funding for it, this message is a clear campaigning aspect; the film is not only raising awareness of a problem but providing a potential solution.

Fictionalised truth films are timely, speaking directly to issues in the public consciousness. *Let Him Have It* was released whilst the Bentley family were campaigning for Derek to be posthumously pardoned. *County Lines* was released within a year of the Home Office adding county lines crime response

122 A Popular Criminology of Youth Justice

into its serious crime strategy (HM Government, 2018) and in the same year as the launch of the County Lines Programme (Home Office, 2023). The fictionalised truth films advocacy requires that it be released in a timely manner, otherwise its purpose is negated. This means that many fictionalised truth films are smaller productions with lower budgets. The greenlighting process for many large film studios is time-consuming, and if this would undermine the activist/campaigning aspect of the work, taking the independent route is often more attractive. Being an independent production also usually means less pressure to make the story commercially attractive through use of sensationalism. The sensationalised truth films discussed here were all produced by major studios. This creates an element of financial pressure, the film *has* to make its money back to be seen as successful, and to allow the director/writer/cast to maintain their career trajectory. This financial pressure may be a contributing factor to sensationalism, as it is clear that violence, gore, and sex all draw in audiences, and are seen as attractive aspects of crime stories in particular (Jewkes, 2015). If a true youth crime film heightens these aspects, there is a better chance of being profitable. For fictionalised truth films, choosing the independent route lessens these pressures, meaning they can emphasise more on the "true" aspects relating to the overall message. However, this also means that these films tend to be more serious. There is not the same drive to make them commercially attractive and as the purpose is linked to activism, the tone tends to be more serious. Given these films are specifically based upon timely stories and intend to persuade audiences on social issues, having anything other than a serious tone would seem dismissive.

Consuming Truth

The true youth crime film has not been given the same level of attention as other types of true crime. True crime documentaries' quest to uncover corruption, declare innocence, and/or identify the "real" guilty parties (Hernandez, 2019) has allowed them to develop a cult following, with viewers then taking part in their own investigations, turning passive consumption into "research" (Bruzzi, 2016). True crime films focusing on adults raise questions about violence and our relationship to the media (Clayton, 2015), particularly in relation to gender dynamics and the celebritisation of mass killers (Yardley et al., 2019). However, true youth crime media isn't considered or critiqued in the same way, these stories are viewed as a way of blaming children for their actions. There isn't the same quest for truth, as it is frequently clear *what* happened in these cases, and there isn't the same humanisation of perpetrators as occurs with adults (Bruzzi, 2016). Because the perpetrators in these cases are children, they are tainted with the identity of "young offender" (Creaney, 2012). Whereas true crime focuses on adults

"Thank You for Respecting Me and My Family's Privacy" **123**

views their behaviour through the lens of childhood trauma (Wiltenburg, 2004), true youth crime does not view contemporary traumatic childhood experiences in the same way. The underlying message of these films is that these children should have known better and should have made other choices. Holly in *Badlands* had a stable homelife and a bright future, had she not agreed to go out with Kit. Similarly, Derek Bentley in *Let Him Have It* is portrayed as having a potentially bright future if he did not become friends with Chris. In both sensationalised truth and fictionalised truth films we see the blaming of "bad seeds" who have corrupted otherwise innocent children. This is also the message when the crime is not violent; Marc in *The Bling Ring* is corrupted by Rebecca, and Connor in *County Lines* is exploited by Simon. The protagonists in these films are innocents who have been drawn into criminality by others. Whilst the films may portray these protagonists sympathetically, there is not the same level of compassionate understanding given to the characters who lure them into criminality, despite them also being children.

In this regard the true youth crime film upholds the message of many other youth crime films; that of innocent victims and dangerous offenders. For youth justice and justice-involved children depicted in media there is very little to distinguish what is presented as truth and what is presented as fiction. This means that the fictional narratives can easily be seen as true. For the true youth crime film the impact is that they affirm the narratives from fictional works rather than countering them. For fictionalised truth films this is a problem, as many of these works aim to counter traditional narratives of dangerous offenders. This raises the question of why these films maintain conventional narratives about youth crime, even when they actively disagree with them. A potential answer to this is the mechanisms through which films are financed and made. For a film to gain funding, it must be perceived as being profitable, which means it must be commercially viable or attractive to audiences. Even for independent films, there is a financial pressure that impacts upon what stories are told and how they are presented. In all the films discussed in this chapter the protagonists (who are often the sympathetic characters) are white. There is a clear focus on having stable family backgrounds, access to education, and whilst there may not be unlimited opportunity, the characters have "good" lives. This in essence makes these films more appealing to the target audiences of commercial films, which is primarily middle-class white society (Yardley et al., 2019). Stories of ethnic minority children are presented in the context of urban films (see Chapter 5), stories of girls are presented as bad girl films (see Chapter 4), and stories of redemption are presented only rarely (see Chapter 8). The true youth crime film has to conform to not only the tropes of youth crime films, but the true crime genre more broadly (Lamb, 2019). This makes only a specific type of case suitable for this approach to film, lest the film be seen as unmarketable,

124 A Popular Criminology of Youth Justice

unprofitable, and unappealing. The true youth crime film cannot be considered outside of the context of the capitalist structure in which it is made.

The popularisation of a true youth crime story through a film adaptation can go on to create an ouroboros of subsequent media. *The Bling Ring* is an example of this. The original Hollywood Hills burglaries were reported on in Vanity Fair by Nancy-Jo Sales (2010). This piece gained the attention of Sophia Coppola, who went on to direct the film 2013 adaptation, *The Bling Ring*. This brought much more attention to the case than the article itself did, meaning there was now an audience wanting further information about the case and the individuals involved, in the now classic response to true crime media (Ilan, 2012; Yardley et al., 2019). Mirroring the ending of the film, in which Nikki (Emma Watson) participates in interviews for TV and magazines setting herself up as a celebrity figure; Alexis Neiers (on whom the character is based) became a reality TV personality following her arrest, and in 2019 launched a podcast about her experiences. Other members of the group have participated in documentaries about the case allowing them to share their perspective of events (*The Real Bling Ring: Hollywood Heist*, 2022), echoing the closing lines of the film.

and eventually, when I'm able to tell my story people will know the truth. [...] Anyway, you can follow everything about me and my journey at Nickimooreforever.com

The message of *The Bling Ring* about consumerism and society's emphasis on valuing possessions and fame (Pesce, 2015), is undercut by the film essentially doing publicity work for the individuals it is based upon. The characters in *The Bling Ring* are portrayed as being fame hungry, and the desire for proximity to the celebrities they admire is a driving factor behind their criminal behaviour. In making this film, having the characters played by famous and well-regarded actors, being written and directed by an auteur from a well-established film dynasty, and featuring cameos from one of the victims of the original crimes (Paris Hilton), *The Bling Ring* essentially gives the group what they were aiming for; fame and attention. Whilst not delivering fame in the same explicit way as *The Bling Ring*, other true youth crime films also are clearly linked to capitalism. In *Let Him Have It*, the Bentley family is hounded by the press who want to tell their story as a means to sell papers. *Bully* uses shock and controversy as a means to gain attention for the film, driving ticket sales. Even *County Lines* has an undercurrent of capitalism within the story; Simon gains Tyler's trust through buying him brand name trainers, and his mother uses the money Tyler makes to buy herself a fur-trimmed jacket. Purchasing power and the consumption of goods is an inherent aspect of true crime, whether this is the stories that true crime presents or the commodification of crime itself.

"Thank You for Respecting Me and My Family's Privacy" 125

Of the two types of films discussed throughout this chapter: fictionalised truth and sensationalised truth, only one makes effort to showcase that it is "based on a true story". The sensationalised truth film bears this descriptor proudly, including it in opening credits, posters, and using the true crime trope of having the film end with a postscript outlining the sentences or consequences given to each character. The publicisation of being based on a true story, or based on real events, gives these films a level of believability, and tells audiences that what they are seeing is at its core, not only true, but accurate (Lamb, 2019; Valsesia et al., 2017). Research has shown that being associated with real events heightens the believability of a film (Seltzer, 2007), and that whilst audiences are aware that some aspects may be altered or heightened for entertainment purposes, they still believe the content presented to them, including those heightened aspects. Fictionalised truth films focus on social issues, and their explicit awareness and social activism make them seem much less attractive to audiences in comparison to sensationalised truth films. The colour palettes of these films are less bright, the lives of the characters seem bleak, and their stories are treated with seriousness. There is little fun in fictionalised truth films, and whilst this is aimed at not belittling the genuine concerns that the films depict, it means that characters (and thus justice-involved children) are seen in a purely negative light. That fictionalised truth films depict children from more marginalised backgrounds is telling of the broader conception of class in relation to justice involvement. Children from impoverished backgrounds, single-parent families, with disabilities or additional needs are portrayed in the serious and dour fictionalised truth films. The colour palettes are muted, the endings are sad, and their stories are of a descent into hopelessness. Whereas sensationalised truth films show children who had bright futures and chose to swap this for the excitement of crime. The colours in these films are brighter, whether due to the bright red of blood or the shine of money. The characters get to be funny or witty, laughing at the seriousness of the consequences they face, and the endings of their stories may feature negative consequences, but also feature their immortalisation as pop culture figures. They've "made it", even if they only get to do so from a prison cell.

Whereas many youth crime films are accused of glamourisation and promoting criminal lifestyles (*Little White Lies*, 2023), *The Bling Ring* has seemed to avoid this criticism. However, this is potentially the most aspirational and glamourous of all the films discussed in this chapter. The characters are shown having a great time with their notoriety, enjoying the spoils of their criminal activities, and even after their arrests, they achieve the status and fame that partially motivated their crimes. The message the characters receive is not that their consumption and consumerisation were wrong, but the way in which they went about it was. In other sensationalised truth films, the story ends upon arrest, meaning we frequently don't see the impact of consequences on the characters. As the experience of criminal justice processes can be

126 A Popular Criminology of Youth Justice

traumatic for justice-involved children (McElvaney and Tatlow-Golden, 2016), that this is excluded means that viewers are not seeing the full story. The glamourisation of crime in these films and their marketing as "truth" means that viewers, including young audiences, are given the impression that criminal behaviour is fun, gets you the things you want in life, and the consequences are negligible. For children who have little social capital and a lack of social opportunity (as is the case for many justice-involved children), this can seem highly attractive. However, the reality of crime for many of these individuals will be more like *County Lines* than *The Bling Ring*.

As justice-involved children in reality are better represented by the characters in fictionalised truth stories than sensationalised truth stories, this sends a message about their lives. The assumption that all justice-involved children have hopeless futures is as harmful as the label of "offender" as it means the way adults around these children treat them changes. For children being told that an option is available to them is important, as this makes it seem like a viable pathway (Boudon, 1973). If the options discussed or presented to justice-involved children are all negative or unattractive, this consequently makes alternative pathways like crime seem more attractive (Barry, 2000). Hope is an important notion, and whilst true youth crime films shouldn't be aspirational or glamourise criminality, presenting hopeful stories is necessary. This signals a clear need for positive youth justice stories that recognise the realities of justice-involved children's lives, while also recognising them as individuals rather than caricatures.

Film List

Badlands (1973)
Boy A (2007)
Bully (2001)
Catch Me If You Can (2002)
County Lines (2019)
Donnie Brasco (1997)
Extremely Wicked, Shockingly Evil and Vile (2019)
Fargo (1996)
Kids (1995)
Let Him Have it (1991)
Mean Girls (2004)
Molly's Game (2017)
My Friend Dahmer (2017)
Natural Born Killers (1994)
The Bling Ring (2013)
The Irishman (2019)
Zodiac (2007)

References

Agnew R (1992) Foundation for a general strain theory of crime and delinquency. *Criminology* 30: 47–88.

Barry M (2000) The mentor/monitor debate in criminal justice: 'what works' for offenders. *British Journal of Social Work* 30(5): 575–595.

BFI (2020) Henry Blake on county lines and teenage drug running. Available at: https://www.bfi.org.uk/sight-and-sound/interviews/henry-blake-county-lines-teenage-drug-running-social-work (accessed 7 March 2024).

Boudon R (1973) *Education, Opportunity, and Social Inequality: Changing Prospects in Western Society*. New York: Wiley-Interscience. Available at: http://eric.ed.gov/?id=ED091493 (accessed 14 March 2015).

Boyle K (2001) What's natural about killing? Gender, copycat violence and natural born killers. *Journal of Gender Studies* 10(3): 311–321. Routledge.

Brien D (2009) 'Based on a true story': The problem of the perception of biographical truth in narratives based on real lives. *Text* 13(2): 1–6. Epub ahead of print 1 January 2009. https://doi.org/10.52086/001c.31605

Bruzzi S (2016) Making a genre: The case of the contemporary true crime documentary. *Law and Humanities* 10(2): 249–280.

Burnside AN and Gaylord-Harden NK (2019) Hopelessness and delinquent behavior as predictors of community violence exposure in ethnic minority male adolescent offenders. *Journal of Abnormal Child Psychology* 47(5): 801–810.

Calleja N (2022) Intersectionality and processes of belonging: Thinking critically about sociomaterial entanglements with the voices of upper-primary school-aged young people in youth research. *Journal of Applied Youth Studies* 5(4): 317–334.

Clayton W (2015) "Unnatural, unnatural, unnatural, unnatural" ... but real? The Toolbox Murders (Dennis Donnelly, 1978) and the Exploitation of True Story Adaptations. *Transatlantica. Revue d'études américaines. American Studies Journal* (2). 2. Association française d'études américaines (AFEA). Epub ahead of print 15 December 2015. https://doi.org/10.4000/transatlantica.7901

Creaney S (2012) Targeting, labelling and stigma: Challenging the criminalisation of children and young people. *Criminal Justice Matters* 89(1): 16–17.

Doherty TP (2002) *Teenagers and Teenpics: The Juvenilization of American Movies in the 1950s*. Rev. and expanded ed. Philadelphia: Temple University Press.

Dowler K (2020) Innocence lost (and then found): The depiction of wrongful convictions in prison films. In: Harmes M, Harmes Meredith, and Harmes B (eds) *The Palgrave Handbook of Incarceration in Popular Culture*. Cham: Springer International Publishing, pp. 375–393. Available at: https://doi.org/10.1007/978-3-030-36059-7_22 (accessed 26 April 2023).

Ellis BE (2016) PodcastOne: B.E.E. – Larry Clark – 9/26/16. Available at: https://www.podcastone.com/episode/B.E.E.---Larry-Clark---9/26/16-1677831 (accessed 12 March 2024).

Farrington DP (2020) The integrated cognitive antisocial potential (ICAP) theory: Past, present, and future. *Journal of Developmental and Life-Course Criminology* 6(2): 172–187.

France A (2020) County Lines director tells how throat-slash pupil inspired movie. Available at: https://www.standard.co.uk/culture/film/county-lines-henry-blake-film-director-b153905.html (accessed 7 March 2024).

128 A Popular Criminology of Youth Justice

Giroux HA (1996) Reviews: hollywood, race, and the demonization of youth: The "kids" are not "alright". *Educational Researcher* 25(2): 31–35. American Educational Research Association.

Goldman M and Rodriguez N (2022) Juvenile court in the school-prison nexus: Youth punishment, schooling and structures of inequality. *Journal of Crime and Justice* 45(3): 270–284. Routledge.

Gray RM, Green R, Bryant J, et al. (2019) How 'vulnerable' young people describe their interactions with police: Building positive pathways to drug diversion and treatment in Sydney and Melbourne, Australia. *Police Practice and Research* 20(1): 18–33. Routledge.

Harbord V (1997) Natural born killers: Violence, film and anxiety. In: Sumner C (ed) *Violence, Culture And Censure*. London: Taylor & Francis.

Henderson L (2020) Framing 'The Bling Ring': (Im)material psychogeography and screen technology. *Colloquy* (28): 22–44. Monash University - School of Languages, Cultures and Linguistics.

Hernandez M (2019) True injustice: Cultures of violence and stories of resistance in the new true crime. *IdeaFest: Interdisciplinary Journal of Creative Works and Research from Cal Poly Humboldt* 3(1): 77–89.

HM Government (2018) Serious violence strategy. Available at: https://assets.publishing.service.gov.uk/media/5acb21d140f0b64fed0afd55/serious-violence-strategy.pdf (accessed 19 March 2024).

Home Office (2023) County Lines Programme overview. Available at: https://www.gov.uk/government/publications/county-lines-programme/county-lines-programme-overview (accessed 19 March 2024).

Ilan J (2012) 'The industry's the new road': Crime, commodification and street cultural tropes in UK urban music. *Crime, Media, Culture* 8(1): 39–55. SAGE Publications.

Jewkes Y (2015) *Media and Crime*. London: SAGE.

Kashani JH, Jones MR, Bumby KM, et al. (1999) Youth violence: Psychosocial risk factors, treatment, prevention, and recommendations. *Journal of Emotional and Behavioral Disorders* 7(4): 200–210.

Klenk N (2018) Adaptation lived as a story: Why we should be careful about the stories we use to tell other stories. *Nature and Culture* 13(3): 332–355. Berghahn Journals.

Koch I, Williams P and Wroe L (2024) 'County lines': Racism, safeguarding and statecraft in Britain. *Race & Class* 65(3): 3–26. SAGE Publications Ltd.

Lamb A (2019) Fact to Fiction: The truth behind movies based on true stories. *Teacher Librarian* 45(5): 46–52.

Little White Lies (2023) In defence of The Bling Ring. Available at: https://lwlies.com/articles/bling-ring-10/ (accessed 20 February 2024).

Maltby R (1995) The genesis of the production code. *Quarterly Review of Film and Video* 15(4): 5–32. Routledge.

McAra L and McVie S (2012) Negotiated order: The groundwork for a theory of offending pathways. *Criminology & Criminal Justice* 12(4): 347–375. SAGE Publications.

McElvaney R and Tatlow-Golden M (2016) A traumatised and traumatising system: Professionals' experiences in meeting the mental health needs of young people in the care and youth justice systems in Ireland. *Children and Youth Services Review* 65: 62–69. Elsevier Ltd.

O'Hagan A and Edmundson CJ (2021) County lines: The exploitation of vulnerable members of society. *Forensic Research & Criminology International Journal* 9(2): 47–57. 2. MedCrave Group.

Pavés GM (2023) Unacceptable matters: The Hays Code, Family, Film Noir and RKO Radio Pictures. *Historical Journal of Film, Radio and Television* 43(2): 359–379. Routledge.

Pesce S (2015) Ripping off hollywood celebrities: Sofia Coppola's The Bling Ring, luxury fashion and self-branding in California. *Film, Fashion & Consumption* 4(1): 5–24.

Ringer BS (2012) Based on an almost true story: Providing real life protection to real life characters. *Pittsburgh Journal of Technology Law and Policy* 13(1): 1–19.

Robinson G, McLean R and Densley J (2019) Working county lines: Child criminal exploitation and illicit drug dealing in Glasgow and Merseyside. *International Journal of Offender Therapy and Comparative Criminology* 63(5): 694–711. SAGE Publications Inc.

Rowen L (2017) True Crime as a Literature of Advocacy. *Undergraduate Theses.* Epub ahead of print 28 April 2017.

Sales NJ (2010) The Suspects Wore Louboutins | Vanity Fair. Available at: https://archive.vanityfair.com/article/share/e9cc0cc3-dbf1-4fab-8367-5fc7c05608e6 (accessed 20 March 2024).

Schmid D (2008) 3. Natural born celebrities: Serial killers and the Hollywood Star System. In: *3. Natural Born Celebrities: Serial Killers and the Hollywood Star System.* University of Chicago Press, pp. 105–137. Available at: https://www.degruyter.com/document/doi/10.7208/9780226738703-005/pdf?licenseType=restricted (accessed 12 March 2024).

Seger L (2011) *The Art of Adaptation: Turning Fact And Fiction Into Film.* New York: Henry Holt and Company.

Seltzer M (2007) *True Crime: Observations on Violence and Modernity.* New York: Routledge.

Seltzer M (2017) Wound culture. In: *Oxford Research Encyclopedia of Criminology and Criminal Justice.* Available at: https://oxfordre.com/criminology/criminology/oso/viewentry/10.1093$002facrefore$002f9780190264079.001.0001.002facrefore-9780190264079-e-166 (accessed 12 March 2024).

Stapleton EK (2015) Objects after adolescence: Teen film without transition in spring breakers and the bling ring. In: Dowd G and Rulyova N (eds) *Genre Trajectories: Identifying, Mapping, Projecting.* London: Palgrave Macmillan UK, pp. 183–199. Available at: https://doi.org/10.1057/9781137505484_11 (accessed 6 February 2024).

Steinberg S (2018) When life comes early: Larry Clark's kids (1995) and bully (2001), an enquiry into the loss of innocence. Thesis: University of Witwatersrand, Johannesburg.

Stone N (2018) Child criminal exploitation: 'County lines', trafficking and cuckooing. *Youth Justice* 18(3): 285–293. SAGE Publications.

The Real Bling Ring: Hollywood Heist (2022) *Netflix.* Available at: https://www.netflix.com/gb/title/81349491 (accessed 23 April 2024).

Valsesia F, Diehl K and Nunes JC (2017) Based on a true story: Making people believe the unbelievable. *Journal of Experimental Social Psychology* 71: 105–110.

Watson G (2020) Let him have it: The short, sad life of Derek Bentley. *Bar News: The Journal of the NSW Bar Association* (Summer 2016): 40–43. New South Wales Bar Association.

Wiener T (2002) *The Off-Hollywood Film Guide: The Definitive Guide to Independent and Foreign Films on Video and DVD.* New York: Random House Publishing Group.

Wilkinson M (2017) Leisure/crime, immaterial labor, and the performance of the teenage girl in Harmony Korine's Spring Breakers (2012) and Sofia Coppola's The Bling Ring (2013). *Journal of Feminist Scholarship* 12(12): 20–37.

Willing I (2022) The film kids 25 years on: A qualitative study of rape culture and representations of sexual violence in skateboarding. *Young* 30(2): 149–164. SAGE Publications India.

Wiltenburg J (2004) True crime: The origins of modern sensationalism. *The American Historical Review* 109(5): 1377–1404.

Windle J, Moyle L and Coomber R (2020) 'Vulnerable' kids going country: Children and young people's involvement in county lines drug dealing. *Youth Justice* 20(1–2): 64–78. SAGE Publications.

Wroe LE (2021) Young people and "county lines": A contextual and social account. *Journal of Children's Services* 16(1): 39–55. Emerald Publishing Limited.

Yardley E, Kelly E and Robinson-Edwards S (2019) Forever trapped in the imaginary of late capitalism? The serialized true crime podcast as a wake-up call in times of criminological slumber. *Crime, Media, Culture: An International Journal* 15(3): 503–521. SAGE Publications Ltd.

7

"YOU WON, JUSTICE WAS DONE, WHO CARES?"

Children in the Courtroom

After policing and prisons, the court system is the most well-known aspect of criminal justice. Courts are where many in society perceive justice to be "done"; in that this is the setting for decision making regarding guilt and sentencing. They are also one of the more visible aspects of criminal justice. This is due to having a physical presence in towns and cities in the form of courtrooms and being the setting of many aspects of "justice" iconography, such as the scales of justice, gavels, judges' robes, and so on, all of which are heavily featured in both fictional and factual media. Many news broadcasts about criminal justice take place outside courtrooms, we are familiar with legal representatives, defendants, and complainants giving interviews or being photographed on courtroom steps, and courtroom dramas are a mainstay of popular culture. Most people will not see the inside of a courtroom, so the only exposure to this aspect of criminal justice is through media. The courtroom drama has been frequently discussed by legal experts and is heavily critiqued for a lack of realism (Grossman, 2019; Levi, 2005), courtroom dramas have a clear pattern and only tell specific types of stories (Bergman and Asimow, 2006; Rockell, 2009), sensationalising both the crimes discussed, and the legal process in courtrooms (Corcos, 2002). In reality courtrooms are heavily process-driven with clear routines, guidelines and legal requirements for what is allowed to happen and how this should occur. In the courtroom drama, courts are spectacular, with surprise witnesses, last-minute confessions, and shocking evidence being frequent features (Machura and Ulbrich, 2001). The courtroom film uses the perceived legitimacy of the court system to give gravitas to the more fantastical or dramatic elements of these stories. As many have posited, crime stories have

DOI: 10.4324/9781003403159-7

132 A Popular Criminology of Youth Justice

to include elements of the fantastic to be believed (Corcos, 2002; Levi, 2005; Rafter, 2000). The public cannot countenance perceiving crime as part of the everyday because that would mean having to consider the possibility that crime could enter their own lives. The lure of the crime film is the vicarious enjoyment of the danger of crime, whilst simultaneously knowing you are safe from it (Rafter, 2007).

In the courtroom film, the presentation of children differs subtly from other genres. Whereas other crime films are quite clear in their presentation of justice-involved children as either innocent victims or dangerous offenders, the courtroom film is unique in that it presents both characterisations simultaneously. The courtroom is clearly an adult setting, it is serious, the workplace of not just adults, but dedicated professionals who have trained extensively, the most adult of adults, lawyers and judges. The architecture is formal and sober, the rooms are for the specific purpose of administering justice. In this context children are out of place, heightening their childishness and otherness; they do not belong in this adult world; therefore, their presence means something has gone wrong. This sense of wrongness means that including child characters in courtroom dramas is a way of developing tension; their presence means that either something unpleasant has happened to this child or this child did something unpleasant, and it is part of the characters (and audiences) duty as responsible adults to find out what. This allows courtroom films to present the innocent–dangerous dichotomy differently, transforming this from a dichotomy into a dyad. Whereas the innocent–dangerous dichotomy describes "innocent children" and "dangerous offenders" as two contrasting stereotypes that are applied to children (Case, 2018; Evans, 2005), the dyad utilises both stereotypes at once. The innocent–dangerous dyad is where children are presented as being innocent and dangerous simultaneously. Other films focus on the permanent transformation from innocent to dangerous (see Chapters 2 and 5), or children avoiding this transformation through submitting to conformity (see Chapter 3). But the courtroom drama shows children utilising other's perceptions of them as innocent and/or dangerous to achieve a desired outcome. The innocent–dangerous dichotomy often overlooks justice-involved children being both victims and offenders. The innocent–dangerous dyad doesn't rectify this, instead presenting children as using victimhood as a shield to avoid consequences. The result of this is not recognising that justice-involved children are still children and should be treated as such though. Rather than creating a Child First viewpoint where it is recognised that children can behave in criminal ways and still be considered as children, the innocent–dangerous dyad presents children as sinister and manipulative; dangerous offenders who cynically utilise the innocent child stereotype to gain sympathy and evade justice. The tropes and standards of the courtroom drama are an effective showcase for this.

Youth Court Dramas

The courtroom drama uses the inherently adversarial nature of criminal justice to develop tension. These films are not "whodunits", but about if the criminal will get away with it, or about uncovering the truth in the form of a "whydunit" (Rafter, 2001). The audience becomes invested in deciding what would be "justice" in this case, and whether or not this will be done. Despite being a very popular genre of cinema, courtroom films tend to be uniform (Bergman and Asimow, 2006; Kuzina, 2001). There are set character archetypes, set routines that audiences expect, and set outcomes (Bergman and Asimow, 2006). The courtroom drama has a consistent format, allowing audiences to instantly feel familiar and comfortable with what they are viewing so that the tension and drama come from dialogue and character interactions (Elkins, 2006). We know that the film is building to a decision by either the judge or the jury; the end of the trial is the end of the film, so building to what this outcome will be and developing twists that mean this isn't obvious keeps the audience engaged (Grossman, 2019). Because of the constraints of the format, there are a limited range of reasons why a child would be present in a courtroom; they are a defendant, a witness, or a victim. Courtroom dramas play on these limited reasons to allow the audience to develop a specific perception of child characters, utilising the innocent–dangerous dyad to change this perception and keep audiences guessing. The impact of this for the perception of children is that their presence in a courtroom film signifies something malevolent; the children in courtroom films are not necessarily "normal" children, regardless of their role.

Despite courtroom dramas being centred on the stories of defendants and whether or not they will be found guilty, defendants are very rarely the main characters in courtroom films; the stars are the legal professionals both in terms of being the protagonists and being played by famous and well-regarded actors (Meyer, 2020). Some of the classics of cinema are courtroom dramas, and this type of film has become well-established as a way for actors to show their ability to play serious, complex characters (Levi, 2005). *12 Angry Men* (1957) is a key example of the genre, both establishing and showcasing many conventions of a courtroom film. *12 Angry Men* is also a youth court drama, but audiences frequently do not realise this. The defendant in *12 Angry Men* is 18 years old and accused of murdering his father. We see very little of this character, with the majority of the film taking place in a single room where the titular jurors are deliberating. In *12 Angry Men* we see the transformation of the jurors' opinions, from being convinced of guilt at the start of the film, to recognising a reasonable doubt of guilt. This change is instigated by Juror 8 (Henry Fonda), who focuses on inconsistencies in the evidence presented, taking a critical view of what is being argued and persuading his fellow jurors one by one. But this change also showcases a transformation in

134 A Popular Criminology of Youth Justice

the perception of the defendant, from a dangerous criminal to potentially innocent, and with this changing from being perceived as an adult to a child.

> *You sat right in court and heard the same things we did. The man's a dangerous killer. You could see it.*

12 Angry Men set a precedent for courtroom films; the position at the start is not the position at the end of the film. Whilst many courtroom films end with a declaration of innocence (Grossman, 2019; Meyer, 2020), they often start with a presumption of guilt. The audience is then drawn in by the struggle to change the mind of the jurors. In *12 Angry Men* this persuasion comes from another juror rather than a lawyer, but his approach mirrors one, he is in essence the representation that the boy should have had. The lack of effective representation is even one of the points raised by Juror 8 as part of the discussion. For justice to be done through appropriate sentencing, decisions by judges and jurors have to be made based on the truth, and so the courtroom film is in essence about truth itself. This philosophical undercurrent in these films means the stakes have to be high. Finding the truth of the situation needs to matter, and so small, non-violent crimes don't make for compelling courtroom films. Much like true-crime, courtroom films are about murder. Even when they are comedy, such as *My Cousin Vinny* (1992) and *Legally Blonde* (2001), a murder is the inciting incident for the story. For youth court films, this is also essential, as this is one of the few types of crime that would see a child in a "typical" court, which audiences would be familiar with. The majority of youth crime cases are addressed in a youth court (van den Brink, 2022), which does not conform to the conventions of legal cinema. By focusing only on murder cases, youth court films can utilise the existing framework of a courtroom drama, but also gain the audiences' interest through the spectacle of violence (Casper, 2011). This inadvertently sets the expectation that all youth justice cases are or should be addressed in an adult court though, undermining the variety of reasons for the existence of youth courts.

Youth courts are less formal than adult courts and do not feature juries. They are presided over by magistrates rather than judges, and the robes and wigs that confer status and authority are not worn by magistrates or solicitors (Acker et al., 2001). The language in youth court is less formal, and there is not the same process of calling witnesses, questioning, and cross-examination. The differences between youth courts and adult courts are an active recognition of the need to tailor criminal justice to children, with a need for differing language to ensure everything is understood (Greene et al., 2010), a need to ensure children are safeguarded during the process (Baidawi and Ball, 2023), and a need to maintain children's trust in criminal justice institutions to ensure they do not become further excluded from law-abiding society (Good et al., 2023). Whilst youth courts have been criticised

"You Won, Justice was Done, Who Cares?" **135**

(Acker et al., 2001; Bath et al., 2020; Greene et al., 2010; Ivankovic, 2010) and there is a need for further change, having a clear distinction between processes of justice for adults and children is necessary. However, few people see the inside of a youth court or are familiar with its processes. Youth courts are not open to the public in the way that adult courts are, to protect the privacy of those involved. This means that those making films are often unfamiliar with youth courts as a setting, meaning this is not used in courtroom stories. Having child characters be tried as adults also allows these films to have juries, all of whom must be convinced for an outcome, acting as a proxy for the audience (Grossman, 2019). The courtroom film as a genre is dominated by American works, many of which feature the death penalty as a potential outcome of the trial. This further increases the tension, particularly in films where the defendant is a child; making a life-or-death decision is even more complex when the person is only at the beginning of their life.

The youth court drama takes two forms: a child as a defendant or a child as a witness. Where children are defendants, this is almost always against a charge of murder, frequently of a family member or mentor (often a father figure). Examples of this are: *The Whole Truth* (2016) and *Primal Fear* (1994). This instantly increases the shock value of the crime, not only has a murder occurred, but of someone the accused child should have loved and respected. That a child could be capable of killing a parent presents a strong societal taboo, not only against violence, but the idea of a family unit, and how a child should feel about their family. The child defendants in youth court films are not only potentially dangerous, but this danger goes beyond causing harm, speaking to broader societal concerns about the destruction of the "traditional family" (Knox, 2019). Youth court films that feature children as witnesses also tend to be cases of murder or extreme violence, such as *The Client* (1994), *Sleepers* (1996) and *On Trial* (1939). This also has inherent shock value, as this exposure to violence is something that children should be protected from, again suggesting a breakdown in family values and appropriate parenting (Knox, 2019). In this way the youth court drama speaks to much broader societal fears about children's place in society, how to protect children and prevent them from becoming not only dangerous offenders, but also dangerous adults.

The Innocent–Dangerous Dyad

The societal perception of how children "should" behave defies complexity. The idea that children should be innocent, quiet, obedient and well-mannered has been pervasive throughout history (Brunson and Pegram, 2018; Case, 2016), and is both constructed, reproduced and critiqued by popular media (Driscoll, 2011; Smith, 2017). Where children do not conform to this idea of innocence, through behaving in ways that are labelled as criminal, such as

136 A Popular Criminology of Youth Justice

not obeying authority figures (from parents through to police), participating in sub-culture or counter-culture, or donning physical markers of deviance through dress, they are labelled as dangerous (Creaney, 2012). Regardless of whether they participate in criminal activity or not, those labelled as dangerous are considered as being criminal and capable of violence (Feld, 2009; Fraser and Atkinson, 2014). As the classification of child is culturally bound to the notion of innocence, therefore those who are not innocent cannot be considered as children. This means that "dangerous offenders" are frequently considered as adults regardless of age (Davis and Marsh, 2020). This adultification (see Chapter 5 for further discussion) is harmful for children (Koch and Kozhumam, 2022), and particularly impacts upon minority ethnicity children (Davis and Marsh, 2020). However, the ideas are perpetuated in culture through youth crime films despite their negative impacts. Signalling whether a character is an "innocent child" or a "dangerous offender" on film is often done through costuming; James Dean's T-shirt and red jacket in *Rebel Without a Cause* (1955) showed his defiance; the tracksuits in *La Haine* (1995) and *Kidulthood* (2006) have not only class connotations but suggest deviance; even the candy coloured femme fatal outfits of *Jawbreaker* (1999) suggest that these are not "normal" girls. However, in the youth court drama the setting brings its own dress code which means that dangerousness cannot be visually identified and alters the innocent–dangerous dichotomy into an innocent–dangerous dyad, where children not only signal innocence visually, but also utilise this to avoid consequences for their dangerousness.

There are few courtroom films where children are defendants. This may be due to the inherent sympathy given to children in a formal adult space. This setting means that many of the visual markers used to signal that a child is a "dangerous offender" are not appropriate or would not be believable. In courtrooms everyone is dressed formally, if a young defendant were wearing typical visual markers of deviance, such as a hoodie, bandana, baseball cap, or leather jacket, they would instantly be marked as being out of place, meaning audiences would have to suspend their disbelief that someone would dress like this in a courtroom. Not everyone wears a suit to court in reality, the reasons for which vary. Not everyone owns or has access to a suit or other formal clothing, and the intersection of criminal justice with poverty and class means that justice-involved children are likely to have a smaller range of clothes, and less likely to own formalwear that is only required infrequently (Logan-Greene et al., 2020; Navarro, 2004). In courtroom films, the young characters are dressed formally, so as to not cause audiences to question the reality of the setting. However, this means that these characters also automatically conform more to audiences' expectations of what innocence looks like. A white shirt and a tie when worn by a child project the idea of a well-behaved, controllable, law-abiding citizen, it is inherently easier to believe that someone is innocent when they are dressed smartly

(Navarro, 2004). It is also more difficult to adultify a child when they are dressed in a way that only a child would, such as a school uniform. This means that courtroom films have to utilise other methods to suggest a child is guilty or capable of crime. This is often done through suggesting that this child is internally, psychologically more adult than a child "should" be.

The Whole Truth (2016) is the story of 17-year-old Mike (Gabriel Basso), who is on trial his father's murder. Having confessed to the police, and not spoken since, Mike is facing a likely guilty verdict and the death penalty. The main character of *The Whole Truth* is his lawyer, Richard Ramsay (Keanu Reeves), who also happens to be a close friend of the family, having worked with Mike's father in their early careers. We see very little through Mike's perspective in the film, and we don't hear him speak at all until quite late in the film's run time (56 out of 96 minutes). That Mike is sidelined in this story is reflective of the broader conception of children in criminal justice. They are viewed as being in a liminal state; both adult and child simultaneously, and both fully aware of the harm they caused (presumably on purpose), but also lacking the agency to be consulted on their own defence. The seriousness of the crime means they must be an adult, however, categorisation as a child means that they can be denied agency or voice. Research has highlighted how the experience of youth court is confusing and distressing for justice-involved children (Larner and Smithson, 2023) and the processes are biased against those with complex and intersecting needs (Baidawi and Ball, 2023; Rubino et al., 2021) In courtroom films, children are talked about as objects, rather than talked to. Mike is discussed in terms of his potential future, he is a "legal prodigy" and was applying to law schools in the lead-up to his father's death. Mike's intelligence is used to adultify him, signifying that he is unlike other children and more like the adults around him. He gives a note to a member of his legal team, one of his first direct acts of communication in the film, suggesting a course of action which allows a cross-examination to go successfully. The idea that Mike is highly intelligent and logical is subtly telegraphed throughout the film, leaving the audience to question if a legal mastermind could also be a criminal mastermind.

The idea that a child could be more intelligent than the adults around them and uses this intelligence to manipulate those adults twists the innocent–dangerous dichotomy in a way that doesn't occur in other youth crime films. What is normally a binary becomes a dyad, where a child exists in both categories, switching from one to the other when it suits their agenda. In *The Whole Truth* we initially consider Mike as a dangerous criminal, based on his age (he is 17, almost an adult), his perceived churlishness due to not speaking or engaging with those trying to help him, and the seriousness of the crime. The police officers when questioned admit that they did not pursue other suspects when investigating the case.

it was open and shut. That boy did it.

138 A Popular Criminology of Youth Justice

Upon hearing the testimony of neighbours, it is revealed that Mike's father was abusing his mother, implying that the murder was an attempt to protect his mother from further harm. This softens the audience's perception of Mike, meaning the initial image of dangerous criminal is no longer applicable. However, it is not until Mike chooses to testify and states that his father sexually abused him, and the murder was self-protective that the audience considers him an innocent victim. This changing perception is a way of building surprise into the story, as a courtroom drama largely takes place within a single room and has a set process, twists and shocks are only achievable through dramatic testimony revealing previously unknown information, changing the allocation of guilt or innocence. As youth court films feature murders, it is not a case of if a crime happened or not, it is not a "whodunit", but a "whydunit" (Rafter, 2001). We want to know what has happened to cause a child to carry out such horrific acts, and often the explanation relates to the equally shocking crime of sexual abuse.

Casting children as victims of sexual abuse makes their crimes seem excusable to audiences, as the only thing that is more culturally reviled than a murder is a child abuser. However, this switch to child defendants being codified as innocent victims is short-lived in the courtroom drama. Mike's disclosure of abuse is suggested to be false, that he is only saying this as he knows that this will change how he is perceived by the jury, creating reasonable doubt as to his guilt, and explaining his lack of communication up to that point. It is suggested that Mike's true personality is cutthroat and manipulative, similarly to his father, doing what it takes to secure the legal outcome he wants. The idea that Mike is running his own defence and manipulating not only the jury but those representing him is not said explicitly in the film, but implied, using the trope of child prodigies being inherently evil (Jackson, 2000). This trope is based on the idea that "normal" children should not be equally or more intelligent than adults (particularly authority figures like parents, teachers and lawyers), therefore there must be something sinister about that child and they must be capable of violence. This can be seen in a variety of films across different genres, such as *The Bad Seed* (1956), *Leon: The Professional* (1994), and *Orphan* (2009). This is often explicitly played for horror or shock value, invoking both aspects of the innocent–dangerous dyad at once. This switching back and forth between presenting a child defendant as an innocent victim and a dangerous offender means that audiences view justice-involved children as calculating and aware of how their behaviour will be perceived and responded to by others. This gives a large amount of agency to the child characters, whilst simultaneously sidelining them in their own story in favour of the adult characters defending them. This is the core of the innocent–dangerous dyad; adultifying a child for the purpose of the story, whilst also denying them the role of protagonist in favour of the respectable adult characters fighting a moral crusade on their behalf.

"You Won, Justice was Done, Who Cares?" **139**

In *The Whole Truth* the audience is given another twist, as it is revealed that all along Mike knew that not only was he innocent, but that Ramsay was having an affair with his mother, and they planned the murder together. Mike's fury at the truth shows his true innocence, his confession and refusal to speak was genuinely out of a drive to protect his mother, but he is upset that the adults around him did not do more to protect him. Mike has had to take on the adult role of self-protection and self-preservation, as those supposed to safeguard and protect him, his mother and his legal represent-ative, were ok with him standing trial and potentially receiving the death penalty to disguise their own guilt. This revelation shows the purpose of many courtroom films; to question the legitimacy of legal processes and the idea that there can be any identification of "truth" through this process (Corcos, 2002).

The Whole Truth's use of an innocent–dangerous dyad is implicit, unlike in other youth crime films more explicit stereotyping. Mike is not referred to as a "monster" or "evil" at any point. However, it is clear that the prosecu-tion and defence are invoking these stereotypes. The prosecution refers to him as Mike throughout the case, using a chosen nickname and highlighting his adult nature, his wanting to be a lawyer, being on the debate team, and his intelligence. The defence uses Micheal in their closing statement, full names being more often used by parents regarding their children. Ramsay also implores the jury to "send that boy back home to his mother", further suggesting Mike's child status and need for protection. The jury is swayed by this, finding Mike not guilty, allowing him his freedom and the opportunity to live the rest of his life. However, having been at the centre of a high-profile trial, it is unclear if Mike will be able to return to his life as it was previously. His education and law school applications will undoubtedly have been impacted by his arrest and being held in custody on remand during the trial, and his family is disrupted due to his father's death and mother's affair. For many children any contact with justice systems has a destabilising impact (McAra and McVie, 2007), even if they do not receive formal punishments. The broader impact of this is the application of the label "offender", which has been shown to be damaging on a long-term scale (Creaney, 2012). Whilst the courtroom drama ends upon receipt of a verdict, the ramifications for children are lifelong.

Whereas *The Whole Truth* uses the innocent–dangerous dyad to ultimately cast Mike as an innocent child brought in proximity to but avoiding danger, this is not the trajectory of all youth court films. Despite the general outcome of courtroom dramas being a finding of not guilty (Levi, 2005), the child defendant is still portrayed as dangerous, specifically to call into question the legitimacy of legal systems. An example of this is *Primal Fear* (1996). Based on a William Diehl novel, *Primal Fear* recounts the trial of 19-year-old Aaron Stampler (Edward Norton), accused of the murder of an Archbishop.

140 A Popular Criminology of Youth Justice

The main character is once again the defence lawyer, Martin Vail (Richard Gere), and we see the trial through his perspective rather than that of the young person who the story is arguably about. *Primal Fear*, like *The Whole Truth* is not a whodunit but a whydunit. The film opens with Aaron escaping the scene of the crime covered in blood. He claims to have "lost time" or blacked out and so is unable to recount the events that led up to the death, and so is certain of his own guilt. This certainty, combined with Aaron's perceived vulnerability and youthful looks also convinces the cynical Vail of his innocence. Aaron's appearance and demeanour are key factors in *Primal Fear*; he is described as looking "like a boy scout", speaks with a stutter, and is polite, addressing the adults around him as sir and ma'am. This conformation to the stereotype of an "innocent victim" helps Vail present Aaron as such and is commented on by the lead prosecutor.

> *I've got to admit, that face is great. Are you prepping him to take the stand? That stutter, it's priceless.*

The idea that innocence and guilt have specific visual characteristics is something that courtroom films comment on, in an attempt at critique. However, courtroom films also have partially created and upheld these ideas (Kuzina, 2001; Levi, 2005). Through a narrow focus on the types of stories that are told in film (Jewkes, 2015), the narrative drive to end with not guilty verdicts (Levi, 2005), and constraints on casting meaning that these films tend to depict white, male, telegenic, and well-dressed children, the idea of what "innocent" looks like is further embedded into society, biasing us towards those who fit the stereotype (Gabrieli et al., 2021).

However, *Primal Fear* doesn't just portray innocence, again turning the innocent–dangerous dichotomy into a dyad. Aaron is revealed to have dissociative identity disorder (DID, referred to in the film as multiple-personality disorder). This is a typical Hollywood depiction of DID, being inaccurate and recreating negative stereotypes (Byrne, 2001). For *Primal Fear*, this means it can showcase both aspects of the innocent–dangerous dyad; Aaron representing the innocent child, and his alter-ego Roy representing not just a dangerous offender, but a dangerous adult. *Primal Fear* presents the adultification of children who offend very clearly; Roy swears, smokes, and is open about his violent tendencies. All of which is a very simplistic way of characterising the behaviours of justice-involved children (Harrison et al., 2020). The idea that the "boy scout" Aaron is capable of murder or violence is so unbelievable that he essentially needs to become another person for the audience and the jury to accept his potential guilt. But *Primal Fear* has one final twist; after Roy attacks the lead prosecutor a mistrial is called, leading to a much-reduced sentence of inpatient psychiatric care for Aaron, meaning he will likely be free within a matter of months and will not go to prison at all.

"You Won, Justice was Done, Who Cares?" **141**

As Vail relays this information to Aaron, it is revealed that the DID symptoms displayed were fake and the whole thing was an act purposely created to avoid consequences for the murder. Vail's shock that "there never was a Roy", is met with the retort "there never was an Aaron". The innocent child was an illusion put on by a manipulative, dangerous offender solely for the purpose of evading justice.

In *Primal Fear*, the question of what a just outcome looks like hangs over all the characters. No one is truly innocent; the murdered Archbishop was sexually exploiting altar boys, the state's attorney was profiteering through land acquisition deals, Vail only took Aaron's case for the publicity and renown. If no one is innocent, there can be no justice. The youth court film, like many courtroom dramas, places the justice system itself on trial (Rafter, 2001). However, when paired with the innocent–dangerous dyad, this critique of justice systems and the position that no one is truly innocent becomes applied to all justice-involved children. Given this group is already uniquely vulnerable (Logan-Greene et al., 2020) and can be actively harmed by involvement with justice systems (McAra and McVie, 2007), the cultural idea that all justice-involved children are not only guilty but are also manipulative and using the sympathy gained from being a child to their advantage is particularly inappropriate.

Whilst *The Whole Truth* was not a critical success, featuring big-name stars and being accessible through streaming platforms means it has potentially had a much broader reach than it would have otherwise (Miller, 2016). However, *Primal Fear*'s reception was one of praise (Al-Masykuri, 2017; Vogel, 2005) and acted as a star-making turn for Edward Norton. However, the youth court film is not a well-developed genre, and films with children as defendants remain few. Whilst this could be viewed positively, as it means there are fewer bad examples, it also means that the current poor examples like *The Whole Truth* and *Primal Fear* are the only representations. This highlights the need for better examples, including ones representing actual youth courts as well as children in adult courts.

Innocent Children in Dangerous Situations

As mentioned, there are few examples of youth court films with children as defendants. When children appear in courtroom dramas, they are more likely to be witnesses or victims. Whilst these characters are not being accused of crime, are not on trial, and are unequivocally innocent, they are still not solely portrayed as "innocent victims". The use of the innocent–dangerous dyad in courtroom dramas means that a child character cannot be presented as the stereotype of an "innocent victim", as this does not fit with the established conventions of the genre. Where youth court dramas feature children as witnesses or victims they are presented as roguish delinquents with the

142 A Popular Criminology of Youth Justice

potential to become adult criminals, but ultimately support justice through telling the truth in court. *The Client* (1994) is a key example of this, having gone on to influence the depiction of children in other courtroom dramas (Corcos, 2002). In *The Client*, the titular character is 11-year-old Mark Swain (Brad Renfro), a witness to the suicide of a lawyer, who confesses to Mark details of his involvement with the mafia, including where victims of murders are buried. This leads to police officers, FBI agents and a US attorney all wanting to speak to Mark and find out what he knows. This of itself is not a problem, however, the way these professionals treat Mark is not as a child that has witnessed a violent incident, but as a suspect. A police officer offers Mark a soda solely so that he can get a copy of his fingerprints from the can, the US attorney tries to question Mark without a parent or legal representative present and denies that this is necessary when asked directly. Additionally, Mark's name was released to media who attempt to question and photograph Mark whilst he is visiting his brother in hospital. Because the Swain family are poor, lack knowledge of the legal system, and are perceived as being deviant; powerful, professional adults feel that they can treat Mark and his family as criminals rather than victims.

Particularly for children, their status as victims is overlooked entirely if they do not conform completely to the stereotype a "victim". Justice-involved children often exist across multiple social categories, being victims and offenders simultaneously (Bailey et al., 2020). A high proportion of justice-involved children have been victims of crime (Bailey et al., 2020), are victims of abuse or neglect (Fox et al., 2015), and have experience of environments where victimisation seems to be rife, such as care systems (Staines et al., 2023), or the custodial estate (Puffett, 2016). For children the "ideal victim" (Christie, 1986) categorisation is highly restricted and is often an impossibility, with those from lower class backgrounds, minority ethnicity children, and those with additional needs instantly being excluded (Cater et al., 2016; Marshall, 2023). This makes it harder for these groups to access support for their victimisation (Staines et al., 2023), which more broadly impacts upon overall trust in justice systems (Griffith and Larson, 2016). For many children there is no way to be perceived by broader society as "innocent" due to their ethnicity, family background, or class status. These aspects are explicitly played upon by courtroom dramas as a way of making audiences suspicious of child witnesses or victims. Because Mark Swain smokes, swears, and isn't beholden to authority figures, he is characterised as being suspicious and therefore it is reasonable to treat him as a suspect.

He's a kid. They always lie. Adults are the enemy, remember?

Whilst films like *The Client* include elements of criticism of the structures of justice systems, this seems to be largely aimed at inefficiency, process

"You Won, Justice was Done, Who Cares?" **143**

overriding "common sense", or the fallibility of a system that prioritises the presumption of innocence over the presumption of guilt (Corcos, 2002). This means that whilst the assumptions of characters in these films about children's guilt or innocence may be shown to be incorrect, the broader idea that children are untrustworthy is not. Even if Mark Swain did so out of fear, he still lied to police about what he witnessed. His fear is shown as being out of self-interest, which allows the audience to see him as manipulative and conniving, even if it is understandable given the situation he is in. Mark Swain is a witness to a death, which should trigger safeguarding processes and the criminal justice system to treat him as a victim (Zajac et al., 2012). However, due to the convention of not just youth court dramas, but youth justice films more broadly, this would not fit with audience expectations or provide an entertaining spectacle that is expected of crime films. Therefore, characters like Mark Swain are adultified, and treated as simultaneously innocent and dangerous. The courtroom drama genre is not aimed at being an accurate source of information about criminal justice, however, it is where many people gain their understanding of criminal justice and the individuals within it (Casper, 2011; Kuzina, 2001). Therefore, the lack of accuracy and presentation of justice-involved children as dangerous and manipulative (regardless of their reason for being in a courtroom) is harmful.

Given the lack of accurate courtroom films featuring children, there is a clear need for better representation. Youth court dramas, as they have been termed in this chapter, do not actually take place in youth courts, and actively utilise the inappropriateness of a child being in an adult courtroom as a way of signalling danger to the audience. That these films are ostensibly about children but centre on the narratives of adults is telling of the value placed upon children's perspectives within criminal justice and beyond (Case and Haines, 2015; Papke, 1998). When combined with the use of the innocent-dangerous dyad, it becomes clear that the youth court drama is not representing justice-involved children but using the imagery that justice-involved children have been associated with in film to create tension, spectacle and shock within audiences. Whilst fictional films and filmmakers should not be limited by reality and don't have a responsibility to represent justice-involved children accurately, it is clear that there is a gap in the market for films that present a different view of justice-involved children, showing them as fully formed individuals opposed to caricatures for the purpose of plot development. There is a clear need for Child First films.

Film List

12 Angry Men (1957)
Jawbreaker (1999)
Kidulthood (2006)

144 A Popular Criminology of Youth Justice

La Haine (1995)
Legally Blonde (2001)
Leon: The Professional (1994)
My Cousin Vinny (1992)
On Trial (1939)
Orphan (2009)
Primal Fear (1996)
Rebel Without a Cause (1955)
Sleepers (1996)
The Bad Seed (1956)
The Client (1994)
The Whole Truth (2016)

References

Acker J, Hendrix PN, Hogan L, et al. (2001) Building a better youth court. *Law & Policy* 23(2): 197–215.

Al-Masykuri MZ (2017) *Language style used by Martin Vail in Primal Fear (1996) movie.* diploma. UIN Sunan Gunung Djati Bandung. Available at: https://etheses.uinsgd.ac.id/29511/ (accessed 26 April 2024).

Baidawi S and Ball R (2023) Child protection and youth offending: Differences in youth criminal court-involved children by dual system involvement. *Children and Youth Services Review* 144: 106736.

Bailey L, Harinam V and Ariel B (2020) Victims, offenders and victim-offender overlaps of knife crime: A social network analysis approach using police records. *PLOS ONE* Jackson J (ed.) 15(12): e0242621.

Bath EP, Godoy SM, Morris TC, et al. (2020) A specialty court for U.S. youth impacted by commercial sexual exploitation. *Child Abuse & Neglect* 100: 104041. Child Trafficking: Global Health Care Issues, Perspectives, and Solutions.

Bergman P and Asimow M (2006) *Reel Justice: The Courtroom Goes to the Movies.* Kansas City: Andrews McMeel Publishing.

Brunson RK and Pegram K (2018) "Kids do not so much make trouble, they are trouble": Police-youth relations. *Future of Children* 28(1): 83–102. Center for the Future of Children.

Byrne P (2001) The butler(s) DID it - dissociative identity disorder in cinema. *Medical Humanities* 27(1): 26–29. Institute of Medical Ethics.

Case S (2016) Negative Youth Justice: Creating the youth crime 'problem'. Available at: https://www.cycj.org.uk/negative-youth-justice-creating-the-youth-crime-problem/ (accessed 21 April 2023).

Case S (2018) *Youth Justice: A Critical Introduction.* Abingdon, Oxon; New York, NY: Routledge.

Case S and Haines K (2015) Children first, offenders second: The centrality of engagement in positive youth justice. *The Howard Journal of Criminal Justice* 54(2): 157–175. Wiley-Blackwell Publishing Ltd.

Casper D (2011) Social problem film and courtroom drama. In: *Hollywood Film 1963–1976.* John Wiley & Sons, Ltd, pp. 271–274. Available at: https://onlinelibrary.wiley.com/doi/abs/10.1002/9781444395242.ch18 (accessed 11 March 2024).

Cater ÅK, Andershed AK and Andershed H (2016) Victimized as a child or youth: To whom is victimization reported and from whom do victims receive professional support? *International Review of Victimology* 22(2): 179–194. SAGE Publications Ltd.

Christie N (1986) The ideal victim. In: Fattah EA (ed) *From Crime Policy to Victim Policy*. London: Palgrave Macmillan UK, pp. 17–30.

Corcos CA (2002) Legal fictions: Irony, storytelling, truth, and justice in the modern courtroom drama the Ben J. Altheimer Symposium: Imagining the law: Lawyers and legal issues in the popular culture: Essay. *University of Arkansas at Little Rock Law Review* 25(3): 503–634.

Creaney S (2012) Targeting, labelling and stigma: Challenging the criminalisation of children and young people. *Criminal Justice Matters* 89(1): 16–17.

Davis J and Marsh N (2020) Boys to men: The cost of 'adultification' in safeguarding responses to Black boys. *Critical and Radical Social Work* 8(2): 255–259. Policy Press.

Driscoll C (2011) Modernism, cinema, adolescence: Another history for teen film. *Screening the Past* (32): 2–21. Epub ahead of print 1 January 2011.

Elkins JR (2006) Popular culture, legal films, and legal film critics. *Loyola of Los Angeles Law Review* 40: 745.

Evans K (2005) Young people in the media: A dangerous and anti-social obsession. *Criminal Justice Matters* 59(1): 14–15. Taylor & Francis Group.

Feld BC (2009) Violent girls or relabeled status offenders?: An alternative interpretation of the data. *Crime & Delinquency* 55(2): 241–265. SAGE Publications Inc.

Fox BH, Perez N, Cass E, et al. (2015) Trauma changes everything: Examining the relationship between adverse childhood experiences and serious, violent and chronic juvenile offenders. *Child Abuse & Neglect* 46: 163–173.

Fraser A and Atkinson C (2014) Making up gangs: Looping, labelling and the new politics of intelligence-led policing. *Youth Justice* 14(2): 154–170. SAGE Publications Inc.

Gabrieli G, Lee A, Setoh P, et al. (2021) An analysis of the generalizability and stability of the Halo effect during the COVID-19 pandemic outbreak. *Frontiers in Psychology* 12: 1–9. Frontiers.

Good A, Beaudry A and Day D (2023) Five key learnings from a court-based crossover youth program. *Children and Youth Services Review* 155: 107268.

Greene C, Sprott JB, Madon NS, et al. (2010) Punishing processes in youth court: Procedural justice, court atmosphere and youths' views of the legitimacy of the justice system. *Canadian Journal of Criminology and Criminal Justice* 52(5): 527–544. University of Toronto Press.

Griffith AN and Larson RW (2016) Why trust matters: How confidence in leaders transforms what adolescents gain from youth programs. *Journal of Research on Adolescence* 26(4): 790–804.

Grossman N (2019) Just looking: Justice as seen in hollywood courtroom films. *Law, Culture and the Humanities* 15(1): 62–105. SAGE Publications.

Harrison A, Ramo D, Hall SM, et al. (2020) Cigarette smoking, mental health, and other substance use among court-involved youth. *Substance Use & Misuse* 55(4): 572–581. Taylor & Francis.

Ivankovic L (2010) Confidence and credibility: magistrates and youth offending teams within the youth courts in England and Wales roles within the youth court. *British Journal of Criminology* 8(1): 19–30.

146 A Popular Criminology of Youth Justice

Jackson C (2000) Little, violent, white: The Bad seed and the matter of children. *Journal of Popular Film and Television* 28(2): 64–73. Routledge.

Jewkes Y (2015) *Media and Crime*. London: SAGE.

Knox E (2019) The 400 blows and juvenile courts featured practice perspectives: Review. *Children's Legal Rights Journal* 39(3): 288–293.

Koch A and Kozhumam A (2022) Adultification of Black children negatively impacts their health: Recommendations for health care providers. *Nursing Forum* 57(5): 963–967.

Kuzina M (2001) The social issue courtroom drama as an expression of American popular culture. *Journal of Law and Society* 28(1): 79–96.

Larner S and Smithson H (2023) 'How can you punish a child for something that happened over a year ago?' The impacts of COVID-19 on child defendants and implication for youth courts. *The Journal of Criminal Law* 87(4): 252–265. SAGE Publications Ltd.

Levi RD (2005) *The Celluloid Courtroom: A History of Legal Cinema*. New York, UNITED STATES: Bloomsbury Publishing USA. Available at: http://ebookcentral. proquest.com/lib/leicester/detail.action?docID=495105 (accessed 11 March 2024).

Logan-Greene P, Kim BKE and Nurius PS (2020) Adversity profiles among court-involved youth: Translating system data into trauma-responsive programming. *Child Abuse & Neglect* 104: 104465.

Machura S and Ulbrich S (2001) Law in film: Globalizing the hollywod courtroom drama. *Journal of Law and Society* 28(1): 117–132.

Marshall H (2023) Victims first? Examining the place of 'child criminal exploitation' within 'child first' youth justice. *Children & Society* 37(4): 1156–1170.

McAra L and McVie S (2007) Youth justice?: The impact of system contact on patterns of desistance from offending. *European Journal of Criminology* 4(3): 315–345.

Meyer PN (2020) Reel justice: The films that become Hollywood blockbusters reveal popular skepticism about the rule of law. *ABA Journal* 106(1): 24–24. American Bar Association.

Miller D (2016) Interview: Director Courtney Hunt explores 'The Whole Truth' with Keanu Reeves and Renée Zellweger. In: *Cinephiled*. Available at: https://www. cinephiled.com/interview-director-courtney-hunt-explores-whole-truth-keanu-reeves-renee-zellweger/ (accessed 19 March 2024).

Navarro J (2004) Testifying in the theater of the courtroom. *FBI Law Enforcement Bulletin* 73(9): 26–30.

Papke DR (1998) Conventional wisdom: The courtroom trial in American popular culture essay. *Marquette Law Review* 82(3): 471–490.

Puffett N (2016) Urgent call for staffing overhaul to make youth custody safer. *Children and Young People Now* 2016(2): 8–9. Mark Allen Group.

Rafter N (2001) American criminal trial films: An overview of their development, 1930–2000. *Journal of Law and Society* 28(1): 9–24.

Rafter N (2007) Crime, film and criminology: Recent sex-crime movies. *Theoretical Criminology* 11(3): 403–420. SAGE Publications Ltd.

Rafter NH (2000) *Shots in the Mirror: Crime Films and Society*. Oxford Berlin: Oxford University Press.

Rockell Barbara A (2009) Challenging what they all know: Integrating the real/reel world into criminal justice pedagogy: *Journal of Criminal Justice Education*. *Journal of Criminal Justice Education* 20(1): 75–92. Routledge.

Rubino LL, Anderson VR and McKenna NC (2021) Examining the disconnect in youth pathways and court responses: How bias invades across gender, race/ethnicity, and sexual orientation. *Feminist Criminology* 16(4): 480–503. SAGE Publications.

Smith F (2017) *Rethinking the Hollywood Teen Movie: Gender, Genre and Identity*. Edinburgh: Edinburgh University Press.

Staines J, Fitzpatrick C, Shaw J, et al. (2023) 'We need to tackle their well being first': Understanding and supporting care-experienced girls in the youth justice system. *Youth Justice* 1–19: 14732254231191977. SAGE Publications.

van den Brink Y (2022) Equality in the youth court: Meaning, perceptions and implications of the principle of equality in youth justice. *Youth Justice* 22(3): 245–271. SAGE Publications.

Vogel JE (2005) Primal fear and the elusive truth. *Journal of Creativity in Mental Health*. Taylor & Francis Group. Epub ahead of print 26 July 2005. https://doi.org/10.1300/J456v01n02_12

Zajac R, O'Neill S and Hayne H (2012) Disorder in the courtroom? Child witnesses under cross-examination. *Developmental Review* 32(3): 181–204. Special Issue: Child Witness Research.

8

"NOW THAT I KNOW YOU, I CAN'T REALLY NOT KNOW YOU"

Child First Films

The stereotypes and tropes set up by problem youth films that have become the standard in youth justice film are detrimental, perpetuating the idea that children are dangerous and that once a child has transformed into a "dangerous offender" they are beyond help. Whilst subsequent films have critiqued these stereotypes, they simultaneously maintain their cultural prominence as we have seen in the previous chapters. This means that the youth justice film is generally harmful to real justice-involved children, as it perpetuates the attitudes and labels that support punitive practices, which are ineffective in supporting desistance and positive change in children's lives (Creaney, 2012). However, a new type of youth justice film has begun to emerge, which shows justice-involved children in a different way, presenting them as children.

Presenting children as children is a core tenet of Child First youth justice (Case and Browning, 2021). Emerging from work looking at Welsh youth justice (Drakeford, 2009) and building upon positive youth justice (Case and Haines, 2015), Child First has become the new dominant theoretical and practice approach within youth justice in England and Wales (Case and Hazel, 2023). Having been adopted by the Youth Justice Board as the guiding principle for practice (Youth Justice Board, 2021) and implemented in various ways by practitioners (Burns and Creaney, 2023; Case et al., 2023; Hazel, 2022), Child First is the future of youth justice. Initially termed children first, offenders second (Drakeford, 2009; Haines and Case, 2017), Child First is a minimum-interventionist model that actively critiques and calls for moves away from risk-based frameworks and labelling of children by

DOI: 10.4324/9781003403159-8

criminal justice (Case and Hazel, 2023). The impact of Child First is that children's criminalised behaviours are considered contextually, in relation to both time, setting, and situation, as well as biopsychosocial factors and broader socio-economic contexts. This is a very nuanced view, meaning that the complexity of children's lives is recognised. However, Child First approaches do not view children as powerless or without decision-making agency in their lives, emphasising the need to listen to children's views whilst providing them with appropriate support and care.

Youth justice has historically swung between welfare and justice-oriented approaches (Smith, 2005), both of which have limitations and harmful aspects. Justice-oriented approaches are criminalising and have been found to strengthen criminal identities in children, meaning they are more likely to persist behaving in ways that are counter to the law (Creaney, 2012). Justice-oriented approaches also promote harsh punishments, justifying this as an appropriate response to behaviours framed as an active choice on the part of a child (Cavadino and Dignan, 2006). These punishments have been found to be ineffective at preventing crime or promoting desistance and have actively harmed children, leading to deaths (Baldry et al., 2018; Youth Justice Board, 2014b). In contrast to this, welfare-oriented approaches have generally been viewed as being more appropriate for responding to children's criminal behaviours as they promote providing support for children's needs and view these behaviours as a sign that a child has been failed by those around them rather than viewing the child as actively choosing crime (Whyte, 2015). However, this approach also has limitations, such as denying children agency and framing them as being purely shaped by their circumstances rather than making decisions (Cavadino and Dignan, 2006). Welfare-oriented approaches have also been criticised for overlooking the concerns of communities, parents, and victims who desire to see consequences for harms caused. For professionals within youth justice the contrast between welfare and justice ideas is problematic, as they are required to provide both aspects simultaneously (Whyte, 2015). This contradictory position is an inherent aspect of youth justice, creating tensions and issues in practice (Smith, 2005; Urwin, 2018). These traditional approaches to youth justice either demonise children as "bad kids" choosing crime or infantilise them as victims of circumstance who had no option to behave differently. In effect, this is an operationalisation and institutionalisation of the innocent-dangerous dichotomy. This simplification of how children are viewed by both society and institutions like criminal justice prevents progress and limits opportunities for children themselves. Once they have been typecast by society, it is incredibly difficult to be perceived differently.

That youth justice has cycled between welfare and justice consistently since its inception (Smith, 2005; Whyte, 2015) shows the need for alternative

150 A Popular Criminology of Youth Justice

approaches. Child First has become that alternative. Child First has four key tenets (Case and Hazel, 2023):

- As children
- Building pro-social identity
- Collaborating with children
- Diverting from stigma

Viewing justice-involved children as children is the central aspect of Child First and inspiration for the name. Recognising that criminalised behaviours are not the primary aspect of a child's identity is important for systems to do, due to the harms of labelling and stigma that comes from being considered an "offender". In practice this has meant many aspects of youth justice have undergone renaming and linguistic changes: Youth Offending Teams are being renamed Youth Justice Teams, or Youth Justice Services, and some have removed the term "youth" altogether, becoming Children and Families Justice Service instead (Case and Morris, 2018). The language used to describe a service is important as this implies what the purpose of that service is, and this reframing implies that these services are aimed at delivering justice for children. This can take the form of providing justice to victims of harm through the application of appropriate consequences, but also justice for those who have caused harm by providing appropriate support. As many justice-involved children have been failed or victimised by either others around them, institutions or society more broadly (Pettitt et al., 2013), providing support regarding their health, wellbeing, education, housing etc. is a form of justice, particularly in light of the duty of care regarding children enshrined in society (Hunter et al., 2023). In this way Child First also resolves the welfare vs justice debate. By viewing children as children, it reinforces the duty of care that is required, meaning that providing welfare should not only take precedence, but also *is* a form of justice. As institutions both within and beyond criminal justice begin to view justice-involved children as children, this allows a greater and more explicit recognition of other aspects of children's identities than their behaviours, which professionals can use in promoting pro-social identities.

Identity is a key influence on behaviours both positive and negative and has been found to be a primary driver of both maintenance and desistance from specific behaviours (Breakwell, 2023). This applies to a wide-range of behaviours; such as exercise, alcohol consumption, hobbies, and crime (Hagger et al., 2007). The development of a criminal identity is something that youth justice systems have focused on preventing throughout their history (Baker, 2011), with varying levels of success. However, it is very difficult to prevent or dissolve aspects of identity, and much research suggests an identity shift is more effective in creating change (Breakwell, 2023). Child First approaches actively engage with this work and instead of centring desistance or deconstructing criminal identity, emphasise building pro-social identity. For practitioners, this means work focuses on developing positive aspects of children's lives with the aim of these aspects becoming larger parts of that child's identity and engaging them with pro-social activities that may also build positive relationships, skills, and future opportunities (Chernyak and Kushnir, 2018). This formalises projects or aspects of work that were already occurring within youth justice, such as music programmes (Caulfield and Sojka, 2023), collaborations with sports organisations (Hargreaves et al., 2023), arts workshops (Sharkey et al., 2015), and film courses (Blum-Ross, 2017). Many justice-involved children do not have the resources or opportunity to engage with activities such as sport or the arts as much as they may like to (Sharkey et al., 2015) as programmes frequently have costs that make them inaccessible, entry requirements based on prior experience or academic ability, or logistical aspects that limit who is able to participate. Class, ethnicity, poverty, and location have real impacts of what opportunities are available to children, meaning that pro-social activities cannot be considered without reference to these socio-economic factors. For justice-involved children, this means that building pro-social identities may be more challenging, as they have fewer opportunities to see themselves as musicians/actors/athletes etc. due to factors beyond their control such as class and finances. Aspiration, ambition and hope are linked to identity formation (Hagger et al., 2007). For children who are more likely to become justice-involved, there are fewer social opportunities for aspirational activity, meaning that criminal pathways may appear to be the most achievable option (Boduszek et al., 2021; Hagger et al., 2007; Jackson et al., 2023). This means that Child First's promotion of pro-social identity is essential, and forces youth justice services to actively engage with and provide opportunities for identity shifts to occur and aspiration to develop unrelated to crime. This work also encourages collaboration with children, as it requires understanding of their interests, skills, and identity to work effectively.

Collaboration with children is the third tenet of Child First and defines collaboration quite broadly. This can take the form of children's forums being a vital aspect of institutional level decision making and monitoring (Burns and Creaney, 2023), or it can be on an individual level such as a practitioner asking a child what they would like to happen and responding based not on expectations but their view (Blum-Ross, 2017). This places a responsibility upon the institutions and professionals of youth justice to recognise and be receptive to the views of children. However, this also allows children to be more active in and responsible for their development. Treating children's views as valid and worth consideration is vital in securing their engagement. Children's lives are institutionalised, however, these institutions frequently do not listen to children, instead expecting them to conform to their requirements (Haydon, 2020; Hollingsworth, 2013). From parents/carers deciding

152 A Popular Criminology of Youth Justice

what is appropriate at home, schools framing learning and knowledge development, healthcare providers defining "appropriate" standards of behaviour, to police defining and controlling public spaces, children have very few opportunities to express themselves and exert control over their lives. Child First youth justice systems providing managed and safe opportunities for collaboration recognise the ability and agency of children and create opportunities for building trust.

The fourth aspect of Child First is diverting from stigma. This relates to both the stigma of "offending" labels and the stigma of criminal justice system contact. Research has consistently suggested that contact with criminal justice systems is harmful to children and is the greatest predictor of future criminal behaviours (McAra and McVie, 2007, 2012; Modrowski et al., 2023). When a child becomes involved with criminal justice systems, this frequently impacts all aspects of their life. Youth justice teams are required to complete an assessment of a child with 48 hours of receiving a referral, which involves collecting information from the child themselves, their parents/carers where possible, their school, police, social care etc. (Youth Justice Board, 2014a). This means that very quickly a child's involvement with criminal justice becomes known by everyone they interact with, which impacts how they are perceived and treated. In this way the label of "criminal" is inescapable, which has a profound impact upon children (Creaney, 2012; Wiley et al., 2013). Diverting children from criminal justice systems or using a minimum-intervention model to avoid contact with criminal justice systems is a way of reducing this impact and allows children to remain children opposed to becoming "offenders". One of the criticisms of the minimum-intervention model is that it allows harmful behaviours to occur without consequence (Cavadino and Dignan, 2006), however, this is a misconception. Minimum-intervention approaches, and Child First, suggest that consequences for harmful behaviours should occur, but do not necessarily have to be driven by criminal justice (Smith and Gray, 2019). Instead, where children behave in harmful ways, this could be responded to by other organisations such as social care, schools, or healthcare providers, as well as parents. The negative reinforcement of formalised punishment has been shown to be ineffective as a way of changing behaviour (The Howard League for Penal Reform, 2011), therefore providing positive forms of support for children is a more effective way of achieving the aims of youth justice: preventing and reducing crime.

Child First has been developing as an ideological position since its inception (Drakeford, 2009) and is having clear policy and practice impacts on both a global and national scale (Case and Hazel, 2023; Hazel, 2022). As this is already occurring, it raises the question of why media presentation of justice-involved children matters. However, as has been seen in the preceding chapters of this book, media presentation of justice-involved children cannot

"Now That I Know You, I Can't Really NOT Know You" **153**

be separated from the realities of practice, as both have an intertwined relationship. Media informs and influences public attitudes, which are then used as the basis of policy agendas by those the public elects, which influences practice and the lives of justice-involved children (Jewkes, 2015). From the censoring of 1950s problem youth films in efforts to control children's behaviour (Simmons, 2008), to David Cameron referring to *Kidulthood* (2006) in a speech about youth justice, youth crime films have always been viewed as an accurate reflection of justice-involved children's behaviours and lives and these representations are clearly not presenting characters as children first. This means that there is a need to consider and think critically about these films, but also that there is a need for Child First films, to ensure there is public support for this development in practice is maintained. Fortunately, some filmmakers have created works that present justice-involved children, and show them committing crimes, but are not "crime films" in the same way that the works discussed in previous chapters are. These films are not about crimes committed by children, but films about children who happen to behave in ways labelled as criminal. They are Child First films.

Showing Children as Children

The Child First film is different in style and tone from other youth crime films. Whereas the latter generally uphold the conventions of crime films, where the story centres on a crime or series of crimes and the central conflict is about whether or not the characters will get caught, Child First films centre the experiences or relationships of justice-involved children, with their criminal behaviours being a minor feature or a contextual factor in showcasing their story. The main examples of Child First films that will be discussed in this chapter are *Scrapper* (2023), *Do Revenge* (2022), *The Young Offenders* (2016) and *Attack the Block* (2011). That all these films are comedies is telling of the style of Child First films, this is a clear departure from social realism, gritty dramas, or even black comedies discussed in other chapters. Child First films are confident in presenting justice-involved children in light-hearted ways, and as characters to be empathised with who can be funny and have fun. This genre difference also impacts upon the visual presentation of justice-involved children, these films are bright and colourful; the characters dress in ways that are childlike, and costumes are not defined by symbols of non-conformity or gang involvement. The characters may still live in tower blocks or on estates, but these are not shown as being grey, dangerous, places to be feared, but as homes where children and families are living happy lives. And whilst previous films clearly maintained the innocent-dangerous dichotomy, Child First films show the complexities of children's lives and that these categories are not discrete or distinct. Child First films are not only opposing the stereotypes about justice-involved children that were established in the

154 A Popular Criminology of Youth Justice

1950s and have pervaded both film and society since, but are actively deconstructing them by presenting an alternative view.

Scrapper (2023), directed by Charlotte Regan, tells the story of 12-year-old Georgie (Lola Campbell), who tries to manage her grief and maintain her independence after the death of her mother. Georgie tells the adults around her that her uncle is caring for her when she actually lives alone and sells stolen bikes to pay for rent, utilities, and food. Whilst this is a sad conceit for a film and could have been treated with the same social realist lens as *County Lines* (2019), *Scrapper* is heartwarming, funny, and shows Georgie as a child in need of care and support rather than pity. The opening of the film shows that Georgie, like many justice-involved children (Gowen et al., 2022), has had to take on adult responsibilities for her own care, as the adults and system around her have failed to do so. The phrase "it takes a village to raise a child" appears on the screen, only to be crossed out and replaced with "I can raise myself thanks" in a child's handwriting. Following the death of her mum, Georgie has received intervention from social services, and her school is aware of her circumstances, however, these institutions have not been able to provide appropriate support, meaning Georgie has taken on this responsibility herself. Many films utilise the "heroes journey" format, to show change or development within a character, often depicting them overcoming a problem or challenge (Seger, 2011). In *Scrapper* that development is for Georgie to feel safe to be a child and to trust that the adults around her will manage the responsibility of her care. Following her Mum's death, Georgie is living by herself in their home and trying to keep things exactly as they were, right down to how the sofa cushions are arranged. For Georgie this sameness allows her to feel connection to her Mum still and exert some control over her situation. However, despite the adult responsibilities that Georgie has taken on, she is still shown as a child; the first words she says in the film are asking a friend if he is "playing out", she likes dancing, has named the spiders in her home, and does skits narrating the shopping channel on TV. Play is a frequent feature of *Scrapper*, making it different from almost all other youth justice films. Play is an important aspect of childhood that supports development (Creaney, 2020; HSE, 2009). However, its depiction in films featuring justice-involved characters is limited. This furthers the idea that justice-involved children are different from others and are not really "children". *Scrapper*'s portrayal of play is joyous, marking it out as different from other youth justice films, and a key example of a Child First film.

Scrapper focuses on Georgie's emotional change from desiring control to allowing adults to take on the responsibility of caring for her. The catalyst for this change is the return of her dad, Jason (Harris Dickinson). Jason left when Georgie was born, to work as a ticket seller in Ibiza, and had no subsequent contact with Georgie. She is understandably distrustful of him, and only "allows" him to stay as he threatens to tell social services that she has been

"Now That I Know You, I Can't Really NOT Know You"   **155**

living alone. Whilst clearly inexperienced in caring for children, Jason does try, and his approach to developing a relationship with Georgie is an interesting example of how to build a trusting bond with a child. Jason doesn't judge Georgie for her behaviours, even when they are criminal, but supports her in responding to consequences and tries to protect her from criminalisation. He also carries out the responsibilities of parenting but doesn't insist to Georgie that this is his role now in the way that other authority figures might. These are simple and small actions, such as making Georgie wash her clothes, or cooking a meal for them. Jason also protects Georgie in more significant ways, through diverting her from criminalisation and institutional involvement. When Georgie's social worker calls their home, Jason answers and doesn't say that Georgie has been living alone or that he isn't the "uncle" she has been claiming to live with. He does the responsible thing by giving the social worker his phone number, so that he can be the point of contact going forward meaning Georgie no longer has to lie, but he also doesn't alert services to the fact that she has been lying, allowing her to avoid punishment or further involvement in social care. Similarly, when Georgie goes to "work" (stealing bikes) one day, Jason comes with her offering to act as a lookout. However, he constantly interrupts her as she is trying to break a bike lock, meaning that they aren't successful, and he runs away from the police with her meaning she avoids criminalisation. Jason is non-judgemental of Georgie but allows her the opportunity to change and develop without forcing her to submit to authority or control.

In *Scrapper* Georgie is portrayed with many of the hallmarks of justice-involved characters. She is working class, lives on an estate, isn't doing well at school, doesn't have many friends, and is somewhat "chavvy". She wears football shirts, carries bolt cutters, and is described by the other girls in the neighbourhood as a "proper weirdo". However, simultaneously, Georgie has characteristics that conflict with the "dangerous offender" stereotype. She has a hearing aid, she may not be academic but knows the names and biographies of many world leaders throughout history (having named spiders after them) and develops a plan that outsmarts her social worker by using pre-recorded voice notes of generic statements to act as her "uncle's" responses in phone calls. Georgie is creative, funny, and sensitive. The depiction of Georgie doesn't airbrush or shy away from her problematic behaviours, but also doesn't judge her for it, showing her as a nuanced person. Her choices are often childlike; before Jason's arrival the food she made for herself was chocolate spread and sprinkles on toast. However, Georgie has not been given the opportunities that other children have, particularly regarding expressing her grief. Her teacher is outraged at her requiring a full day off school, saying "it doesn't take a whole day to grieve!", and she finds private spaces in which to cry. Georgie hasn't been supported in processing her mum's death to the point that she builds a tower in her room to try and reach the sky, which is where her mum said she was going when she fell ill, to be with her again. Georgie understands that her mum has

156 A Popular Criminology of Youth Justice

died, but she holds on to the literal interpretation of what she has been told to try to regain that sense of safety. This is clearly a child's understanding of grief and allows the audience to empathise with Georgie, seeing her as a child in need of support and protection. It is only when Jason breaks the lock on the door and sees Georgie's tower and plans to break the ceiling written on the walls, that he fully understands the level of support that she needs. Georgie has developed a stoic exterior and her insistence that she is fine means that the adults around her have started to believe this and practically treat her like an adult.

> *You can't keep living by yourself*
> *Why can't I? I'm doing fine*

The visual grammar of *Scrapper* is different from other youth justice films; *Scrapper* is bright, colourful and sunny. Georgie lives in a South London estate, but the homes are painted in pastels, the graffiti is in the form of murals, and the playground is filled with children playing football. This is a marked contrast from the urban films of the 2000s, which were grey, dour, and only showed children playing as a prelude to their moral decay. *Scrapper* actively shows working-class realities as joyful, which is counter to the narratives of other media (Clarke, 2023). The film was influenced by director Charlotte Regan's own childhood, wanting to present a film that was more representative of her experience (*BFI*, 2023; Dazed, 2023). The idea that estates are dangerous places and working-class people are frightening has become pervasive in media, therefore counter narratives are necessary. This contrast also emphasises Georgie's childishness. She likes silly jokes, dancing to pop songs, and playing games. Even though Georgie has taken on a lot of adult responsibilities such as paying rent and utility bills, and reassuring social care of her wellbeing, she is still a child and *Scrapper* does not shy away from emphasizing these aspects. The adultification of children in media has historically reinforced the idea that those who commit crimes no longer fit in the category of "child", instead becoming a "dangerous offender". However, *Scrapper* explicitly shows that Georgie is still a child. Even though she steals, lies, and is capable of managing adult responsibilities, Georgie is presented as needing and deserving the support of adults. At the end of *Scrapper* Georgie has accepted that she needs some support, and Jason has formally taken on responsibility for her care. The relationship that has built up between them is an essential factor in this and has shown Georgie that not all change is as catastrophic as the death of her mum. She acknowledges that she should not have to do everything herself and that children should be supported by adults. She may not accept that it takes a village to raise a child, but she now realises that she shouldn't have to raise herself.

> *I don't need someone to replace Mum. But I need someone.*

"Now That I Know You, I Can't Really NOT Know You"   **157**

Georgie addressing her grief and allowing others to take responsibility for her means that she is free to purely be a child again. This is commented on by her teachers and social worker, who seem somewhat dismayed by this, as Georgie is now being louder and more childish, which makes their job of managing her behaviour more involved. The social worker's comment almost implies that Georgie's adultification was a good thing for her, saying "she was on a good path" before Jason returned. This is indicative of the larger social response to not only justice-involved children but working-class children, that their needs are perceived as difficult, and that it would be better if they were quiet and controllable (Macleod, 2006; Yates, 2012). This echoes the Victorian ideal of children being seen and not heard (Antolak, 2020), and shows the way in which this has shaped societal views of children. However, *Scrapper* counters this narrative, showing that viewing children as children is important and necessary.

Building Pro-Social Identity

Many films prior to the Child First era portrayed a simplistic view of intersectional factors that impact upon children's experiences of youth justice. As discussed in Chapter 4, consideration of gender was simplified into portrayals of middle-class bad girls who used the perception of femininity to manipulate the adults around them to avoid consequences. Consideration of ethnicity was intertwined with inner cities and led to a portrayal of a criminality as inescapable, as explored in Chapter 5. Youth justice films have not frequently considered true intersectionality, focusing instead on individual demographics. However, this is changing in film as it is in practice. *Do Revenge* (2022), directed by Jennifer Kaytin Robinson, is a teen black comedy in the mould of *Heathers* (1989). However, this is a truly modernised version of the bad girl film, which emphasises girls' agency, whilst also acknowledging the pressures of class and relative wealth, ethnicity and minority status, patriarchy, and mental health. *Do Revenge* centres on the friendship between Drea (Camila Mendes) and Eleanor (Maya Hawke) that is based in helping each other get revenge on those who have wronged them. For Drea, this is the ex-boyfriend who leaked an explicit video of her to the whole school. For Eleanor this is the classmate who started a rumour that not only outed Eleanor as LGBT, but implied she forcibly kissed another girl. Their revenge plots involve framing classmates for drug use and possession, spiking a meal with magic mushrooms, stealing classmates' phones, and disseminating their personal data. These plans have varying levels of success in the film, and it is clear that whilst Drea and Eleanor are calculating, they are largely acting in the moment based on opportunity rather than having a grand plan. There are clear deviations from the bad girl template set out by *Heathers* and *Jawbreaker* (1999). Their plans involve forcing those who have hurt them to face consequences socially rather than through physical harm.

158 A Popular Criminology of Youth Justice

They want others to recognise the hurt that has been caused, to recognise that they are victims. Particularly for Drea, seeking revenge is due to the lack of formal consequences through legitimate channels. Because she punches Max (Austin Abrams) when he denies leaking the video, she is cast as an aggressor and Max avoids all consequences. This speaks to the broader culture of victim blaming and the difficulty for women to receive justice regarding gender-based crimes (Davies, 2018).

I'm the slut on probation and he and his tiny little dick get away scot-free

Do Revenge immediately subverts the innocent-dangerous dichotomy by highlighting that both girls are victims as well as behaving criminally. It does not present their victimhood as excusing their negative behaviours, simply as part of the context in which it occurs. This contextualisation of criminal behaviour is a key aspect of Child First films and allows justice-involved characters to be portrayed as complex and nuanced as opposed to shallow stereotypes. This allows characters to have multiple aspects to their identities, in ways that characters in previous youth justice films would not. For example, in *Heathers* Veronica is portrayed as innocent, with plausible deniability of her crimes in contrast to the villainous J.D. (see Chapter 4 for further discussion). She is clever, pretty, and trapped by the social circumstances of her high school. This characterisation overrides her wish to see the titular Heathers dead, and the actions she takes to achieve this. Contrastingly, Drea in *Do Revenge* is also clever, pretty, and confined by social hierarchies, but the audience is allowed to see her personality also can be controlling, manipulative, and childish. Drea's social circumstances are complicated by the fact that she does not come from the same privileged background as her peers, being of a minority ethnicity and less economically well-off means that she perceives injustices more keenly than those around her, as she has more to lose, specifically a college scholarship. Audiences automatically sympathise with the stereotype of Veronica as she is presented as innocent. But with Drea, we empathise with her and whilst we may not approve of her actions, the context makes it clear why she feels this is necessary, which is much more nuanced than the prior presentation of girlhood. Child First films recognise the difference between behaviour and identity, allowing characters that behave in anti-social ways to be shown as simultaneously having pro-social identities and aspirations. This is moving beyond the innocent-dangerous dichotomy and victim/offender labels, to seeing the entirety of a child's personality, including the complexities inherent within this.

Do Revenge is not alone in presenting a pro-social view of anti-social characters, or recognising the intersectional factors that impact upon children's identity formation. *Attack the Block* (2011) is from the era of "urban" films (see Chapter 5), and bears many of the hallmarks of the genre. Set in a

"Now That I Know You, I Can't Really NOT Know You" **159**

South London estate, *Attack the Block* is about a group of 15-year-old boys who wear hoodies and bandanas, carry flick knives, are linked to a local drug dealer, and are in conflict with local police. Featuring a garage-influenced soundtrack and with the script using youth-specific slang (Jablonski, 2011), there are many similarities between *Attack the Block* and films like *Kidulthood* (2006) or *Ill Manors* (2012). However, what sets *Attack the Block* apart is genre. *Attack the Block* is a science-fiction comedy film, where aliens invade Wyndham Estate, and the children who live there have to defend their home. This choice of genre allows relatively stereotypical characters to be perceived in a different way and gives these characters the opportunity to be heroic. Whilst subtle in the film, the idea of giving justice-involved children opportunities to develop separately from the expectations placed upon them is a recurring theme and makes *Attack the Block* an early example of Child First media. Given the cultural climate regarding justice-involved children at the time was steeped in risk-based frameworks (Case et al., 2015; McAlister and Carr, 2014) and there was a clear negative public perception of children, particularly seen in the aftermath of the 2011 London riots (Moxon, 2011), *Attack the Block*'s subverting stereotypes of justice-involved children, and portraying them as heroes was a potentially risky proposition for a film (Korte, 2018). This can be seen in the American release of the film, which was limited due to concern that the film would not be well-received, with the accents of the characters and the use of multicultural London English being difficult to understand for American audiences (Jablonski, 2011). However, the film became a cult favourite, showing that there is a commercial appetite for positive and nuanced portrayals of justice-involved children (*BBC News*, 2021).

Attack the Block's main character is Moses (John Boyega), a 15-year-old Black British boy who at the start of the film appears to be on the pathway to a criminal lifestyle. He and his friends steal from people, he carries a knife, and views the estate (and particularly the tower block in which he lives) as his territory. This territorialism extends to not just the physical space, but the people who live on the estate also. At the start of the film Moses and his friends intimidate and steal from Sam (Jodie Whittaker), a nurse who is walking home from work, threatening her with a knife in the process. Later when Moses realises Sam lives in the same block as him, he apologises saying he wouldn't have done that if he knew she lived there. Whilst this logic is questionable (as is pointed out by Sam), it shows Moses's empathy for those he views as his part of his community, and his ability to recognise the impact of his actions. Many of the films featuring characters like Moses at the time only showed emotional growth in the characters when it was triggered by fear or revenge, whereas *Attack the Block* shows the child-like understanding of the world the characters have and the way in which new situation or experience can change and develop this.

160 A Popular Criminology of Youth Justice

The character of Sam is often the one representing the audience's viewpoint throughout the film. In the opening scene we see her fear as she walks home from work and sees a group of teenage boys in the distance. Her continued anger at the group throughout the film is justified, as she is unaware of why they are behaving as they are, and initially disbelieves their claims of an alien invasion. Having her character be sympathetic; a nurse, wanting a safe home, and trusting in the police; allows the audience to change their opinion of Moses and his friends as she does; whilst Sam still dislikes the group, at the end of the film she is no longer afraid of them and has sympathy for their situations. Sam develops empathy for Moses, as she learns he is much younger than she thought, and that he is an orphan living with his uncle, but largely has to care for himself. This comes not though exposition or being told this, but through Sam seeing Moses's home. The child-like qualities of his bedroom, such as a spiderman duvet, force her to confront the fact that the monstrous character she had created in her mind is actually a child. Her changing perception of Moses and his friends mirrors the expectations of the audience, that they too will perceive Moses differently. In this way the film reflects processes of restorative justice, showing that this can be a two-way relationship. Sam is victimised by Moses, but by having the opportunity to speak to each other they develop empathy and understanding, which leads to both parties feeling less aggrieved by the situation, reflecting research findings on restorative practices (Choi et al., 2012; McVey, 2016). The links to alternative forms of justice in *Attack the Block* are further highlighted by the way police and traditional justice systems are portrayed in the film; as ineffective and unjust.

Police and authority are constantly on the edges of *Attack the Block* and are almost as much of an invading force as the aliens. The characters fall into two distinct camps; those who want further police presence and authority in the area, and those who are anti-police and actively trying to avoid them. Deviant behaviour is a clear factor influencing which camp a character will fall into, but race and ethnicity also play a role. The film is very aware of the setting it is using and the real-life experience of characters like Moses, which is one of police harassment (Flacks, 2020; Francis et al., 2020). Black children in South London have continually been victims of over-policing and criminalisation (Jackson et al., 2019; Myhill and Bradford, 2013). Not only this but ethnic minority groups also report being treated unfairly by police when reporting crimes or having been victim of a crime (Cao et al., 1996; Rosenbaum et al., 2005). *Attack the Block* is explicitly aware of this, and the minority ethnicity characters call this out when Sam (who is white) continually wants to seek help from police regarding the aliens.

You think the police are going to help them? They'll help you, but not them

The narrative of racial injustice is further emphasised by how police treat Moses in the film. Acting on Sam's report of the mugging, a police van chases Moses whilst he is on his bike, knocking him down in the pursuit to make an arrest. This could be considered purely as an exaggerated chase sequence for the purpose of making a film entertaining, however, this is indicative of real police actions. There have been high-profile cases of police vehicles chasing children on bicycles with the result being injuries and deaths (*BBC News*, 2023; Weaver et al., 2023). There is a clear lack of consideration by police that the person riding a bicycle is a child and that the use of full force or tactical driving techniques may not be necessary. The police in *Attack the Block* are consistently heavy-handed, forceful, and only view the young characters in the film as criminals. Whilst the aliens are a threat due to their violence, the police are the real source of fear for Moses and his friends, and one that has been ongoing throughout their lives. Authority figures like police are so distrusted that Moses even suggests that the alien invasion may be staged by those in power as a method of removing poor people from the area, citing the influx of drugs and weapons as failed previous attempts. Whilst this is a conspiracy, the "ghettoisation" of certain areas is well documented (Pattillo, 2009; Wacquant, 1993), and shows that those in power do not consider all groups equally, or view injustices as acceptable when impacting minorities (Hall, 2011). For justice-involved children, their lack of political agency or ability to create change also impacts upon this distrust, as their views and voices are not considered (Arthur, 2015; *Crest Advisory*, 2022; Price et al., 2023).

Attack the Block's novelty as a Child First film comes from its subversion of stereotypes and display of how opportunity is key in developing pro-social identities. At the start of the film Moses and his friends are portrayed very simplistically, as violent, criminal, thugs, and it is clear that is how they are perceived by those around them, even being referred to as "monsters". However, the alien invasion gives the boys an opportunity they have not had previously, to be leaders. The adults around them do not believe that the creatures are aliens, and so continually underestimate their threat, instead believing that Moses and his friends are the cause of the trouble, essentially leaving these children to respond to the threat themselves. Looking out of the windows of the tower block and expecting help to come is a frequent feature of the film, but the characters are always surprised by the lack of response. The national guard isn't called, there is only 1 police helicopter, and rather than storming in to help, the police blockade the estate, containing the problem rather than responding to it. Therefore, Moses and his friends have to think of a plan to save themselves and their home. The subversion of stereotype, from hoodie to hero, was an explicit aim of *Attack the Block*, with director Joe Cornish wanting to write a film which was fun but with a clear social justice subtext about children (Ilott, 2013; Marin-Lamellet, 2022). Making Moses the main character and allowing the audience to see his

162 A Popular Criminology of Youth Justice

development was a main driver for the film, and there is an explicit Child First ideology underpinning this.

> Just because they're in hoods or whatever and doing their thing, they're still children. I think society is pretty cruel and forgets that often these kids are just kids
>
> *(Jablonski, 2011)*

In practice, the process of building pro-social identity is complex and difficult. But films like *Attack the Block* allow for a different social perception of justice-involved children to emerge within society. Identity is complex, multi-faceted and bound to context (Breakwell, 2023), however, giving the opportunity for different aspects of identity to be developed is a clear and practical way to facilitate change. An alien invasion is an extreme and unlikely scenario but developing opportunities for justice-involved children to see themselves as heroes (even if only in media) is important in building pro-social identity.

Diverting from Stigma

The impact of labelling has long been a concern within youth justice (Creaney, 2012; Fraser and Atkinson, 2014), with research showing that being labelled as an "offender" is harmful. However, labelling itself is not inherently negative. Labels can provide access to required services, for example through diagnosis. It is only when a label is associated with a social stigma that it becomes harmful. The negative stigma associated with being an "offender" or "criminal" is what makes this label harmful, leading to individuals being treated by others differently, being denied opportunities, or other social impacts (Liebenberg and Ungar, 2014; MacDonald, 2006). This stigma can become internalised, leading children to feel like they are excluded from society and criminal pathways are the only option available to them (Gray, 2007). From a justice perspective this creates a social aspect to punishment (Cavadino and Dignan, 2006). These social punishments are implicit and unregulated. This additional level of punishment can itself be unjust, as it does not end with formal punishment and can have long-term impacts on individuals (Armstrong et al., 2005). This is one of the reasons that Child First has actively focused upon diversion from stigma rather than solely considering labels. The language of Child First youth justice is explicitly moving away from labels that are heavily stigmatised such as "offender" and "juvenile" (Day, 2023), however, social stigma takes time to deconstruct and it is unlikely that simply renaming services to remove these labels will also remove the stigma associated with justice-involvement. Therefore, the active diversion from stigma is a positive aspect of Child First, allowing

"Now That I Know You, I Can't Really NOT Know You"   **163**

children to not only be perceived as children by criminal justice systems, but by children themselves.

Ironically, one of the best examples of diversion from stigma in fictional film actively uses stigmatised terminology. *The Young Offenders* (2016) is an Irish production written and directed by Peter Foott. Focusing on the relationship between 15-year-olds Conor (Alex Murphy) and Jock (Chris Walley) the film shows their journey to find a bale of cocaine after seeing news reports about a drug trafficking boat crashing on the south coast of Ireland. This plot could be the basis of a conventional crime film, where the boys become involved in drug dealing and are hunted by police, culminating with either their success or arrest, similarly to *Badlands* (1973). It could also be the basis of a social issue film, showing their descent into criminality, and exploitation in a similar vein to *County Lines* (2019). However, *The Young Offenders* is a buddy comedy, a coming-of-age film, and a sensitive portrayal of two children trying to live better lives. Conor and Jock are never judged by the film; in terms of its writing, staging and direction they are portrayed sympathetically, however, the audience does not pity them. Conor and Jock are allowed to be funny and silly, naive but hopeful, and cunning but sensitive. They are allowed by the film to be fully realised characters, and children. They devise a plan to find drugs with the idea of selling them, fully knowing this is criminal, however, they are not shown as being devious masterminds planning a crime spree. Conor describes their trip as a "holiday", they travel by bicycle as this is the transport available to them, and their plans for the money they hope to make are to buy mansions "like Batman". Their criminal plans are still quite child-like, and whilst they show critical thinking and planning, this is clearly not the full-developed skill that would be expected of adults.

Early in the film the label of "young offender" is discussed explicitly. Conor is concerned that their plan will get them into trouble, and Jock (an experienced bicycle thief) quells his fears by outlining that their status as children means they will be treated differently.

If you're younger than sixteen you're classified as a young offender which basically means you can't get in trouble.

For some reason they thought our brains wouldn't be developed or something, like we wouldn't know what we were doing. I know, stupid isn't it?

That Conor and Jock view this as "stupid" is reflective of the societal narrative that children (particularly those below the age of criminal responsibility) are committing crimes and "getting away with it" due to the perceived softness of youth justice, particularly in relation to the use of the welfare approach (Case and Bateman, 2020; Muncie, 2008). However, throughout the remainder of *The Young Offenders* we see a proponent of harsh treatment in the

164 A Popular Criminology of Youth Justice

form of Sergeant Healy (Dominic MacHale). His dogged pursuit of two somewhat hapless children and his refusal to overlook low-level crime in the form of bike thefts is shown to be both absurd and ineffective. Healy's superintendent even chastises him for this focus, highlighting that there are bigger priorities for police. Healy's argument about bike thefts leading to larger crimes ("It starts with a bike, then a car, then…a bus"), shows how this is an oversimplified view of crime, and the that the demonisation of justice-involved children assumes they have no capacity for change. That *The Young Offenders* places Healy as one of the antagonists of the film shows the diversion from previous youth justice narratives, this is a clear move away from authority figures as heroes such as Bell in *The Young Savages* (1961) (see Chapter 2 for further discussion). However, much like all the other characters, Healy is also allowed to be nuanced and not a stereotype. Towards the end of the film, he arrives at Jock's home to arrest him. Upon seeing the abuse Jock receives from his father, he instantly develops sympathy for him and realises that his view of justice-involved children has been over zealous, leading to a change in his approach to policing practice. *The Young Offenders* shows the audience the standard societal narratives that have endured through time regarding justice-involved children. But it also lampoons these as being ridiculous, and in showing the context of Conor and Jock's lives makes clear that these simplistic ideas of "monstrous" children needing harsh punishment to "set them straight" is ineffective at best and harmful at worst. In doing so, *The Young Offenders* makes clear the need to divert justice-involved children from stigma and to ensure they receive other opportunities to develop pro-social identities.

One of the factors that *The Young Offenders* emphasises is the importance of social mobility and opportunities offered to justice-involved children. The hope for a better future or an improvement in circumstances is important in children's social development (Burnside and Gaylord-Harden, 2019). If there is a sense that things will not improve and adulthood will be filled with the same level of hardship, this makes it easier for children to become apathetic or feel disillusioned with the state, and thus more susceptible to viewing criminal behaviour as acceptable (McVey, 2016). Conor and Jock don't have high hopes for their futures. They both intend to leave school as soon as possible as they find it difficult, have limited employment options, and both imagine that their adult lives will be similar to those of their parents. For Jock in particular this is an upsetting proposition as his father is an alcoholic, and abusive. The boys' goal is to be able to move out of their parent's homes and to live independent lives, but the prospect of finding €7 million worth of cocaine gives them the possibility of attaining something more than this. There is little hope that the institutions around them would provide support, opportunity, or the ability to change the lives that are expected for them, meaning that alternative means such as crime are the only feasible hope they have of change.

> *This could be the difference between having an amazing life, or a really shit one*

Throughout Conor and Jock's trip we see other ways in which they have not had the opportunity to learn about the world around them or perceive themselves differently from the expectations of others. It is the first time they have been in countryside or outside of their home city, and they take full advantage of it in ways that show their child-like nature, by chasing birds, stroking caterpillars and swimming in the sea. At one point, they hide from Sergeant Healy in the house of a farmer, who has mistaken them for his sons (possibly due to dementia). He invites them to stay for dinner, which requires killing one of the chickens kept on the farm. Chicken is Conor's favourite food; however, he has never encountered the realities of meat production and is saddened and horrified by this. Seeing a live chicken for the first time and feeling empathy for it shows Conor as a sensitive child, who has had limited exposure to the world around him. During dinner the farmer is drinking whiskey, reminding Jock of his father, and the situation escalates to a fight quickly. The two boys restrain the farmer, tying him to his chair in an effort to keep him from assaulting Jock. They stay with him, watching TV, which Conor describes as "the closest we'd get to a normal night in for a long time", showing how their home lives are far from what would be expected as "normal". Whilst this is essentially a hostage situation, it also shows the vulnerability of Conor and Jock, and the extremes to which they need to go to gain some control over their lives.

Within *The Young Offenders* we see Conor and Jock engage in a variety of crimes, including bike theft, criminal damage (smashing a car window), and the aforementioned hostage-taking. However, they are not portrayed as hardened criminals, despite Sergeant Healy viewing them as such. Conor and Jock's status as "criminal" is questionable in contrast to two other characters: Billy Murphy (Shane Casey) and Ray the Drug Dealer (PJ Gallagher). Billy Murphy, described as "the local nutjob", is violent, threatening and a supplier of drugs. He victimises Conor, beating him up and stealing his phone. Ray the Drug Dealer is similarly violent, using a nail gun to assault multiple characters whilst trying to find his cocaine. In contrast to these two characters, Conor and Jock seem harmless and their crimes insignificant. Many youth justice films only show justice-involved adults as gang leaders, encouraging children's criminal behaviour or manipulating them into it (e.g. *County Lines* (2019), *Ill Manors* (2012), *Kidulthood* (2006)). This essentially portrays justice-involved children as miniature versions of these adults, allowing audiences to view them equally negatively. However, *The Young Offenders*

166 A Popular Criminology of Youth Justice

contrasting justice-involved children and adults allows a clear distinction between the two to be drawn, meaning that Conor and Jock can be shown committing crimes, but also clearly as children. Whilst this raises the question of how justice-involved adults are portrayed and the harm caused by these stereotypes, it clearly places *The Young Offenders* as a Child First film, that is actively trying to reduce the stigma of children's justice-involvement.

The stigma of justice involvement goes beyond individual children, impacting on their families also (McMickens et al., 2024). This is particularly the case for single-parent families like Conor and Jock's, with parents frequently receiving blame for raising delinquent children, or failing to control them (Aldridge et al., 2011). These narratives around parenting have been reflected in youth justice policy and legislation such as Parenting Orders (Evans, 2012) but are also reflected in media presentation of youth justice. Many youth justice films use one of two approaches to portraying parents of justice-involved children: as absent or neglectful. Where parents are portrayed as absent, this doesn't always mean that they have literally abandoned their child, but rather that they are only on the fringes of the story and are unaware of their child's activities. Alternatively, parents tend to be portrayed as neglectful, either being abusive, or unable to appropriately provide for their child. *County Lines* (2019), discussed in Chapter 5, is an example of both parental stereotypes simultaneously; the mother character is absent due to working long hours and nights but is also neglectful due to not noticing that her son has become involved in trafficking drugs. This stereotyping of parents of justice-involved children acts as a form of scapegoating, speaking to the societal view of why children commit crimes, blaming the parents for a lack of control over their children, which is often also pared with narratives about working class families and relative poverty. This also links to the stereotype of criminality being inevitable for certain groups of children. However, Child First films deviate from this media standard, breaking down the stigma applied not only to justice-involved children, but their families and the circumstances of their lives as well. *The Young Offenders* is a good example of this, showing Conor's mother Mairead (Hilary Rose) as being caring and attentive, which is not a frequent way of depicting working-class single mothers (Littler, 2020; Walters and Harrison, 2014). Mairead is concerned about and makes herself aware of where Conor is, unlike the depictions of parents in 2000s "urban films"; she ensures he attends school, she encourages him to have ambition for employment, and is clearly trying to support him into developing into an adult. She does not approve of his friendship with Jock, seeing him as a bad influence, but ultimately recognises that Jock is impacted by his family circumstances and needs support as well. Mairead clearly cares about her child and is a model of a supportive parent. Mairead does not always get things right, such as describing Conor in ways that upset him. However, she does listen to his view and agrees to change.

"Now That I Know You, I Can't Really NOT Know You" **167**

Mairead is a clear example of "good enough" parenting (Choate and Engstrom, 2014) and highlights the need for middle-class values not to be considered as the standard regardless of context. This also emphasises the need for diversion from stigma and the broader impacts this has beyond the individual. The stigma of the label "young offender" impacts upon parents of these children as well, with policy responsibilising parents for the behaviours of their children through measures such as fines (Walters and Woodward, 2007). Child First's call for diversion from stigma goes beyond stigma against justice-involved children, including their families, communities and the services that support them.

Throughout film history clothing has been used symbolically to showcase character's motivations, allegiances, and morality (Bauman, 2022). This has held true for representations of justice-involved children as well, with clothing being used as a signifier of non-conformity, gang involvement, and "otherness", as seen throughout this book. *The Young Offenders* uses clothing to tell the audience things about the characters, but simultaneously confronts and subverts the stereotypes that are being telegraphed. Conor and Jock both have ear piercings, shaved eyebrows, wear chunky jewellery, trainers, and tracksuits. This is commented on by Mairead as Conor copying Jock and a sign of peer pressure, indicative of Jock encouraging Conor to behave criminally, despite Conor's insistence that this is not the case.

Mam's always going on about me mimicking Jock. I mean, yeah, we have similar haircuts, but that's just the fashion. Aside from that we have our own individual shit going on

There are socio-economic connotations of this style of dress separate from it being reflective of youth culture; connotations of being poor, working class and criminal (Boldison, 2006). The social stereotype of "chavs" frequently overlaps with stereotypes of justice-involved children, leading to assumptions that people who dress this way are criminal (Hayward and Yar, 2006). However, Conor himself states that this is simply the style of the time, which is both accurate of the film's 2007 setting and the time of its release. Sportwear and athleisure have been a consistent trend during this period, but whether this is considered as stylish or "chavvy" is dependent on who is wearing it. The class connotations in this characterisation cannot be ignored, but neither can the demonisation of youth culture. Children's style and fashions have consistently been criticised by adults throughout history. From James Dean's t-shirts in *Rebel Without A Cause* (1955), to Conor and Jocks tracksuits, youth style has always been seen as symptomatic of their behaviour (Ilan, 2017). That a particular style of dress can lead to an individual being considered as criminal by those around them further emphasises the need to divert children from stigma and to deconstruct stigmatised stereotypes throughout

168 A Popular Criminology of Youth Justice

society. Child First films can support this by developing audience empathy for characters who visually appear in ways that may not immediately suggest positive portrayals.

A Child First Future

Film is a form of representation of public attitudes, but also a forum in which people vicariously learn about the world (Jewkes, 2015). In this way film can act as a bellwether signifying shifts in public opinion. The development of Child First films suggests that the public is more open to viewing justice-involved children in a different way than previously, moving away from punitive attitudes.

The films discussed in this chapter are not necessarily commercial success-stories but have developed cult-followings, are developed into TV series (*The Young Offenders*, 2018), and have maintained enough interest for sequels to be considered (*BBC News*, 2021). This suggests that the characters and ideas within these films capture the public's imagination and are something they want to engage with. Child First films may not have the same initial commercial impact as a traditional "crime film", but they appear to have longevity and an enduring appeal. For youth justice, this is a positive, suggesting that the public view of Child First justice is favourable, indicating public support for this in practice. As youth justice has been greatly impacted by populism (Green, 2008) which has traditionally resulted in the demonisation of children and more punitive practices (Muncie, 2008), seeing populism in the form of a commercial film potentially advocating for Child First values is heartening.

The films discussed in this chapter are examples of Child First narratives in media, which is a highly positive development and shows that there is both public and institutional support for this type of story and representation. However, who is making these films must be considered. *Scrapper, Attack the Block, Do Revenge* and *The Young Offenders* are all written and directed by white creatives. Whilst the casts may be diverse, and the stories recognise the need for intersectionality, Child First ideas emphasise collaboration and creating opportunities for justice-involved children (Burns and Creaney, 2023). *Scrapper* and *The Young Offenders* were both based upon the childhood experiences of their writers, who wanted to create films that were more representative of the children they were and knew (*BFI*, 2023; Devine, 2017). This is worthy of praise, and the funding of these films shows that there is support for this. The National Lottery and BFI contributed funding to *Attack the Block* and *Scrapper*, and *The Young Offenders* received funding from the Irish Film Board. However, as discussed in Chapter 5, not all filmmakers have equal access to funding and may have to compromise the stories they tell in order to secure this. That the films created by minority ethnicity filmmakers tend to conform to stereotypes, whereas their white contemporaries

"Now That I Know You, I Can't Really NOT Know You" **169**

can create more hopeful works that subvert these stereotypes suggests that there is a disparity in who gets to tell what stories (Nwonka and Malik, 2018). Film funders need to recognise this disparity and allow stories of minority ethnicity children not to be characterised as "crime films". Child First as a project is focused upon youth justice, however, it's true success will be if it is applied in other areas, for example when the "youth justice film" becomes a "Child First film".

Youth justice is not the end point of Child First. For this to be truly effective, it should be adopted by all institutions working with and supporting children (Case and Morris, 2018; Case and Smith, 2023). It is not only justice-involved children who are impacted by negative stereotypes, stigma, and a lack of support. Minority ethnicity children are impacted by this (Medina Ariza, 2014), as are working-class children (Arnež, 2022), those in care (McElvaney and Tatlow-Golden, 2016), neurodiverse children (Day, 2022), and more. If the whole range of services provided to children adopted a Child First approach, this would be beneficial for all children. However, youth justice is an excellent starting point as many of those who are impacted across a range of intersecting factors are justice-involved (Baidawi and Ball, 2023; Liebenberg and Ungar, 2014; Peguero and Popp, 2012), and criminal justice involvement has a profound impact upon children's futures (McAra and McVie, 2007; McFarland et al., 2019). Expanding Child First beyond youth justice into other sectors such as policing would be beneficial in reducing the criminalisation of children, and the harmful aspects of policing which disproportionately impact children such as stop and search (Alliance for Youth Justice, 2022). In education, this could encourage practice developments allowing those who are not naturally academic to still engage and providing better support for those with additional learning needs who are often siloed out of mainstream classes (Shafi, 2019). For social care, Child First would prioritise safeguarding and the need to avoid adultification of children in care (Staines et al., 2023). Child First is a social justice ideology, meaning that for it to be truly successful, it should support *all* children. Whilst film cannot achieve this itself, by telling a more diverse range of stories about justice-involved children and presenting this in a Child First way, it can help to counteract the social narratives and stereotypes that have impacted the individuals, institutions and systems that support children.

The main aim of Child First is for justice systems and beyond to see children as children, rather than as offenders. For this to be truly successful, the general public also need to see all children as children, regardless of their behaviour, circumstances, or involvement with statutory agencies. This is a complex task to achieve but can be supported by Child First media. Films like *Scrapper, Do Revenge, The Young Offenders and Attack the Block* that tell different types of stories are a way of developing the public's understanding of and empathy for justice-involved children. By presenting their stories and

170 A Popular Criminology of Youth Justice

lives with the context and nuance that we know occurs, we as a public can understand and perceive these children beyond cultural stereotypes. Child First films help us get to know who justice-involved children are and to recognise that they are children, and such knowledge cannot be undone. As Georgie in *Scrapper* states;

Now that I know you, I can't really NOT know you

Film List

Attack the Block (2011)
Badlands (1973)
County Lines (2019)
Do Revenge (2022)
Kidulthood (2006)
Ill Manors (2012)
Scrapper (2023)
The Young Offenders (2016)
The Young Savages (1961)

References

Aldridge J, Shute J, Ralphs R, et al. (2011) Blame the parents? Challenges for parent-focused programmes for families of gang-involved young people. *Children & Society* 25(5): 371–381.

Alliance for Youth Justice (2022) The neglected realities of child stop and search - StopWatch. Available at: https://www.ayj.org.uk/news-content/stopwatch-child-stop-and-search (accessed 27 June 2023).

Antolak -Saper Natalia (2020) The adultification of the youth justice system: The Victorian experience. *Law in Context* 37(1): 99–113. La Trobe University Law School.

Armstrong D, Hine J, Hacking S, et al. (2005) *Children, Risk and Crime: The on Track Youth Lifestyles Surveys*. Home Office D and SD (ed.). London: Home Office, Development and Statistics Directorate.

Arnež J (2022) *Negotiating Class in Youth Justice: Professional Practice and Interactions*. Oxon: Taylor & Francis.

Arthur R (2015) Recognising children's citizenship in the youth justice system. *Journal of Social Welfare and Family Law* 37(1): 21–37.

Baidawi S and Ball R (2023) Child protection and youth offending: Differences in youth criminal court-involved children by dual system involvement. *Children and Youth Services Review* 144: 106736.

Baker K (2011) Antisocial behaviour orders: A culture of control? By Jane Donoghue. *British Journal of Criminology* 51(6): 3.

Baldry E, Briggs DB, Goldson B, et al. (2018) 'Cruel and unusual punishment': An inter-jurisdictional study of the criminalisation of young people with complex support needs. *Journal of Youth Studies* 21(5): 636–652. Routledge.

"Now That I Know You, I Can't Really NOT Know You" **171**

Bauman R (2022) 'Now you are one of us': Mafia fashion on-screen. *Film, Fashion & Consumption* 11: 155–168 (Masculinities on Screen). Intellect.

BBC News (2021) Attack the block sequel: Cult movie had 'timely' message about race. 18 May. Available at: https://www.bbc.com/news/newsbeat-57157066 (accessed 4 June 2024).

BBC News (2023) Cardiff riots: Police refer themselves to watchdog after crash deaths. 23 May. Available at: https://www.bbc.com/news/uk-wales-65687785 (accessed 27 June 2024).

BFI (2023) Charlotte Regan on Scrapper: "I'd love to see more working-class films that are happier". Available at: https://www.bfi.org.uk/interviews/charlotte-regan-scrapper (accessed 20 March 2024).

Blum-Ross A (2017) Voice, empowerment and youth-produced films about 'gangs'. *Learning, Media and Technology* 42(1): 54–73.

Boduszek D, Debowska A, Sharratt K, et al. (2021) Pathways between types of crime and criminal social identity: A network approach. *Journal of Criminal Justice* 72: 101750.

Boldison L (2006) *'Hoodies': A New Moral Panic?: An Examination of Media Representations of Crime, Youth Subcultures, Moral Panics and the Application of the Moral Panic Theory to Media Reporting of 'Hoodies' in Britain's National Newspapers*. Leicester: University of Leicester.

Breakwell GM (2023) *Identity: Unique & Shared*. London; Thousand Oaks, California: SAGE Publications.

Burns S and Creaney S (2023) Embracing children's voices: Transforming youth justice practice through co-production and child first participation. In: Case S and Hazel N (eds) *Child First: Developing a New Youth Justice System*. Cham: Springer International Publishing, pp. 333–365. Available at: https://doi.org/10.1007/978-3-031-19272-2_12 (accessed 15 April 2024).

Burnside AN and Gaylord-Harden NK (2019) Hopelessness and delinquent behavior as predictors of community violence exposure in ethnic minority male adolescent offenders. *Journal of Abnormal Child Psychology* 47(5): 801–810.

Cao L, Frank J and Cullen FT (1996) Race, community context and confidence in the police. *American Journal of Police* 15(1): 3–22.

Case S and Bateman T (2020) The punitive transition in youth justice: Reconstructing the child as offender. *Children and Society* 34(6): 475–491.

Case S and Browning A (2021) *The child first strategy implementation project: Realising the guiding principle for youth justice*. report, 7 October. Loughborough University. Available at: https://repository.lboro.ac.uk/articles/report/The_child_first_strategy_implementation_project_Realising_the_guiding_principle_for_youth_justice/16764124/1 (accessed 15 April 2024).

Case S and Haines K (2015) *Positive Youth Justice: Children First, Offenders Second*. London: Policy Press.

Case S and Hazel N (eds) (2023) *Child First: Developing a New Youth Justice System*. Cham: Palgrave Macmillan.

Case S and Morris R (2018) Promoting children first youth work in the youth justice system and beyond. In: *The SAGE Handbook of Youth Work Practice*, pp. 241–254.

Case S and Smith R (2023) Child first and the end of 'bifurcation' in youth justice? *Journal of Children's Services* 18(3/4): 180–194. Emerald Publishing Limited.

Case S, Creaney S, Deakin J, et al. (2015) Youth justice: Past, present and future. *British Journal of Community Justice* 13(2): 99–110.

Case S, Browning A and Hampson K (2023) The child first strategy implementation project – translating strategy into practice. *Youth Justice* 24: 204–230. SAGE Publications.

Caulfield L and Sojka B (2023) Exploring the impact of music on children at risk of contact with the criminal justice system. *Safer Communities* 22(2): 121–132. Emerald Publishing Limited.

Cavadino M and Dignan J (2006) *Penal Systems: A Comparative Approach*. London: SAGE.

Chernyak N and Kushnir T (2018) The influence of understanding and having choice on children's prosocial behavior. *Current Opinion in Psychology* 20: 107–110. Elsevier.

Choate PW and Engstrom S (2014) The "good enough" parent: Implications for child protection. *Child Care in Practice* 20(4): 368–382. Routledge.

Choi JJ, Bazemore G and Gilbert MJ (2012) Review of research on victims' experiences in restorative justice: Implications for youth justice. *Children and Youth Services Review* 34(1): 35–42.

Clarke C (2023) 'A lot of working-class cinema is so joyless': Charlotte Regan on her candy-coloured debut Scrapper. *The Guardian*, 24 August. Available at: https://www.theguardian.com/film/2023/aug/24/a-lot-of-working-class-cinema-is-so-joyless-charlotte-regan-on-her-candy-coloured-debut-scrapper (accessed 20 March 2024).

Creaney S (2012) Targeting, labelling and stigma: Challenging the criminalisation of children and young people. *Criminal Justice Matters* 89(1): 16–17.

Creaney S (2020) "Game playing" and "docility": Youth justice in question. *Safer Communities* 19(3): 103–118.

Crest Advisory (2022) Forgotten voices: Policing, stop and search and the perspectives of Black children. Available at: https://www.crestadvisory.com/post/forgotten-voices-policing-stop-and-search-and-the-perspectives-of-black-children (accessed 27 June 2023).

Davies P (2018) Tackling domestic abuse locally: Paradigms, ideologies and the political tensions of multi-agency working. *Journal of Gender-Based Violence* 2(3): 429–446. Policy Press.

Day A-M (2022) Disabling and criminalising systems? Understanding the experiences and challenges facing incarcerated, neurodivergent children in the education and youth justice systems in England. *Forensic Science International: Mind and Law* 3: 100102.

Day A-M (2023) 'It's a hard balance to find': The perspectives of youth justice practitioners in England on the place of 'risk' in an emerging 'child-first' world. *Youth Justice* 23(1): 58–75. SAGE Publications.

Dazed (2023) Scrapper director Charlotte Regan is breaking class ceilings. Available at: https://www.dazeddigital.com/film-tv/article/60689/1/scrapper-film-review-charlotte-regan-director-interview-harris-dickinson-2023 (accessed 20 March 2024).

Devine P (2017) The young offenders (Peter Foott, 2016). *Estudios Irlandeses - Journal of Irish Studies* (12): 269–273. AEDEI.

Drakeford M (2009) Children first, offenders second: Youth justice in a devolved Wales. *Criminal Justice Matters* 78(1): 8–9.

Evans R (2012) Parenting orders: The parents attend yet the kids still offend. *Youth Justice* 12(2): 118–133. SAGE Publications.

Flacks S (2020) Law, necropolitics and the stop and search of young people. *Theoretical Criminology* 24(2): 387–405. SAGE Publications Ltd.

Francis S, Welsh T and Adesina Z (2020) Met Police 'four times more likely' to use force on black people - BBC News. Available at: https://www.bbc.co.uk/news/uk-england-london-53407560?intlink_from_url=https://www.bbc.co.uk/news/topics/c48yrnxgd7rt/black-lives-matter&link_location=live-reporting-story (accessed 11 August 2020).

Fraser A and Atkinson C (2014) Making up gangs: Looping, labelling and the new politics of intelligence-led policing. *Youth Justice* 14(2): 154–170. SAGE Publications Inc.

Gowen SM, Sarojini Hart C, Sehmar P, et al. (2022) '..It takes a lot of brain space': Understanding young carers' lives in England and the implications for policy and practice to reduce inappropriate and excessive care work. *Children & Society* 36(1): 118–136.

Gray P (2007) Youth justice, social exclusion and the demise of social justice. *The Howard Journal of Criminal Justice* 46(4): 401–416.

Green DA (2008) *When Children Kill Children: Penal Populism and Political Culture.* OUP Oxford. Available at: https://books.google.com/books?id=QIvp2Jg7yRkC&pgis=1 (accessed 13 November 2015).

Hagger MS, Anderson M, Kyriakaki M, et al. (2007) Aspects of identity and their influence on intentional behavior: Comparing effects for three health behaviors. *Personality and Individual Differences* 42(2): 355–367.

Haines K and Case S (2017) The context of children first, offenders second positive youth justice: In: Haines K and Case S (eds) *Positive Youth Justice.* Bristol: Policy Press, pp. 81–124.

Hall S (2011) The neo-liberal revolution. *Cultural Studies* 25(6): 705–728.

Hargreaves F, Carroll P, Robinson G, et al. (2023) County Lines and the power of the badge: The LFC Foundation's approach to youth intervention. *Safer Communities* 22(2): 91–105. Emerald Publishing Limited.

Haydon D (2020) Detained children: Vulnerability, violence and violation of rights. *International Journal for Crime, Justice and Social Democracy* 9(4): 16–30. Queensland University of Technology.

Hayward K and Yar M (2006) The 'chav' phenomenon: Consumption, media and the construction of a new underclass. *Crime, Media, Culture* 2(1): 9–28. SAGE Publications.

Hazel N (2022) Putting child first into practice. Available at: https://www.gov.uk/government/news/putting-child-first-into-practice (accessed 15 April 2024).

Hollingsworth K (2013) Theorising children's rights in youth justice: The significance of autonomy and foundational rights. *The Modern Law Review* 76(6): 1046–1069.

HSE (2009) Childrens play and leisure- promoting a balanced approach [online] Available from: https://www.hse.gov.uk/entertainment/childs-play-statement.htm (accessed 05 June 2024).

Hunter K, Fitzpatrick C, Staines J, et al. (2023) A difficult balance: Challenges and possibilities for local protocols to reduce unnecessary criminalisation of children in care and care leavers. *Youth Justice.* Epub ahead of print 2023. https://doi.org/10.1177/14732254231154153

Ilan J (2017) *Understanding Street Culture: Poverty, Crime, Youth and Cool.* New Delhi: Bloomsbury Publishing.

Ilott S (2013) "We are the Martyrs, you're just squashed tomatoes!" Laughing through the fears in Postcolonial British Comedy: Chris Morris's Four Lions and Joe Cornish's attack the block. *Postcolonial Text* 8(2). 2.

Jablonski S (2011) Joe Cornish discusses attack the block. Available at: https://thequietus.com/culture/film/joe-cornish-interview-attack-the-block/ (accessed 4 June 2024).

Jackson DB, Fahmy C, Vaughn MG, et al. (2019) Police stops among at-risk youth: Repercussions for mental health. *Journal of Adolescent Health* 65(5): 627–632. Elsevier USA.

Jackson LA, Kyriakopoulos A and Carthy N (2023) Criminal and positive identity development of young male offenders: Pre and post rehabilitation. *Journal of Criminal Psychology* 13(3): 173–189. Emerald Publishing Limited.

Jewkes Y (2015) *Media and Crime*. London: SAGE.

Korte B (2018) In the Ghetto: Inequality, riots and resistance in London-based science fiction of the twenty-first century. In: *Resistance and the City*. Brill, pp. 130–148. Available at: https://brill.com/display/book/9789004369313/BP000012.xml (accessed 20 March 2024).

Liebenberg L and Ungar M (2014) A comparison of service use among youth involved with juvenile justice and mental health. *Children and Youth Services Review* 39: 117–122. Elsevier Ltd.

Littler J (2020) Mothers behaving badly: Chaotic hedonism and the crisis of neoliberal social reproduction. *Cultural Studies* 34(4): 499–520. Routledge.

MacDonald R (2006) Social exclusion, youth transitions and criminal careers: Five critical reflections on 'risk'. *Australian & New Zealand Journal of Criminology* 39(3): 371–383. SAGE Publications Ltd.

Macleod G (2006) Bad, mad or sad: Constructions of young people in trouble and implications for interventions. *Emotional and Behavioural Difficulties* 11(3): 155–167. Routledge.

Marin-Lamellet A-L (2022) Generic confluence as the art of ideological peddling: Attack the Block (Joe Cornish, 2011). *Film Journal* (8). 8. SeERCIA - Société pour l'Enseignement et la Recherche du CInéma Anglophone. Epub ahead of print 1 July 2022. https://doi.org/10.4000/filmj.331

McAlister S and Carr N (2014) Experiences of youth justice: Youth justice discourses and their multiple effects. *Youth Justice* 14(3): 241–254.

McAra L and McVie S (2007) Youth justice?: The impact of system contact on patterns of desistance from offending. *European Journal of Criminology* 4(3): 315–345.

McAra L and McVie S (2012) Negotiated order: The groundwork for a theory of offending pathways. *Criminology & Criminal Justice* 12(4): 347–375. SAGE Publications.

McElvaney R and Tatlow-Golden M (2016) A traumatised and traumatising system: Professionals' experiences in meeting the mental health needs of young people in the care and youth justice systems in Ireland. *Children and Youth Services Review* 65: 62–69. Elsevier Ltd.

McFarland MJ, Geller A and McFarland C (2019) Police contact and health among urban adolescents: The role of perceived injustice. *Social Science and Medicine* 238: 112487. Elsevier Ltd.

McMickens CL, Jackson N, Williams K, et al. (2024) Justice-involved youth: Support for community and family interventions. *Child and Adolescent Psychiatric Clinics.* https://www.childpsych.theclinics.com/article/S1056-4993(24)00024-5/abstract. Elsevier.

McVey M (2016) Re-engaging disconnected youth: Transformative learning through restorative and social justice education. *International Review of Education* 62(5): 647–649. Springer Netherlands.

Medina Ariza JJ (2014) Police-initiated contacts: Young people, ethnicity, and the 'usual suspects'. *Policing and Society* 24(2): 208–223. Routledge.

Modrowski CA, Chaplo SD and Kerig PK (2023) Youth dually-involved in the child welfare and juvenile justice systems: Varying definitions and their associations with trauma exposure, posttraumatic stress, & offending. *Children and Youth Services Review* 150: 106998.

Moxon D (2011) Consumer culture and the 2011 'riots'. *Sociological Research Online* 16(4): 1–5.

Muncie J (2008) The 'punitive turn' in juvenile justice: Cultures of control and rights compliance in Western Europe and the USA. *Youth Justice* 8(2): 107–121.

Myhill A and Bradford B (2013) Overcoming cop culture? Organizational justice and police officers' attitudes toward the public. *Policing: An International Journal of Police Strategies & Management* 36(2): 338–356.

Nwonka CJ and Malik S (2018) Cultural discourses and practices of institutionalised diversity in the UK film sector: 'Just get something black made'. *The Sociological Review* 66(6): 1111–1127. SAGE Publications Ltd.

Pattillo M (2009) Revisiting Loïc Wacquant's urban outcasts. *International Journal of Urban and Regional Research* 33(3): 858–864.

Peguero AA and Popp AM (2012) Youth violence at school and the intersection of gender, race, and ethnicity. *Journal of Criminal Justice* 40(1): 1–9.

Pettitt B, Greenhead S, Khalifeh H, et al. (2013) *At Risk, Yet Dismissed The Criminal Victimisation of People with Mental Health Problems.* London: Victim Support.

Price J, Wilkinson D and Crossley C (2023) Children and young peoples' lyrics and voices capturing their experiences within youth justice services. *Safer Communities* 22(3): 186–199.

Rosenbaum DP, Schuck AM, Costello SK, et al. (2005) Attitudes toward the police: The effects of direct and vicarious experience. *Police Quarterly* 8(3): 343–365. Sage Publications Sage CA: Thousand Oaks, CA.

Seger L (2011) *The Art of Adaptation: Turning Fact And Fiction Into Film.* New York: Henry Holt and Company.

Shafi AA (2019) The complexity of disengagement with education and learning: A case study of young offenders in a secure custodial setting in England. *Journal of Education for Students Placed at Risk (JESPAR)* 24(4): 323–345. Routledge.

Sharkey JD, Stifel S and Mayworm A (2015) How to help me get out of a gang: Youth Recommendations to Family, School, Community, and Law Enforcement Systems. *Journal of Juvenile Justice* 1(4): 64–83. Epub ahead of print 11 December 2023.

Simmons J (2008) Violent youth: The censoring and public reception of The Wild One and The Blackboard Jungle. *Film History: An International Journal* 20(3): 381–391. Indiana University Press.

Smith R (2005) Welfare versus Justice- Again! *Youth Justice* 5(2): 3–16.

Smith R and Gray P (2019) The changing shape of youth justice: Models of practice. *Criminology & Criminal Justice* 19(5): 554–571. SAGE Publications.

Staines J, Fitzpatrick C, Shaw J, et al. (2023) 'We need to tackle their well being first': Understanding and supporting care-experienced girls in the youth justice system. *Youth Justice* 24(2): 185–203. SAGE Publications.

The Howard League for Penal Reform (2011) *Response to Breaking the Cycle, Effective Punishment, Rehabilitation and Sentencing of Offenders*. London: Criminal Justice Alliance.

The Young Offenders (2018) *BBC*. Available at: https://www.bbc.co.uk/programmes/p05v9qqg (accessed 23 July 2022).

Urwin J (2018) *A Return to Social Justice: Youth Justice, Ideology, and Philosophy*. London: Palgrave Macmillan UK.

Wacquant LJD. (1993) Urban outcasts: Stigma and division in the Black American Ghetto and the French urban periphery*. *International Journal of Urban and Regional Research* 17(3): 366–383.

Walters R and Woodward R (2007) Punishing 'poor parents': 'Respect', 'responsibility' and parenting orders in Scotland. *Youth Justice* 7(1): 5–20. SAGE Publications.

Walters SD and Harrison L (2014) Not ready to make nice: Aberrant mothers in contemporary culture. *Feminist Media Studies* 14(1): 38–55. Routledge.

Weaver M, Morris S and Grierson J (2023) Police admit following e-bike before crash that killed Cardiff teenagers. *The Guardian*, 23 May. Available at: https://www.theguardian.com/uk-news/2023/may/23/south-wales-police-van-was-pursuing-teenagers-in-cardiff-force-admits (accessed 13 July 2023).

Whyte B (2015) Values in youth justice: Practice approaches to welfare and justice for young people in UK jurisdictions. In: *Youth Justice Handbook*. Oxon: Willan, pp. 221–230.

Wiley SA, Slocum LA and Esbensen FA (2013) The unintended consequences of being stopped or arrested: An exploration of the labeling mechanisms through which police contact leads to subsequent delinquency. *Criminology* 51(4): 927–966.

Yates J (2012) What prospects youth justice? Children in trouble in the age of austerity. *Social Policy & Administration* 46(4): 432–447.

Youth Justice Board (2014a) Case management guidance. Available at: https://www.gov.uk/government/collections/case-management-guidance (accessed 22 February 2015).

Youth Justice Board (2014b) Deaths of children in custody: Action taken, lessons learnt [online] Available from: https://assets.publishing.service.gov.uk/media/5a7d5bf5ed915d28e9f39cff/deaths-children-in-custody.pdf (accessed 01 May 2024).

Youth Justice Board (2021) Strategic Plan 2021–2024. Available at: https://assets.publishing.service.gov.uk/media/603f6d268fa8f577c44d65a8/YJB_Strategic_Plan_2021_-_2024.pdf (accessed 8 April 2024).

9
CONCLUSION

Film is one of the most popular modern forms of art and entertainment. Society uses film to engage with ideas and experiences that individuals would not normally have access to, to tell stories that are both fantastical and realistic, and to develop shared understanding (Rafter, 2000). Whether factual or fictional, it is inarguable that film influences our thinking and understanding of the world (Rafter, 2017). This means that film is important, and what films say matters. This is particularly true for criminal justice, as most people will not experience this aspect of society at all, with their closest exposure being crime films. Whilst we should not expect film to be truthful and realistic all the time, it is important to pay attention to the "sins of omission and commission" (Wilson and O'Sullivan, 2004) committed by crime films and how this influences the public's view of criminal justice. There is not a direct line between a film's depiction of criminal justice, and the realities of practice, however, there is a clear relationship between the two. This can be seen in the cycle of media, public opinion, policy makers actions, and their practice implementation (Jewkes, 2015). For justice-involved children, this cycle is more impactful. As children have limited agency and power in society, they are more impacted by the views and actions of the adults around them. They have fewer opportunities to voice their opinions, or have their views acted upon by those in power, and their lives are largely controlled by the adults around them, whether that is parents, family, teachers, health care providers, or criminal justice professionals such as police, youth justice team workers, and magistrates. Children are frequently targets of both media and political discussion (Jowett et al., 1996) which tends to be reductive, framing children as innocent victims or dangerous criminals (Mejias and Banaji, 2019). As these stereotypes have been so longstanding within society and are deeply

DOI: 10.4324/9781003403159-9

embedded in the social understanding of childhood and youth (Panelli, 2007), it is difficult for individual children to overcome these expectations, meaning their behaviours are frequently viewed in a simplified way separated from the context of their lives. That media has played a role in both establishing and maintaining these stereotypes is indicative of its social importance, but also shows that it is necessary to critically engage with media that presents these ideas, as it has a real impact upon children's lives.

The clearest example of the cycle of media, policy and practice and its impact on children is the 1998 Crime and Disorder Act. This legislation was a landmark change for youth justice in England and Wales, ushering in a new era of punitive populism (Case and Bateman, 2020). This legislation fundamentally reformed the structure and approach of youth justice practice, establishing youth offending teams in place of youth justice teams that had been operating previously (Muncie, 1999). This also brought in a risk management approach, based upon actuarial assessments of children's needs, framing children as inherently "risky" (Briggs, 2013). This was widely criticised both at the time and since, being referred to as a "zombification" of youth justice (Pitts, 2001), with critics arguing that this approach and structure meant that justice-involved children would come to identify themselves as "offenders" making paths to desistance more difficult (Smith, 2001). This was in addition to removing the presumption of *doli incapax*, meaning that criminal justice was able to respond to more and younger children. The 1998 Crime and Disorder Act was clearly populist legislation, acting on public concerns about children committing crimes and "getting away with it" (Fitz-Gibbon, 2016). But these concerns had been fuelled by media both factual and fictional. The culture at the time was very focused on protecting children from the corrupting influence of violent and/or explicit films, with concerns that viewing these works would cause children to copy the violence they had viewed (Frey, 2006), with films being denied distribution rights due to their content, regardless of rating or intended audience (Cloarec, 2013; Green, 2008). This moral panic regarding media influence reached a nadir in 1993 following the death of James Bulger and the subsequent trial of his killers, who were both 10 years old. The media coverage of this case was unprecedented, due to the age of the children involved, the level of violence involved, and the reporting media's use of sensationalist language (Franklin and Petley, 1996). This case acted as a catalyst for growing concerns regarding youth crime and the language used in tabloid newspapers in particular acted as a form of permission for the public to describe and perceive justice-involved children in increasingly vitriolic ways (Franklin and Petley, 1996). The moral panic following the James Bulger case also encompassed the prior concerns regarding violent films, as newspaper reports suggested the perpetrators were influenced by the film *Childs Play 3* (1991), leading to calls for this to be banned from video distribution. However, there was no evidence to support the claim that the two boys had watched this film, or had access to it at all (Hay, 1995). Politically, this public concern about youth crime and media was seized upon by the Labour party in the lead-up to the 1997 general election. Declaring that Labour would be "tough on crime and tough on the causes of crime" was a key part of their campaign, and reforming youth justice in particular was a running policy theme, with then party leader Tony Blair speaking specifically about the "disintegration" of law and order in relation to the James Bulger case (Petley, 2007). The Crime and Disorder Act being enacted as legislation was seen as a success for Labour and a delivery of their campaign promises. For justice-involved children, these social and political developments had a real impact. The reforms to youth justice systems led to an increase in the number of children being arrested, an increase in the use of custody, and an increase in reoffending (Bateman, 2011; Muncie, 1999; Smith, 2010). This change, fuelled by media discussion impacting on public concerns, effectively meant that youth crime rates rose, and children were further embedded within the criminal justice system. Whilst this can't be directly related to the depiction of justice-involved children in film, it clearly shows the impact of media upon real children's lives. The James Bulger case and the media response surrounding it re-cemented the image of justice-involved children as dangerous to society. Prior to this youth justice practice had become increasingly welfare-oriented, being referred to as the decade of diversion (Case, 2018). However, without media calling children monsters, the punitive turn may not have been as punitive, and the public may not have been as accepting of the violent hopelessness of the urban films that followed (see Chapter 5). However, as we have seen throughout this book, the concern regarding youth justice in media and film in particular has not been limited to this period, as long as there have been crime films, there have been crime films about children.

The Youth Crime Film

Many of the tropes and visual signifiers of deviance that have been used in youth justice films were established by the problem youth films of the 1950s (Doherty, 2002). As discussed in Chapter 1, these films told stories of children struggling with the transition to adulthood, with some behaving in ways labelled as "delinquent". The enduring example of this is James Dean in *Rebel Without A Cause* (1955). However, Dean's *Rebel* also embodied another standard of the problem youth film, the transformation to conformity. To appease censors and production codes, these films could not show rebellious behaviour going unpunished; this was seen as detrimental to the stability of society (Biltereyst, 2007; Simmons, 2008). So problem youth films often centred on a character who recants their ways by the end of the film, reforming into a law-abiding, norm conforming, young adult. This transformation is

180 A Popular Criminology of Youth Justice

contrasted with the alternative: death. The subtext of problem youth films was that non-conformity is dangerous, bringing harm to both individuals and the world around them, and that the responsible thing to do is to accept one's responsibilities, grow up, and become an adult that contributes to society through work, having children, and consumerism. Whilst this message was very specific to the culture of the middle-class white American audience these films were aimed at, their success and popularity meant that aspects of problem youth films became the standard way of depicting justice-involved children on film.

Problem youth films centred on the dangers of subculture, non-conformity, and difference. This impacted upon public perceptions of youth culture more broadly, suggesting that any engagement with this was potentially dangerous. For children, this made their lived experience of public space more difficult, particularly if they displayed visible markers of subculture. Despite "hanging out" in public spaces being a recognised and common-place childhood behaviour throughout history (MacDonald and Shildrick, 2007), due to societal concerns regarding youth subculture, this became increasingly policed. There are few spaces children have free access to, meaning that parks, streets, and other public places are valuable. The increasing policing of these spaces, particularly when children engage in subculture, increases distrust and dislike of police and associated authority figures. This distrust strongly intersects with class and ethnicity, as lower-class and minority ethnicity children are more frequently targeted by police than their middle-class and/or white counterparts (Bowling and Phillips, 2007). As discussed in Chapter 2, *La Haine* (1995) exemplified these issues, showing the experience of lower-class minority ethnicity teenagers and their relationship with local police. Whilst films like *La Haine* using social realism to develop cultural understanding of children's experiences is positive, films depicting these issues often display a level of hopelessness that echoes the conformity vs death narratives of "problem youth" films. At the end of *La Haine* the three main characters are involved in an armed standoff with police, with at least one of the group being killed. The remaining message of this is that "justice" will be restored (Wilson and O'Sullivan, 2004) and for working class, minority ethnicity children this means that they will not experience social change. Similarly, films showing the consequences of criminal or deviant behaviours also reinforce the idea that authority will prevail. Whilst created with a welfare-oriented intention to highlight injustice, *Scum* (1979) reiterates the message that the way for children who are deviant, criminal, or just different to survive in the world is by doing as they are told and accepting the role that they are given by society, even if that means accepting a hopeless life marked by a lack of opportunity. *Scum*'s underlying message is that for children, criminal justice is brutal and they are powerless to change it.

Conclusion **181**

This message of the status quo being maintained that comes from films depicting the policing and imprisonment of children is challenged somewhat by films featuring justice-involved girls. By depicting a demographic that is less associated with the societal stereotype of "criminal" (instead being stereotyped as victims), these films were able to subvert some of the messages and tropes that permeated youth justice films. However, this was not necessarily positive, as many of these films still showed girls as being devious, but that this was focused on harming other girls and gaining social power rather than challenging authority or societal expectations. *Jawbreaker* (1999) showed girls killing a friend, staging a rough-sex murder, and manipulating the adults around them for the purpose of gaining and maintaining social status. Whilst the characters in bad girl films like *Jawbreaker* are witty, stylish and interesting, they are still portrayed as deviant. However, this deviance is not the same as the "dangerous offender" stereotype that typically depicts working-class minority ethnicity boys. Girls' deviance is portrayed as being cunning, sadistic, and manipulative. This is relational rather than physical aggression (Cecil, 2008). This portrayal of teenage girls as Machiavellian is interwoven with expectations of femininity in these films as well. Even though they may acknowledge and critique the pressures of social expectations regarding appearance and femininity through the use of makeover montages, they still reinforce the idea that being successful means being stylish and conforming to societal standards of femininity (Smith, 2017). Whilst presenting justice-involved girls as anti-heroes and style icons counters societal stereotypes, that this only exists in teen-comedies that focus on white, wealthy, American girls who escape the consequences of criminal justice, ultimately means that this is not a representation of the stories of the majority of real justice-involved girls. Because these bad girl films have become cultural icons, they have impact upon what is expected of girls in reality, reinforcing impossible standards of what a justice-involved girl "should" be like, which only contributes to further feelings of exclusion.

Whereas films about justice-involved girls dismiss the realities of their lives to focus on heightened femininity, films about minority ethnicity children dismiss the realities of their lives to create fear. Frequently using the existing narratives about cities as places of fear as a way of implying that minority ethnicity (particularly Black) boys are dangerous. By building on ideas of urban outcasts (Wacquant, 1993) and existing crime film narratives about cities (King, 2003; Quinn, 2005) and combining this with "dangerous offender" stereotypes present in society, urban films have a clear implication that minority ethnicity children are uncontrollable, criminal, and unchangeable. Whereas other types of youth crime films offer redemption from criminality for some characters, to show impressionable audiences the value of living a law-abiding life, urban films show criminal justice involvement as inescapable and permanent. However, these films make clear that this

182 A Popular Criminology of Youth Justice

hopeless situation only applies to certain groups; minority ethnicity children in cities. *Kidulthood* (2006) set the tone for this type of film, showing growing up in a city as being dangerous, frightening, and hopeless. This used existing tropes of crime films and stereotypes of justice-involved children, showing them as being thieving, drug-taking, violent, and callous. The cultural impact of *Kidulthood* meant that many other filmmakers used this as a template, highlighting the similarities to get funding for their projects (Nwonka and Malik, 2018). *Blue Story* (2019) is a key example of the legacy of urban film, again showing criminal gangs as an unavoidable feature of city life, leading to children being forced to choose between criminality or death. Whilst these films aimed to showcase the harms of criminal activity, and particularly knife crime, their underlying message is not that this type of behaviour is avoidable or can be recovered from, which ultimately undermines their intended purpose. This means that these films then become a spectacle for predominantly white middle-class audiences, who raise moral concerns about the acceptability of this type of film, whilst also engaging the fear of minority ethnicity children that these films depict for the purpose of entertainment. These films make urban children's crimes into spectacle, in the process unwittingly reaffirming racist narratives about cities, crime, and minority ethnicity people.

The notion of spectacle and using crime media as a way of vicariously enjoying harmful behaviours is well established (Alexandrescu, 2022; Cohen, 2011; Jarvis, 2007). But it is less considered how this can impact upon those that are depicted in these media. Much as urban films maintain negative perceptions about minority ethnicity children, true crime films further the narrative that children are dangerous. True crime films that focus on children highlight the most extreme crimes and show children as calculating, manipulative, and without remorse. These films focus on the details of the crime itself, showing audiences how it was done, whether this includes violence or not (but more often it does). The other feature is the psychological state of the children perpetrating these crimes, in an effort to try to understand why they did it. Because this is an unanswerable question without collaborating with those at the centre of these stories (which these films very rarely do) this often leads to these children being characterised as uncaring and concerned only with their own reputation or notoriety. True youth crime films fall into one of two categories: sensationalised truth or fictionalised truth. Sensationalised truth films utilise the innocent-dangerous dichotomy to contrast the perception of how the child characters would be expected to behave (obedient, respectful), with how these children actually behaved (violent, callous). This presents the real people the characters are based on, and thus justice-involved children in general, as being different from other children, and having transgressed standards in such a way that they can no longer be classed as children. *Badlands* (1973) is an example of this, where Holly (Sissy Spacek) is shown

Conclusion **183**

as being unfeeling in the face of death and only concerned with her romantic relationship. Similarly, but with less violence, *The Bling Ring* (2013), shows characters only concerned with their own status and fame rather than the harm they have caused. There are many concerns about how true crime films impact upon real individuals (Ringer, 2012), which is why some true youth crime films have utilised a fictionalised truth approach. By creating fictional characters based on a true story, films have more flexibility to protect real individuals, or to raise public awareness of a specific issue. *County Lines* (2019) is a key example of this, showcasing the impact of child criminal exploitation (CCE). Fictionalising true stories to create a social issue film often leads to using a social realist style, meaning fictionalised truth films inadvertently share similarities with urban films. Fictionalised truth films aim to convince audiences of the harms of a particular issue, whether this is CCE, unfair sentencing, or the dangers of weapon carrying. However, these films rarely offer a clear solution to the issues they discuss, meaning that these films echo the message of the inescapability of criminality, and the idea that some children will always become involved in crime.

Due to the ongoing narratives within youth crime films about the inevitability of children becoming criminal, it would be expected that there would be a high number of courtroom films showing these "dangerous offenders" receiving justice under the law. However, there are surprisingly few showing children as defendants or even witnesses. The formality of the courtroom setting instantly frames this as an adult space, meaning that when children are in this space, it means that something has gone wrong. Courtroom films' reliance on twists and shock revelations (Bergman and Asimow, 2006) means that the innocent-dangerous dichotomy is too simplistic and characterising a child as either an "innocent victim" or a "dangerous offender" would not lead to a satisfying story for audiences as it does not leave room for ambiguity. Instead, youth court films use an innocent-dangerous dyad. The dyad characterises children as simultaneously both innocent and dangerous, often drawing on cultural narratives about psychopathy (Oosterhuis and Loughnan, 2014). This allows child characters in courtroom films to switch between the two positions without confusing audiences. The best example of this is Aaron Stampler in *Primal Fear* (1996), who literally has an innocent personality and a dangerous one, switching between the two when appropriate throughout the film. However, the innocent-dangerous dyad also includes aspects of manipulation. The child characters in courtroom films are portrayed as being very aware of how they are perceived by others and how to utilise that to their own advantage. This leads to child defendant characters using the image of "innocent victim" to hide their "dangerous offender" side and avoid justice. It is a standard of the genre that defendants in courtroom films are found not guilty (Corcos, 2002), with the main tension of the film being about why the crime occurred and if the explanation is sympathetic or not.

184 A Popular Criminology of Youth Justice

But for youth court films, the final twist is often that the child defendant is not the "innocent victim" they portrayed themselves as having fooled both jury and audience, and are able to live their lives without receiving consequences for their wrongdoing, and feeling no remorse for their manipulation of justice systems. The innocent-dangerous dichotomy has been a mainstay of society and youth crime films throughout history. That youth court films developed this would arguably be a positive, showing potential move away from traditional stereotypes of justice-involved children. However, in moving to a dyad, this only heightens the negative aspects of the "dangerous offender" stereotype, as a seemingly innocent child may only be pretending. This means that audiences are only further impelled to fear justice-involved children.

The youth justice film in general presents something of a grim picture of the lives of justice-involved children; that they are dangerous, their lives are hopeless, they manipulate others, they cannot be controlled, and that this life was inevitable for them. However, more recently there have been works that show a potential change in attitudes that mirrors developments in youth justice practice. Child First (Case and Hazel, 2023) has been adopted in youth justice practice as the main ideological approach, aiming to divert children from the stigma of "offending" labels, build pro-social identities, develop approaches where children's views are considered, and promote the idea that all children regardless of age, race, class, gender, ethnicity or justice-involvement, should be considered by society as children and treated as such (Case and Haines, 2014). Whilst this has largely been confined to youth justice thus far, some films show children in this way and can be classed as Child First films. Scrapper (2023) is a key example of this. Showing a 12-year-old girl who is not only behaving in criminal ways, but also sees this as her job, Scrapper's main character is someone who would likely be demonised by many other films. However, Scrapper is not a film about crime, it is a film about Georgie (Lola Campbell). Both the film and the characters have a non-judgemental approach, whilst not encouraging Georgie's criminal behaviours, they do not treat her harshly instead offering support to develop in pro-social ways. Scrapper also shows aspects of children's lives that other youth crime films do not. Play is a frequent feature of Scrapper and this is shown as being childlike and fun. There are not sinister undertones to Scrapper, implying that Georgie will manipulate others to evade justice, there is the sense that she can develop into a law-abiding adult but only if she receives the appropriate support from the adults around her. In this way Scrapper is revolutionary; instead of responsibilising and criminalising Georgie for her behaviours, it places emphasis on the need for adults and institutions to act appropriately in supporting children to allow them to be children.

This message is not something frequently seen in youth crime films and that Scrapper and others with positive messages about justice-involved

Conclusion **185**

children exist is heartening. However, these films are a minority in comparison to those showing simplistic, stereotyped, and harmful portrayals of justice-involved children. Throughout this book the issues of audience reactions, funding structures, and film standards have all been considered in relation to the films discussed. It is clear that these aspects have profound impacts upon which stories get told in this space (Nwonka and Malik, 2018). This may have been a contributing factor to the persistence of harmful narratives regarding justice-involved children; differing stories or differing perspectives are potentially less marketable and profitable. Whilst criminology does not have the power to change these factors, we can do the work of highlighting the problematic aspects of representations of youth justice on film, by further developing a popular criminology of youth justice that critically considers these media.

A Popular Criminology of Youth Justice

There are multiple benefits to developing a popular criminology of youth justice. Since Rafter and Brown's (2011) seminal work on popular criminology researchers have been developing understanding of a variety of fields through media analysis (Atherton, 2013; Kort-Butler, 2022; Silva, 2019). Popular criminology is a way to understand not the impact or relationship that media has on crime itself, but how crime is represented in society, and thus perceived (Akrivos and Antoniou, 2019). Understanding how an issue is represented in media, whether this is factual or fictional is important, as this has a profound impact upon the opinions and understanding of the general public (Jewkes, 2015). Criminology has always considered media in its work, but regarding youth justice, this has primarily focused on factual media such as newspapers and news websites (Mejias and Banaji, 2019). Overlooking the influence of popular films is a gap in this, as this clearly does play a role in influencing the public, and popular criminology is well placed to examine and understand this. The way in which media influences public attitudes has been well documented, as has the relationship this subsequently has with policy making (Bornter, 1984; Cohen, 2011; Hu and Dittmann, 2019). Whilst there is not a direct line from films to laws, there is an established connection. This has always been the case regarding youth crime films, from politicians' concerns regarding how *Blackboard Jungle*'s (1955) international release would impact perceptions of American discipline (Golub, 2009), to Jean-Marie Le Pen citing *La Haine* (1995) in relation to rioting (Vincendeau, 2012), to David Cameron saying children's lives shouldn't be like those depicted in *Kidulthood* (2006) (Featherstone, 2013). Film is a powerful communication tool, and how this is used by the political establishment to discuss youth justice has a real impact upon the policies that are selected and how they are received. To truly understand the relationship between public

186 A Popular Criminology of Youth Justice

opinion, policy, and practice, we must consider how justice-involved children and youth justice systems are represented in media, including film.

Given the importance and impact of film upon public attitudes and policy makers, it becomes essential to not only understand how youth justice is represented in film, but what this means in the context of broader society, and how this changes over time. Achieving this has been one of the aims of this book, and the chapters have considered different time periods, contexts, and concerns. But understanding these issues and discussing them explicitly can allow scholars of youth justice to develop theoretical perspectives. The mythologising of the "young offender" as a label is clearly a concern within the subject, as almost all theories discuss labelling in some way. However, this is often discussed in a limited way, that being required to attend a Youth Offending Team means the label of "offender" is applied (Creaney, 2012). However, we know there are broader aspects to this, such as social impacts which are laden with the stereotypes of "offender" that have been established, mythologised, and maintained in film media. These aspects of labelling are more likely to have impacts upon justice-involved children as these labels are the ones that the people around them; friends, family etc. are likely to have been exposed to, have understanding of, and therefore apply to others. There is a clear difference in what the experience of being labelled an "offender" would be like if this label is based on Conor (Alex Murphy) from *The Young Offenders* (2016) than if it was based on Carlin (Ray Winstone) from *Scum* (1979). This means that popular criminology's work of analysing, understanding, and critiquing the messages, symbols, and ideas that enter society through film is necessary to help understand and develop work about the lived experiences of the children to who these labels are applied to.

Another benefit of a popular criminology of youth justice is that by developing this area of study, we can develop clear messages and support for filmmakers about how youth justice stories can be told in ways that do not cause harm. As some films about youth crime have been deemed to be harmful or dangerous in some ways which has led to censorship (Biltereyst, 2007), limited their release (Ilott, 2013), or impacted on what stories are or are not told (Nwonka and Malik, 2018), filmmakers clearly have an interest in ensuring their works are appropriate. But filmmakers also do not set out to cause harm or detriment to real children in their works, the impact of labelling, stereotyping, and the mythologising of youth crime is an unintended side effect. But popular criminology can provide support for filmmakers, by reiterating that there is a highly limited and overexaggerated relationship between films about crime and actual crime levels (Rafter, 2000), that any harms that do occur are likely to negatively impact justice-involved children rather than inciting them to further criminality, and that there are ways of telling youth justice stories that are positive and don't utilise harmful stereotypes. Popular criminology of youth justice can support change in film,

Conclusion **187**

by developing as an area of study, and emphasising the need for Child First approaches in film as well as youth justice practice.

There are existing examples of Child First films (see Chapter 8), however, these are currently outweighed by the number of youth crime films that do not portray children as children. For Child First approaches to be truly reflected in film, all four aspects of Child First need to be considered. Representing children as children can be achieved through storytelling, scripting, costuming, and set design. Similarly, diversion from stigma can be achieved through which stories are told and how. But the collaborative aspects of Child First approaches can be achieved by consideration of the filmmaking process itself. Who is given the opportunity to make films, and what stories they are allowed to tell has been a continuing theme in this book and shows the importance of developing a diverse film industry. Diversity shouldn't be simply for its own sake, but to allow opportunity to those who might not otherwise receive it, to tell new stories, and to allow audiences to see themselves better represented (Corcoran, 2017). Many filmmakers have spoken about their work being based upon aspects of their own childhood experiences, but for those making films about youth crime and justice, it is rare that they have direct experience of this themselves. Filmmaking has been found to be a diversionary activity (Blum-Ross, 2017), therefore supporting more children who have experience of justice-involvement into filmmaking would be beneficial in not only providing purposeful activity, but also supporting the development of pro-social identities, seeing themselves not as offenders but as filmmakers.

Popular criminology's calls for diversity in film do not end at the filmmaking process itself. Whilst this book has made efforts to include diverse perspectives and works from around the world, there are clear limitations to this (as discussed in Chapter 1), and this book largely focused on Western film. A popular criminology of youth justice needs to include scholars globally, reflecting differences in representation. The symbols used in film to denote deviance will differ with culture; biker jackets and hoodies are not universal symbols, there are linguistic differences that will impact how justice-involved children are spoken about, and differing justice systems will impact upon how consequences are shown in film. A popular criminology of youth justice should take all these factors and more into consideration, welcoming contributions from a diverse range of scholars around the world. This book has aimed to act as a starting point for this, but it is clear that there is more work to be done.

Throughout the chapters of this book it has been reiterated that the broad cultural conception of how justice-involved children are perceived and represented within society needs to change. Previous representations have shown justice-involved children as being inconsiderate, manipulative, violent, selfish, and dangerous. Whilst elements of this may be based in truth, that this forms

188 A Popular Criminology of Youth Justice

the majority of representations means a broadly inaccurate message is being given to the public. Audiences are not expected to interpret fictional films as entirely true, and on the whole people do not (Chiricos et al., 1997). However, film does have a clear influence on people's views and attitudes regarding criminal justice, if only because they have a lack of information about the realities of this system, as a majority of people never interact with it. This makes the messages given to the public through film important, and regarding justice-involved children, these messages are primarily negative. Showing children's transformation into criminals as unavoidable, and the prospect of change as hopeless, these films implicitly hinder opportunities for real justice-involved children, as they are not expected to achieve beyond the stereotypes or escape the labels that have been placed upon them. This is an active harm committed without intent or even awareness that it has occurred. There needs to be a change. This is not to say that crime stories involving children as perpetrators should not be told, or that these stories must all be resolutely positive. However, a simple change that would be beneficial and reduce some of these harms would be to portray children as children, regardless of their level of justice-involvement. To tell stories that are not about crime first but are about children first.

Film List

Badlands (1973)
Blackboard Jungle (1955)
Blue Story (2019)
Childs Play 3 (1991)
County Lines (2019)
Jawbreaker (1999)
Kidulthood (2006)
La Haine (1995)
Primal Fear (1996)
Rebel Without A Cause (1955)
Scrapper (2023)
Scum (1979)
The Bling Ring (2013)
The Young Offenders (2016)

References

Akrivos D and Antoniou AK (2019) Conclusion: Popular criminology revisited. In: Akrivos D and Antoniou AK (eds) *Crime, Deviance and Popular Culture*. Palgrave Studies in Crime, Media and Culture. Cham: Springer International Publishing, pp. 335–338. Available at: https://link.springer.com/10.1007/978-3-030-04912-6_14 (accessed 4 January 2023).

Alexandrescu L (2022) Violence, crime dystopia and the dialectics of (dis)order in The Purge films. *Crime, Media, Culture* 18(4): 561–577. SAGE Publications.

Atherton M (2013) Teaching through film: Utilizing popular criminology in the classroom. *Journal on Excellence in College Teaching* 24(2): 77–99.

Bateman T (2011) 'We now breach more kids in a week than we used to in a whole year': The punitive turn, enforcement and custody. *Youth Justice* 11(2): 115–133.

Bergman P and Asimow M (2006) *Reel Justice: The Courtroom Goes to the Movies.* Kansas City: Andrews McMeel Publishing.

Biltereyst D (2007) American juvenile delinquency movies and the European censors: The cross-cultural reception and censorship of the wild one, blackboard jungle, and rebel without a cause. In: Timothy Shary and Alexandra Seibel (eds) *Youth Culture in Global Cinema.* Austin: University of Texas Press, 9–26.

Blum-Ross A (2017) Voice, empowerment and youth-produced films about 'gangs'. *Learning, Media and Technology* 42(1): 54–73.

Bornter MA (1984) Media Images and public attitudes toward crime and justice. In: Ray Surrette (ed) *Justice and the Media: Issues and Research.* Springfield, Illinois: Charles C. Thomas, pp. 15–30.

Bowling B and Phillips C (2007) Disproportionate and discriminatory: Reviewing the evidence on police stop and search. *Modern Law Review* 70(6): 936–961. Wiley/ Blackwell (10.1111).

Briggs DB (2013) Conceptualising risk and need: The rise of actuarialism and the death of welfare? Practitioner assessment and intervention in the youth offending service. *Youth Justice* 13(1): 17–30. SAGE PublicationsSage UK: London, England.

Case S (2018) *Youth Justice: A Critical Introduction.* Abingdon, Oxon; New York, NY: Routledge.

Case S and Bateman T (2020) The punitive transition in youth justice: Reconstructing the child as offender. *Children and Society* 34(6): 475–491.

Case S and Haines K (2014) Children first, offenders Second positive promotion: Reframing the prevention debate. *Youth Justice* 15(3): 226–239. SAGE Publications.

Case S and Hazel N (eds) (2023) *Child First: Developing a New Youth Justice System.* Cham: Palgrave Macmillan.

Cecil DK (2008) From Heathers to mean girls: An examination of relational aggression in film. Journal of criminal justice and popular culture, 15(3), 262–276.

Chiricos T, Eschholz S and Gertz M (1997) Crime, news and fear of crime: Toward an identification of audience effects. *Social Problems* 44(3): 342–357.

Cloarec N (2013) From the banned telefilm to the feature film: The two versions of Alan Clarke's Scum (1977-1979). *Revue LISA/LISA e-journal. Littératures, Histoire des Idées, Images, Sociétés du Monde Anglophone – Literature, History of Ideas, Images and Societies of the English-speaking World* (Vol. XI-n°3). Vol. XI-n°3. Presses Universitaires de Rennes. Epub ahead of print 26 November 2013. https://doi.org/10.4000/lisa.5549

Cohen S (2011) Whose side were we on? The undeclared politics of moral panic theory. *Crime, Media, Culture* 7(3): 237–243. SAGE Publications.

Corcoran T (2017) Are the kids alright? Relating to representations of youth. *International Journal of Adolescence and Youth* 22(2): 151–164. Routledge.

Corcos CA (2002) Legal fictions: Irony, storytelling, truth, and justice in the modern courtroom drama The Ben J. Altheimer symposium: imagining the law: Lawyers and legal issues in the popular culture: Essay. *University of Arkansas at Little Rock Law Review* 25(3): 503–634.

Creaney S (2012) Targeting, labelling and stigma: Challenging the criminalisation of children and young people. *Criminal Justice Matters* 89(1): 16–17.

Doherty TP (2002) *Teenagers and Teenpics: The Juvenilization of American Movies in the 1950s.* Rev. and expanded ed. Philadelphia: Temple University Press.

Featherstone M (2013) "Hoodie horror": The capitalist other in postmodern society. *Review of Education, Pedagogy, and Cultural Studies* 35(3): 178–196. Routledge.

Fitz-Gibbon K (2016) Protections for children before the law: An empirical analysis of the age of criminal responsibility, the abolition of doli incapax and the merits of a developmental immaturity defence in England and Wales. *Criminology & Criminal Justice* 16(4): 391–409. SAGE Publications Sage UK: London, England.

Franklin B and Petley J (1996) Killing the age of innocence: Newspaper reporting of the death of James Bulger. In: Jane Pilcher and Stephen Wagg (eds) *Thatcher's Children?* Bristol: Routledge, pp. 136–157.

Frey M (2006) Benny's video, caché, and the desubstantiated image. *Framework: The Journal of Cinema and Media* 47(2): 30–36. Wayne State University Press.

Golub A (2009) They turned a school into a jungle! How The blackboard jungle redefined the education crisis in Postwar America. *Film & History: An Interdisciplinary Journal of Film and Television Studies* 39(1): 21–30. Center for the Study of Film and History.

Green DA (2008) *When Children Kill Children: Penal Populism and Political Culture.* OUP Oxford. Available at: https://books.google.com/books?id=QIvp2Jg7yRkC& pgis=1 (accessed 13 November 2015).

Hay C (1995) Mobilization through interpellation: James Bulger, Juvenile Crime and the Construction of a Moral Panic. *Social and Legal Studies* 4(2): 197–223.

Hu X and Dittmann L (2019) How does print media describe gang members? Analysis of newspaper reports and policy implications. *Journal of Criminal Justice and Popular Culture* 19(1): 19–36.

Ilott S (2013) "We are the martyrs, you're just squashed tomatoes!" Laughing through the Fears in Postcolonial British Comedy: Chris Morris's Four Lions and Joe Cornish's Attack the Block. *Postcolonial Text* 8(2). 2.

Jarvis B (2007) Monsters Inc.: Serial killers and consumer culture. *Crime, Media, Culture: An International Journal* 3(3): 326–344. Sage PublicationsSage UK: London, England.

Jewkes Y (2015) *Media and Crime.* London: SAGE.

Jowett G, Jarvie IC and Fuller-Seeley K (1996) *Children and the Movies: Media Influence and the Payne Fund Controversy.* Cambridge Studies in the History of Mass Communications. Cambridge [England]; New York, NY, USA: Cambridge University Press.

King L (2003) Review of Black City Cinema: African American urban experiences in film. *African American Review* 37(2/3): 445–447. [Indiana State University, Saint Louis University, African American Review, African American Review (St. Louis University)].

Kort-Butler L (2022) The brain and the bat: A popular criminology of the brain in the Batman Animated Universes. *Deviant Behavior* 43(5): 623–645. https://doi.org/10 .1080/01639625.2021.1879604

MacDonald R and Shildrick T (2007) Street corner society: Leisure careers, youth (sub)culture and social exclusion. *Leisure Studies* 26(3): 339–355. Routledge.

Mejias S and Banaji S (2019) Backed into a corner: Challenging media and policy representations of youth citizenship in the UK. *Information Communication and Society* 22(12): 1714–1732. Routledge.

Muncie J (1999) Institutionalized intolerance: Youth justice and the 1998 Crime and Disorder Act. *Critical Social Policy* 19(2): 147–175.

Nwonka CJ and Malik S (2018) Cultural discourses and practices of institutionalised diversity in the UK film sector: 'Just get something black made'. *The Sociological Review* 66(6): 1111–1127. SAGE Publications Ltd.

Oosterhuis H and Loughnan A (2014) Madness and crime: Historical perspectives on forensic psychiatry. *International Journal of Law and Psychiatry* 37(1): 1–16.

Panelli C (2007) 'Preppy-jocks', 'rednecks', 'stoners', and 'scum': Power and youth social groups in rural Vermont. In: Ruth Panelli, Samantha Punch, Elsbeth Robson (eds) *Global Perspectives on Rural Childhood and Youth*. New York: Routledge.

Petley J (2007) New labour, old morality. *Index on Censorship* 36(2): 132–140.

Pitts J (2001) Korrectional Karaoke: New Labour and the Zombification of Youth Justice. *Youth Justice* 1(2): 3–16.

Quinn L (2005) Review of migrating to the movies: cinema and Black urban modernity. *Film Criticism* 29(3): 73–78. Allegheny College.

Rafter N (2017) Crime films and visual criminology. In: Michelle Brown and Eamonn Carrabine (eds) *Routledge International Handbook of Visual Criminology*. Oxon: Routledge, pp. 79–88.

Rafter NH (2000) *Shots in the Mirror: Crime Films and Society*. Oxford Berlin: Oxford University Press.

Rafter NH and Brown M (2011) *Criminology Goes to the Movies: Crime Theory and Popular Culture*. New York: New York University.

Ringer BS (2012) Based on an almost true story: Providing real life protection to real life characters. *Pittsburgh Journal of Technology Law and Policy* 13(1): 1–19.

Silva JR (2019) Mass shooting films: Myths, academic knowledge, and popular criminology. *Victims & Offenders* 14(2): 239–264.

Simmons J (2008) Violent youth: The censoring and public reception of The Wild One and The Blackboard Jungle. *Film History: An International Journal* 20(3): 381–391. Indiana University Press.

Smith F (2017) *Rethinking the Hollywood Teen Movie: Gender, Genre and Identity*. Edinburgh: Edinburgh University Press.

Smith R (2001) Foucault's Law: The Crime and Disorder Act 1998. *Youth Justice* 1(2): 17–29.

Smith R (2010) Children's rights and youth justice: 20 years of no progress. *Child Care in Practice* 16(1): 3–17.

Vincendeau G (2012) La haine and after: Arts, Politics, and the Banlieue. Available at: https://www.criterion.com/current/posts/642-la-haine-and-after-arts-politics-and-the-banlieue (accessed 14 June 2023).

Wacquant LJd (1993) Urban outcasts: Stigma and division in the Black American Ghetto and the French Urban Periphery. *International Journal of Urban and Regional Research* 17(3): 366–383.

Wilson D and O'Sullivan S (2004) *Images of Incarceration: Representations of Prison in Film and Television Drama*. Winchester, UK: Waterside Press.

INDEX

Access to public space 48, 50, 53, 55
Adultification 61, 81, 100, 113, 119,
  136–137, 140–141, 154–156
Adults: as mentors 35; relationships
  with 24, 26, 33–34, 37–38, 55–56,
  80, 155–157
Alcohol *see* Substance Misuse
Aspiration 54–55, 80
Attack The Block (2011) 158–162
Authority Figures 24, 37–39, 41, 55, 61,
  118

Bad Girl films 75–80, 157
Banlieue Films 58–59
Becoming 5, 29, 36, 41
Blackboard Jungle (1955) 28–33
The Bling Ring (2013) 116–117,
  124–125
Blue Story (2019) 103–104
Bullet Boy (2004) 92–94, 102
Bully (2001) 114–116

Capitalism 24, 30, 39, 57, 112, 124
Censorship 25, 28–29, 33–34, 37, 59
Child Criminal Exploitation 52, 95–96,
  98–99, 120–123
Child First 6, 53, 82, 148–153, 163,
  168–170
Child First films 153–169, 187–188
Children in Need 8, 32, 72, 118, 142
Cities 24, 90–97, 99, 101–103

Class 3, 6, 22, 33, 38–39, 56–57, 71,
  80–83, 95, 101, 156, 166–167;
  Underclass 22, 26, 57, 91
The Client (1994) 142–143
Clothing 1, 24, 27, 29, 31, 39, 76, 136,
  167
Commodification 80, 112, 124
Compliance 28, 33, 36, 61–62
Conformity 7, 24–25, 28–29, 31, 33, 36
Consequences 73, 82–84, 125,
  157–158
Consumerism 24, 116–117, 124–126
Consumption 24–26, 113, 116, 122
Corruption 47, 116, 123
County Lines 95, 120, 122
County Lines (2019) 120–122, 166
Courts 131, 134–135, 137
Courtroom Dramas 131–135, 141
Criminal Pathways 39, 49
Criminalisation 6–9, 26, 34, 48–49,
  142, 155
Critical Discourse Analysis 10–13
Cultural Criminology 3, 5–6
Custodial Estate: Borstal 59–61; Prisons
  47–48; Prison Camps 61–64; Young
  Offender Institutions 60, 92

Death 27–29, 36, 58, 77, 93, 96,
  102–103, 155–156
Delinquency 25–26, 31, 36
Demonisation 7, 149, 164, 167–168

Desistance 93, 100, 151
Deviance 3, 6, 9, 29, 142
Do Revenge (2022) 157–158
Drugs *see* Substance Misuse

Education 22, 28–34, 41, 78
Employment 31
Ethnic Minority Children 49, 54, 82,
  89, 91, 94, 100, 103–104, 158–161

Family 34–36, 41, 55, 119, 135,
  154–155, 166–167
Fear 90–92, 96–98, 161
Femininity 71, 74, 84
Fictionalisation 60, 111, 119
Fictionalised Truth 113–114, 117–122,
  125
The 400 Blows (1959) 35, 40–42
Funding 11, 92, 94, 112–114, 168–169

Gangs 23, 38, 93, 95, 98, 101, 112
Genre 73, 81, 89, 112–113, 116–117,
  123, 133, 153, 159
Girlhood 71–72, 74, 80, 83, 117
Graffiti 24, 37, 54, 56–57
Grooming *see* Child Criminal
  Exploitation

Hays Code 28, 102
Heathers (1988) 75–76, 82–83, 158
Hierarchy 62, 74–76, 83
Holes (2003) 61–64
Hope 30, 93, 102, 118, 126, 164–165
Housing 24, 91, 101, 156

I Was A Teenage Werewolf (1957)
  27–30
Ill Manors (2012) 95–96, 102
Injustice 49, 119, 158, 162
Innocent-Dangerous Dichotomy 7, 22,
  28, 37, 47, 81, 113, 123, 132, 153,
  158
Innocent-Dangerous Dyad 132,
  135–141, 143
Intersectionality 22, 71, 81–82, 96,
  157–158

Jawbreaker (1999) 77–78, 83
Judges 62, 119
Juries 113–114, 139
Justice-involved children 15–16,
  178–179

Ken Loach 90, 101–102, 117
Kidulthood (2006) 97–98, 102–103

La Haine (1995) 54–59
Labelling 6, 16, 82, 96–97, 135–136,
  152, 162–163
Let Him Have It (1991) 118–119

Masculinity 27, 120
Monstrous Youth 28, 41, 74, 161, 164
Moral Panic 8, 72, 100
Morality 47, 104, 115
Murder 76–77, 112, 114, 118, 134–135,
  139
Music 23, 91

Outsiders 29, 94–95
Opportunity 54, 56, 97–98, 103–104,
  117–118, 151, 161–162, 164–165

Parents *see* Family
Police 38, 48–59, 160–161, 163–164
Popular Criminology 3–9, 185–188
Populism 4, 7, 9, 53, 168–169
Poverty 32, 38, 79, 91–93, 120
Power 8, 75–76, 83
Primal Fear (1996) 139–141
Problem Youth Films 1, 22–30
Punitiveness 49, 53, 99–100, 178–179

Race 22, 31–32, 55–56, 96, 168–169
Racism 31, 55, 91, 96, 100, 105,
  160–161
Rebel Without a Cause (1955) 23,
  26–27, 35–36, 39
Relational Aggression 74–76
Representation 25, 46, 78, 89, 94–95,
  141
Responsibilisation 53, 63–64, 71,
  104–105, 143
Riots 54, 57
Risk 91–92, 97, 178
Risk Based Frameworks 90, 92, 94, 97,
  99–100, 148

Schools *see* Education
Scrapper (2023) 154–157
Scum (1979) 59–61
Sensationalised Truth 113–117, 125
Sensationalism 8, 40, 79, 90–91, 98,
  104–105, 113–114, 121
Sexualisation 52, 72–73, 114–115

194 Index

Sexuality 29, 39, 114
Social Construction 2–3, 12, 16, 112
Social Control 6–7, 25, 30, 32–33, 114
Social Exclusion 8, 29, 32, 37, 49, 62, 101, 103, 118
Social Fears 2, 9, 23, 50, 74, 76, 135
Social Realism 40, 58–59, 61, 89–90, 98, 101
Societal Expectations 22–33, 36, 70–71
Stereotypes 25–26, 30, 50–51, 59, 61, 138–139, 142, 148–149
Stop and Search 38, 48–49
Subculture 5, 7, 27
Substance Misuse 8, 51, 55, 90, 101, 120–122
Sugar & Spice (2001) 79–80, 83
Sweet Sixteen (2002) 101–102

Teenager 22, 24
Thirteen (2003) 81–82, 84
Transformation 5, 27–30, 34, 73, 77, 95
Transitions 22, 63
True Crime 3–4, 111–113, 116, 122–123

Trust 36, 38, 59–60, 155
Truth 112–113, 117–118, 125–126, 134, 139
12 Angry Men (1957) 133–124
21 Jump Street (2012) 51–53

Unhappy endings 29, 36, 41, 58, 102–103
Urban Films 89–92, 94–97, 99, 125, 158–159

Violence 4, 8, 27, 30, 51–52, 57, 60, 62–63, 72–80, 95, 121
Vulnerability 7–8
Victimisation 142–143, 158

Weapons: Guns 29, 36, 55, 58, 93; Knives 1, 23, 25, 27, 104–105
The Whole Truth (2016) 137–139
Wound Culture 112–113
Witnesses 141–143

The Young Offenders (2016) 163–167
The Young Savages (1961) 1, 37–39
Youth 2–3, 6–7

Printed in the United States
by Baker & Taylor Publisher Services